AMERICAN VISTAS
1607–1877

American Vistas
1607-1877

Fourth Edition

Edited by
LEONARD DINNERSTEIN
UNIVERSITY OF ARIZONA

and

KENNETH T. JACKSON
COLUMBIA UNIVERSITY

New York   Oxford
OXFORD UNIVERSITY PRESS
1983

LIBRARY OF CONGRESS CATALOGING IN PUBLICATION DATA

Main entry under title:
American vistas.

   Contents: [1] 1607-1877—[2] 1877 to the
present.
   1. United States—History—Addresses, essays,
lectures.   I. Dinnerstein, Leonard.   II. Jackson,
Kenneth T.
E178.6.A426   1979   973   82-2160
ISBN 0-19-503164-4 (pbk. v. 1.)   AACR2
ISBN 0-19-503166-0 (pbk. v. 2.)

Printing (last digit): 9 8 7 6 5 4 3 2 1

For
Myra Dinnerstein
and
Barbara Jackson

PREFACE TO THE FOURTH EDITION

It is now more than a decade since we first embarked upon our project of bringing together a series of historical essays that combined interest with readability and which could be used in conjunction with a survey text or a wide variety of other books. We have been gratified by the initial reader response as well as the enthusiasm with which our subsequent editions were received. The testaments that we have read indicate that there are a large number of instructors who find the combination of traditional and off-beat essays on the American past suitable to their own teaching styles. We are particularly pleased that *American Vistas* has been used by a wide diversity of people in every region of the country as well as in Canada and overseas. It reaffirms our belief that the American past can be both enlightening and instructive to all people who are fascinated by the development of societies.

For this revision we have retained a larger number of articles from the previous edition than has been our wont in the past. Letters from users and comments from other colleagues and scholars clearly indicated which pieces were most suitable for college classes. We have tried to follow this collective advice whenever possible. Almost all of the respondents believed that historiographical essays were out of place in *American Vistas*. We agreed. Many other selections were so highly praised that we felt it would be an injustice to students and teachers alike if we eliminated them. On the other hand, more recent scholarship and the changing emphasis of societal and classroom interests have resulted in the addition to this volume of selections on the restrictions of freedom in colonial America, women and work in the Jacksonian era, and political leadership during the Civil War.

For this fourth edition we would like to thank the following people who provided us with candid analyses of previous selections

and/or suggested possibilities for our consideration: Karen Ander-
son, Kent Anderson, Gottlieb J. Baer, Paul A. Carter, Juan Ramon
Garcia, Sidney H. Kessler, Oliver Krug, Constance M. Jones, James
M. Morris, Glenn Miller, James Richardson, and Robert E. Smith.
Phyllis Deutsch was also particularly helpful in evaluating the
book.

We would also like to thank the office staff at the University of
Arizona History Department who facilitated the preparation of the
manuscript: Dawn Polter, Marilyn Bradian, Dorothy Donnelly,
Nikki Matz, Maudie Mazza, and student assistant David Romero.

As in the past, both of us would be grateful for individual comments and suggestions from readers. We also hope that articles included in this edition are as useful for classes as those that were
chosen for our earlier volumes.

L.D.
K.T.J.

November 1981

CONTENTS

I COLONIAL ORIGINS

I

The Man Behind Columbus

EDWARD T. STONE

• Christopher Columbus, a weaver's son, was born in Genoa
in 1451. He took to the sea as a boy and remained a mariner
for the rest of his life. Although he was in Portugal in 1488
when Bartholomeu Días returned from his voyage around the
southern tip of Africa with the sensational news that there
was an eastern water route to the Indies, Columbus was convinced that a western route as well was feasible. When King
John II of Portugal refused to finance an exploratory voyage,
Columbus turned to the Spanish Court. He finally persuaded
Queen Isabella to equip a tiny fleet, and he set out from the
port of Palos in August 1492. A little more than two months
later, on the morning of October 12, a lookout on the Pinta,
one of his vessels, shouted: "Tierra! Tierra!" That discovery is
generally regarded as the most important event in the history of Western civilization since the birth of Christ.

Columbus's reputation has not fared especially well in recent years. We now concede that he was a mediocre administrator and an impractical dreamer who never realized that he
had found anything more than a new route to the Orient.
We also believe that it was Leif Ericson, who reached the
shores of Labrador about the year 1000, who was the first
European to set foot in the New World—though there are
other contenders for the honor, St. Brendan the Navigator
and Madoc the Welshman among them.

The following article continues this tradition by suggesting
that if Columbus had been left to his own devices his ships
would never have sailed. According to its author, it was the
Pinzón brothers, and especially Martín, who enlisted a crew
and who got things moving. If only Martín Pinzón had lived

From *American Heritage* 27 (October 1976): 46–53. Copyright © 1976 by
American Heritage Publishing Co., Inc. Reprinted by permission.

a bit longer (Stone suggests), historians might have credited
him with his critical role in the Columbus expedition.

As you approach the village of Palos de la Frontera, some fifty miles
west of Seville in Spain's Andalusía, the squat little church of San
Jorge looms in the foreground at the base of a rocky cliff that overlooks
the tidal flats created by the mingling of the rivers Tinto and Odiel.
The shallow estuary where the two rivers converge, known of old as the
Saltés, is undistinguished scenically, an obscure corner of Spain virtually
unknown to American tourists.

But a visitor mounting the steps to the plaza of the seven-hundred-
year-old church from the road below soon becomes aware of a dusty
marble plaque affixed to the crumbling brown façade of the sanctuary.
Now chipped and broken, it is a sad remnant of a long-forgotten burst
of civic pride. Chiseled on it are these words:

A LOS PINZONES
IMORTALES HIJOS DE ESTA VILLA
CODESCUBRIDORES CON COLON
DEL NUEVO MUNDO
3 AGOSTO 1910 EL PUEBLO DE PALOS

(to the Pinzóns: Immortal sons of this town, codiscoverers with Columbus of the New World; August 3, 1910; the community of Palos).

But didn't Columbus discover America all by himself? And who
were the Pinzóns anyway? Good questions—and not one American in
ten thousand probably knows the correct answers. Yet the role of the
brothers Pinzón in the discovery of America, and particularly that of
the eldest, their redoubtable leader, Martín Alonso Pinzón, can fairly
be equated with that of Columbus himself.

Pinzón organized the expedition of 1492 after Columbus had failed
to enlist a crew. Pinzón not only helped to finance the voyage but also
advanced funds from his own pocket to the families of the sailors so
they would not be in need during the absence of their breadwinners.
One of the great sailors and navigators of his day, he contributed
the maritime skill and knowledge necessary for the success of the
expedition.

The *Pinta*, under Pinzón's command, invariably led the fleet, and it
was her crew who first sighted land in the predawn hours of October
12. Pinzón was the discoverer of the island of Haiti, where the Span-

iards established their first New World colony, and he was the first European to strike gold in America.

Pinzón was, in fact, the de facto leader of the expedition, since the crews looked to him for direction rather than to Columbus, whom they mistrusted as a foreigner.

It is not difficult to assess the reasons for history's neglect of Martín Pinzón. He died obscurely in Palos within two weeks after the return of the fleet of discovery on March 15, 1493. (Only two ships returned; Columbus's flagship was wrecked on the north shore of Haiti on Christmas Eve.) Columbus and Pinzón quarreled bitterly in the West Indies, and only Columbus's own version of the voyage has survived in conventional histories of the Discovery. He was a prolific writer of journals and letters; even if he and Pinzón had not quarreled, his incessant portrayal of himself as the lone discoverer of the New World would have prevailed because there was no other version.

After the quarrel Columbus's complaints against his fellow argonauts were endless: the seamen of Palos were a bad lot, lawless and disobedient; the Pinzón brothers were greedy and insolent. The theme was picked up by two major contemporary historians, Father Bartolomé de Las Casas, an ardent admirer of Columbus, and Ferdinand Columbus, the illegitimate son of Christopher, who wrote a laudatory biography of his father. Subsequent histories of the Discovery were based almost exclusively on these three sources—Columbus himself, his son Ferdinand, and the partisan Las Casas.

But lying virtually forgotten for nearly three hundred years in the Archive of the Indies in Seville was a mass of unique historical data that revealed the great part Martín Pinzón played in the discovery of America. Preserved in the cramped handwriting of sixteenth-century court reporters are hundreds of thousands of words of sworn testimony about the first voyage that offer a considerably different view of the Enterprise of the Indies from that of the Columbus tradition.

Only gradually, in the last century and this, has this mine of historical evidence yielded its treasure through the work of successive Spanish scholars. Known as the *Pleitos de Colón* (litigation of Columbus), the transcripts of these extraordinary proceedings embody the eyewitness recollections of nearly a hundred residents of the *comarca*, or countryside, of the Tinto-Odiel, men who had been personally acquainted with both Pinzón and Columbus and who had witnessed or participated in the events in Palos immediately before the departure of the expedition of 1492 and after its return seven months later. At least five of the witnesses had been on the voyage.

The *Pleitos* were initiated by Diego Columbus, elder son of Christopher and the latter's successor as admiral of the Indies. Diego brought suit in 1508, two years after his father's death, to have restored to the Columbus family the titles and authority of viceroy and governor of the New World colonies, which King Ferdinand and Queen Isabella had revoked in 1499, deposing Columbus and appointing a new governor. Defending the case for the Crown, the *fiscal*, or royal attorney, chose to base his defense not on the grounds of Columbus's dubious record as governor but on the allegation that he was not the exclusive discoverer of America.

Testimony was presented in an attempt to prove that not only did Martín Pinzón organize and lead the expedition but that it was his idea in the first place. The latter claim, however, had so little evidence to support it that the Council of the Indies, before which the suit was tried, rejected it out of hand.

But the depositions relating to Pinzón's predominant part in organizing the fleet and his role as partner and collaborator in the Discovery were abundant and explicit and were never challenged or denied by the attorney, and witnesses for Diego. Indeed, at least one witness for the plaintiff, Juan Rodríguez de Mafra, a veteran pilot, volunteered in his sworn statement, made in 1515, that if it had not been for Pinzón, Columbus never could have enlisted a crew.

The proceedings dragged on for twenty-five years, with periodic hearings over wide intervals of time and in widely separated places. In the end Luis Colón, wastrel grandson of Columbus, was conceded a dukedom in lieu of the viceroyalty demanded in the suit. Meanwhile descendants of Martín Pinzón were granted a coat of arms by the emperor Charles V in belated recognition of Pinzón's contribution to the Discovery.

Thus but for the court records of the *Pleitos* the knowledge of Pinzón's great role would have vanished forever. Aside from those records the documentary history of the Pinzón family is scanty.

Traditionally 1441 is given as the year of Martín's birth in Palos. Nothing is known of his parents, but evidently the family had been settled in the Palos area for generations. Martín and his younger brothers, Vicente Yáñez and Francisco Martín, lived together in a large house on Calle de la Nuestra Señora de la Rábida, the main street of Palos. Presumably they had inherited the house together with a *finca*, or farm estate, located upriver near Moguer.

Over the years Pinzón built up a prosperous deep-sea shipping business in which his brothers participated. His ships—he owned as many as three at a time—ranged far into the Atlantic and Mediterranean, particularly in the Guinea trade down the West African coast.

Las Casas, whose father later accompanied Columbus on the second voyage in 1493, described the Pinzón brothers as "wealthy mariners and principal persons to whom nearly everyone in their town deferred." And Martín Pinzón, he went on, was the "chief and most wealthy and most honored, very courageous and well versed in matters of the sea."

But it is in abundant testimony presented in the *Pleitos* that the full measure of Pinzón's influence in his community is realized. Witness after witness, without a dissenting voice, told of the admiration and respect in which he was held by his fellow citizens as a sea captain and as a civic leader. And it was precisely Pinzón's influence in the Tinto-Odiel *comarca* that was to be decisive in the discovery of America.

The declaration of Francisco Medel, *regidor* (magistrate) of Huelva, made in Seville in 1535, is typical of many:

> The said Martín Alonso Pinzón was very knowledgeable in the art of navigation in all the seas and was a man than whom in all the kingdom there was no other more courageous in warfare nor more determined . . . for whatever he set his mind to, and at times he had one ship and at others two or three and this witness saw that he had them . . . and he had many honorable relatives and friends and superb equipment . . . to make the said discovery.

From the *Pleitos* we learn the name of Pinzón's wife, María Alvarez, but little else about her. She was probably the daughter of one of the deep-sea mariners of Palos who formed an elite fraternity in a town devoted to the sea. The men who sailed the swift caravels of Andalusía to the far ports of Europe and Africa considered themselves a cut above the humbler fishermen whose daily forays into salt water were confined to the immediate area.

The couple were probably married in 1469, when Pinzón was about twenty-eight. This may be inferred from the testimony of their eldest son, Arias Pérez Pinzón, who was forty-five years old when he testified in 1515.

The world in which Martín and María began their married life was not a tranquil one. Palos was a tough little frontier seaport in a turbulent land. Andalusía was the bloody battleground for the hatreds and ambitions of feudal nobles who maintained private armies and even fleets of war. Bands of robbers nested in strongholds in the mountains and made periodic forays on villages and towns, returning with impunity to their lairs. Also, along the Andalusían coast the towns were prey to raids by Moslem corsairs from North Africa. The area around Palos, situated at the head of the estuary of the Saltés, an open door to the ocean, was particularly vulnerable to forays.

According to tradition in Palos, Pinzón's two younger brothers continued to live with him on Calle de la Rábida after María moved in as a bride, and she kept house for all three. At the end of her first confinement she and Martín, attired in their Sabbath best and accompanied by two sponsors, carried their infant son to the baptismal font in the church of San Jorge, where a friar from the monastery of La Rábida solemnly christened him Arias Pérez Pinzón. In subsequent years came Juan Martín, Catalina, Diego Martín, Mayor, Leonor, and Francisco Martín.

Most of the children were reasonably healthy, but there was a distressing exception. One of the little girls—which one is not known—was subject to violent convulsions. Her malady was diagnosed as the dreaded *gota coral*—epilepsy in its most acute form. This melancholy ordeal in the married life of the Pinzóns is revealed in a curious document brought to light by the Spanish historian Navarrete. Couched in archaic Castilian legalese, it is a mandate issued by Ferdinand and Isabella on December 5, 1500, ordering the authorities of Palos to act on a petition by Arias Pérez Pinzón that his brothers be compelled to take their turns in caring for their epileptic sister in their respective homes.

Martín and María had been married five years when the wretched reign of Enrique IV, the last of the Trasámara dynasty, which had ruled Castile for a hundred years, ended with his death in Madrid in 1474. The throne was seized immediately by his young half sister Isabella and Prince Ferdinand of Aragon, whom she had secretly married five years before. Isabella had the support of a powerful faction of Castilian nobles who were profoundly disturbed by the moral degeneracy of Enrique's court.

Their accession precipitated a war with Portugal, whose king, Afonso V, claimed the Castilian throne on behalf of his niece, Juana. Afonso sent an invading army into Castile to enforce her claim, but it was routed by the forces of Ferdinand and Isabella in a battle on the Duero River in 1476.

Afonso did not attempt a second invasion, but the war continued at sea with singular ferocity. Martín Pinzón and his fellow seamen of Palos were in the forefront of the naval fighting that ranged up and down the Atlantic coast from Lisbon to Guinea in West Africa. In the *Pleitos* a number of witnesses testified to Pinzón's personal prowess. Commanding his own ship on privateering expeditions, he won the admiration of his contemporaries by his valor and daring.

"At the time of the war with Portugal, all the Portuguese feared him because each day he captured some of them," declared Gonzalo Martín of Huelva in his deposition in 1532. Fernando Iáñes Montiel, also of Huelva, said that "he knew very well the said Martín Alonso Pinzón and he was the most valorous man in all this land and with his ship he was feared by the Portuguese." Ferrán Yáñez described Pinzón as being "as courageous a man as there was in this land . . . and there was no Portuguese ship that dared face him."

Because of past irritations the fighting was especially bitter. The Spanish seamen resented the Portuguese claim to a monopoly of the African trade; the Portuguese were incensed by the Spaniards' incursions into what they considered their exclusive domain. The war finally ended with the Treaty of Alcáçovas in September 1479. Afonso gave up his claim to the Castilian throne; Ferdinand and Isabella recognized the exclusive right of the Portuguese to West African trade.

This last provision put a severe crimp in the economy of Palos. The shipowners and their crews henceforth had to depend largely on less lucrative trade with the Canaries and with Mediterranean and northern European ports.

So things went until one day in the winter of 1484–85 an indigent foreigner appeared at the gate of the monastery of La Rábida and begged for bread and water for his small son. It was a minor event that later was to have unimaginable consequences for Pinzón and for the whole world: the stranger was Christopher Columbus.

It was probably two or three years after this that María died and Pinzón took a second wife, Catalina Alonso, who was hated by her new stepchildren. There is no surviving record as such either of María's death or of the second marriage. But both events are implicit in two curious documents in the royal archives of Spain, both bearing the same date and marking another intervention by the Catholic sovereigns in the Pinzón family affairs.

They were discovered by the American scholar Alicia B. Gould y Quincy in the archive of Simancas. Both documents, signed by Ferdinand and Isabella, bear the date October 12, 1493, exactly one year after the discovery of America and six and a half months after the death of Pinzón. The first is a mandate to the authorities of Palos to take appropriate action on a petition by five of the Pinzón children—Arias Pérez, Juan Martín, Mayor, Catalina, and Leonor—to have their stepmother evicted from the family home. The second, directed to the woman herself, instructs her to comply with the wishes of the Pinzón heirs or show cause to the royal magistrates in Palos why she should not.

Thus when Pinzón first met Columbus some time in the latter half of 1491, the Pinzón household, with an epileptic daughter and with a second wife at swords' points with her stepchildren, was anything but happy.

Columbus had spent six bitter years, much of the time in dire poverty, trying to persuade the sovereigns to underwrite his expedition. They were mildly interested, but they were engaged in a costly war with the kingdom of Granada, the last stronghold of the Moors in Spain. Moreover, a commission appointed to examine Columbus's proposal, headed by the queen's most trusted adviser, Father Talavera, reported on it unfavorably. The queen informed Columbus he could not count on royal support.

Heartsick, Columbus returned to La Rábida, where, several years earlier, he had been too poor to care for his son and had left him in the care of the monks. He was determined to try his fortunes in France. But the guardian of the monastery, Father Juan Pérez, had become interested in the project and persuaded him to delay his departure until a new appeal could be made to the queen. Father Pérez at one time had been a *contador* (accountant) in the queen's household and had served as her confessor.

It is clear from testimony in the *Pleitos* that the new application to the queen was contingent on inducing Martín Pinzón to join the enterprise. The shrewd priest must have suspected that a weak point in Columbus's case was the lack of an experienced navigator and fleet organizer.

Unfortunately, at the moment Pinzón was on a voyage to Italy with a cargo of sardines. Once there, he and his twenty-one-year-old son, Arias Pérez, visited Rome and were taken on a tour of the library of Pope Innocent VIII. Their host is described as a "familiar" of the pope and an old acquaintance of Pinzón. He is not otherwise identified, but it is likely that he had once been a monk àt La Rábida.

In the *Pleitos* the legal battery for the Crown made much of this visit of the Pinzóns to the Vatican in attempting to prove that Pinzón and not Columbus had initiated the voyage of discovery. Responding to Question XI in the interrogatory of October 15, 1515, Arias testified to the conversation he and his father had had with the papal servant, whom he described as a "great cosmographer."

"And there this witness and his said father were informed of these lands that awaited discovery," Arias continued. He further said that his father was so impressed by the evidence of undiscovered lands that he was determined to go in search of them himself.

There is a great deal of eyewitness testimony relating to the first meeting between Columbus and Pinzón on the latter's return from Italy. Typical was that of Hernando de Villareal, who said that he "knows that on arrival of the said Martín Alonso from Rome, the said Admiral [Columbus] reached an agreement with him and the said Admiral sent to court a friar of La Rábida and he made relation thereof to Their Highnesses. . . ."

The evidence in the *Pleitos* dovetails with the accounts of the renewed negotiations between Columbus and the sovereigns as related by Father Las Casas and Ferdinand Columbus in their respective histories. Father Pérez wrote to the queen from La Rábida. His letter was so effective that she replied within two weeks, summoning both Pérez and Columbus to the royal encampment of Santa Fe on the *vega*, or lowland, of Granada, where the Spanish armies were besieging the Alhambra. The queen sent 20,000 maravedis (about $140) to Columbus so he could shed his threadbare clothes and make a decent appearance at court.

The Alhambra surrendered on January 2, 1492. Three and a half months later the monarchs signed the Capitulations of Santa Fe, authorizing the voyage and making extraordinary grants of titles and perquisites to Columbus. By a stroke of their pens the erstwhile Knight of the Ragged Cape, as some of the courtiers had scoffingly dubbed Columbus in his years of travail, was transformed into the Very Magnificent Lord, Don Cristóbal Colón, Admiral of the Ocean Sea. Along with the Capitulations the sovereigns issued a directive to the town authorities of Palos to furnish and equip two caravels and to supply the necessary manpower for them.

Columbus returned in triumph to Palos, and the royal directives were read in the church plaza to a small knot of Palos officialdom. Unfortunately for Columbus, his new admiral's uniform and the decrees from the sovereigns did little for him in the jaundiced eyes of the local citizens. To them he was still the indigent foreigner without money or credit who was trying to force them to go on a desperate journey to God knew where.

To Alonso Pardo, town notary of Moguer, fell the task of seeking two caravels in accordance with the royal mandate. He managed to commandeer a couple of ships of dubious vintage whose owners were either unlucky or indifferent. Pardo, a witness years later in the Columbus family litigation, testified that "this witness saw that everyone scorned the said Christopher Columbus and believed he would die and everyone who went with him."

The hostile state of mind of the people of Palos is abundantly revealed in uncontroverted testimony presented in the *Pleitos*. Witness after witness, in interrogatories taken over a period of twenty years and in widely separated places, testified to the universal lack of confidence in Columbus when he tried to man and equip the fleet on his own.

"Everyone said the enterprise of the said Don Cristóbal was vain and they made a mockery of it," declared Martín Gonzalo Bisochero in the 1515 hearing in Moguer.

The villagers' hostility toward Columbus was even confirmed by witnesses sympathetic to Diego Columbus. One of them was Juan Rodríguez de Cabezudo, a Moguer farmer who had rented a donkey to Columbus when the latter went to court after his first interview with Pinzón. "Many persons made fun of the said Admiral," Cabezudo testified. "They . . . even reproached this witness for lending him a mule and publicly they scorned the enterprise."

Week after week the embargoed caravels swung idly at anchor in the Rio Tinto while Columbus strove in vain to enlist a crew. Apparently he must have given the sovereigns the idea that the villagers' stolid resistance portended a full-scale revolt. On June 20, nearly a month after the reading of the ordinance impounding the caravels, Their Highnesses sent a stern letter to the Palos authorities ordering Columbus's ships manned by any means necessary. And they sent an officer of the royal household named Juan de Peñalosa to see that the order was carried out. At the same time the *alcaide* (governor) of the castle was summarily ousted and replaced by the *corregidor* (royal magistrate), Juan de Cepeda, who armed it to repel any rebellion.

These drastic measures only hardened the passive resistance of the villagers. The boycott was complete.

The reader may well wonder whatever happened to the understanding Columbus had reached with Pinzón. The question has never been satisfactorily answered. There is only one reasonable conclusion: with the mandates of the sovereigns in hand, Columbus had decided he had no need for Pinzón's collaboration, no necessity to share the glory and profits of the expedition. Professor Manuel Sales Ferre of the University of Seville, who did extensive research in the transcripts of the *Pleitos*, believes the boycott was actively abetted by a resentful Pinzón, who used his powerful influence in the community to thwart Columbus at every turn. Thus the enterprise was caught in a riptide of contention between two stubborn wills—the one armed with the authority of the Crown, the other with Pinzón's moral authority in the *comarca*.

In the end Columbus had to go to Pinzón. Father Pérez was probably an active mediator in the impasse. Once Columbus had accepted the reality that all the king's horses and all the king's men couldn't put together a crew for him, there remained the task of winning Pinzón to a reconciliation. This probably was not as difficult as it might seem. Pinzón was now fifty years old, well past the life expectancy of those days. Undoubtedly he yearned for one more great adventure to crown his distinguished maritime career. Even more compelling, perhaps, was his longing to escape from his unhappy household.

It is not difficult to imagine the scene as the two protagonists faced each other, Columbus now conciliatory and expansive in his promises, Pinzón dour and still suspicious as he stated his conditions for undertaking the voyage. What were those conditions? No one knows for sure. If there was a written agreement, it has not survived. However, there was considerable testimony by witnesses in the *Pleitos* on this point.

The import of the sworn evidence is that the two partners agreed to share equally the rewards of the expedition. Obviously such an understanding could relate only to the material profits and not to grants of high office made to Columbus by the sovereigns.

The eldest of the Pinzón sons, Arias Pérez and Juan Martín, testified that Columbus had pledged half. So did Diego Hernández Colmenero, who after the voyage married Pinzón's daughter Catalina. Their testimony might be considered suspect because of their close relationship. On the other hand, unless one makes the gratuitous assumption that they were lying, who would be in a better position to know the facts than the immediate members of the Pinzón family?

However, there was strong corroboration from other witnesses. Alonso Gallego of Huelva said he heard Columbus tell Pinzón: "Señor Martín Alonso we will go on this voyage and if God grants that we discover land, I promise you . . . I will share with you as I would my own brother." Gallego added that he heard Columbus make that pledge "many times." Francisco Medel, *regidor* (alderman) of Huelva, testified that "Martín Alonso Pinzón said to this witness that Columbus agreed . . . to give him all that he asked for and wanted."

Father Las Casas, who was strongly partial to Columbus, nevertheless has left a fair assessment of the situation. "Christopher Columbus began his negotiation with Martín Alonso Pinzón," Las Casas wrote in the *Historia de las Indias*,

> begging that he come with him and bring along his brothers and relatives and friends and without doubt he made some promises because no one is moved except in his own interest. . . . We believe that Martín Alonso principally and his brothers aided Christopher Columbus greatly . . . because of their wealth and abundant credit, mainly Martín Alonso Pinzón who was very courageous and well experienced in seamanship . . .
> . . . And as Christopher Columbus had left the court in a very needy condition . . . it appears from accounts of expenses

made before a notary public in the said town of Palos that the
said Martín Alonso . . . himself advanced to Christopher Columbus a half million [maravedis], or he and his brothers . . .

With the decisive intervention of Pinzón, most of Columbus's difficulties vanished. Time was short if the expedition was to sail that
summer, and the energetic Pinzón went all out in organizing the voyage. He discarded the embargoed caravels and substituted two of his
own choice, the *Pinta* and the *Niña*. For a third vessel he and Columbus chartered a somewhat larger ship from the Bay of Biscay that happened to be in the Palos harbor with her owner, Juan de la Cosa of
Santona. Columbus chose her for his flagship. Although she has gone
down in history by the name *Santa María*, Columbus himself never referred to her by that name in his *Journal of the First Voyage*, invariably calling her *La Capitana*, or "the flagship."

With the ships in hand, Pinzón began the task of manning them.
His recruiting was little short of spectacular. He had a vast reservoir of
friends and relatives in the *comarca*, most of them seamen. When
word got out that the Pinzón brothers themselves would sail on the
voyage, many volunteers came to the recruiting table.

But Pinzón didn't leave it at that. He went up and down the little
main street and the waterfront of Palos, exhorting his fellow citizens
with all the fervor of a street evangelist. "Friends, you are in misery
here; go with us on this journey," he exclaimed to the men who gathered around him. "We will, with the aid of God, discover land in
which, according to report, we will find houses with roofs of gold and
everything of wealth and good adventure."

This lively eyewitness account of Pinzón's recruiting was given in a
deposition by Fernan Iáñes Montiel of Huelva. Alonso Gallego testified that Pinzón advanced money out of his own pocket to some of the
families of the sailors he induced to go on the voyage so they would not
be in need.

In the faint light of predawn on August 3, 1492, the little fleet glided
slowly down the Tinto toward the wide ocean and its rendezvous with
history. Columbus commanded the flagship, Martín Pinzón the *Pinta*,
and Vicente Pinzón the *Niña*, smallest of the three.

Twice during the outward crossing Pinzón again came to the rescue
of the expedition. As the voyage grew longer and longer a crisis oc-

curred on the flagship. A disgruntled and fearful crew openly threatened a mutiny.

Testimony concerning this episode is copious and explicit, much of it bearing an air of credibility. The consensus is that it was Martín Pinzón who silenced the grumblers and encouraged Columbus to continue the voyage. One of the most circumstantial of the many witnesses was Hernán Péres Mateos, a veteran pilot of Palos and a cousin of the Pinzóns, who said:

> . . . Having sailed many days and not discovered land those who came with the said Colón wanted to rebel . . . saying they would be lost and the said Colón told the said Martín Alonso what went on and asked what he should do and the said Martín Alonso Pinzón responded: "Señor, your grace should hang a half dozen or throw them into the sea and if you do not venture to do so I and my brothers will come alongside and do it for you, that the fleet which left with the mandate of such exalted princes should not return without good news."

Probably Pinzón bellowed his advice from the rail of his own ship in the hearing of everyone on the flagship. Whatever threat of mutiny may have existed promptly subsided. Mateos added that he had the story of the crisis from the Pinzóns themselves.

Perhaps even more important was the testimony of Francisco García Vallejos of Palos, who was a seaman on the *Pinta*.

"The said Admiral conferred with all the captains," Vallejos explained, "and with the said Martín Alonso Pinzón and said to them 'What shall we do?' [This was the sixth day of October of 92.] 'Captains, what shall we do since my people complain so bitterly to me? How does it appear to you that we should proceed?' And then said Vicente Yáñez [Pinzón]: 'We should keep on, Señor, for two thousand leagues and if by then we have not found what we have come to seek, we can turn back from there.' And then responded Martín Alonso Pinzón 'How, Señor? We have only just left and already your grace is fretting. Onward, Señor, that God may give us the victory in discovering land; never would God wish that we turn back so shamefully.' Then responded the said Admiral: 'Blessings on thee.' "

After the crisis had ended on the flagship and the *Pinta* had resumed her usual position far in advance of the other ships, Pinzón wondered if their due westerly course along the 28th parallel was the right one. Then, as sunset approached on October 6, there came a clear indication: birds.

They were land birds that foraged at sea by day and nested on shore at night, and they were flying over the caravel on what appeared to be a homing course—but not in the direction in which the ship was going. They were on the port side, headed southwesterly.

Pinzón reduced sail and waited for the flagship to catch up. As Columbus came alongside, Pinzón shouted his advice for a change of course toward the south. Columbus demurred and that night stubbornly adhered to his westerly course. But the next day he changed his mind and signaled a divergence toward the southwest. Columbus's journal entry for October 6 mentions Pinzón's advice and his rejection of it. The October 7 entry records the change of course, but characteristically it is now Columbus's own idea.

Pinzón's initiative in urging a change of course was confirmed by Seaman Vallejos of the *Pinta* in his testimony later in the *Pleitos*. Vallejos's version differs in minor detail from that of Columbus:

> He [the witness] knows and saw that [Pinzón] said on the said voyage: "It appears to me and my heart tells me that if we deviate toward the southwest we will find land sooner" and that then responded the said admiral don xtóbal colón "Be it so . . . that we shall do" and that immediately as suggested . . . they changed a quarter to the southwest . . .

Within five days after the change of course the fleet made its landfall on the tiny island of Guanahani in the outer Bahamas.

Had it continued due west along the 28th parallel, the voyage would have required many more days to reach the coast of what is now Florida. There is a good question whether the crews' patience would have endured that long.

Pinzón was mortally ill when the fleet returned to Palos on March 15, 1493. He was borne from his ship to the Pinzón family estate near Moguer, where he could rest in seclusion. But he wanted to spend his last days in the sacred precincts of the monastery of La Rábida among his friends the monks. Sorrowing relatives and friends bore him to the sanctuary of his wish, and there he died in the waning days of March.

2

The Puritans and Sex

EDMUND S. MORGAN

• In 1630, after an arduous Atlantic crossing aboard the Arabella, John Winthrop and a small band of followers established the Massachusetts Bay Colony. In their "Holy Commonwealth" the Puritans emphasized hard work, severe discipline, and rigid self-examination and self-denial. Ministers had great political influence in the theocratic government, and profanation of the Sabbath day, blasphemy, fornication, drunkenness, and participation in games of chance or theatrical performances were among their many penal offenses. Even today the term "puritanical" suggests narrow-mindedness and excessive strictness in matters of morals and religion. Yet, as Daniel Boorstin and others have observed, the Puritans were not simply an ascetic group of fanatics who prohibited all earthly pleasures. Actually the severity of their code of behavior has frequently been exaggerated. The Puritans were subject to normal human desires and weaknesses, and they recognized that "the use of the marriage bed" is "founded in Man's nature." Moreover, numerous cases of fornication and adultery in the law courts of New England belie the notion that all Puritans lived up to their rigid moral ideology. In the following essay, Professor Edmund S. Morgan cites numerous examples of men and women, youths and maids, whose natural urges recognized no legal limits. In viewing their enforcement of laws and their judgments of human frailty, we may find that the Puritans do not always conform to their conventional stereotype as over-precise moralists.

Henry Adams once observed that Americans have "ostentatiously ignored" sex. He could think of only two American writers who touched upon the subject with any degree of boldness—Walt Whit-

From *New England Quarterly*, XV (1942), 591–607. Reprinted by permission of the author and the publisher.

man and Bret Harte. Since the time when Adams made this pene-
trating observation, American writers have been making up for lost
time in a way that would make Bret Harte, if not Whitman, blush.
And yet there is still more truth than falsehood in Adams's statement.
Americans, by comparison with Europeans or Asiatics, are squeamish
when confronted with the facts of life. My purpose is not to account
for this squeamishness, but simply to point out that the Puritans, those
bogeymen of the modern intellectual, are not responsible for it.

At the outset, consider the Puritans' attitude toward marriage and
the role of sex in marriage. The popular assumption might be that
the Puritans frowned on marriage and tried to hush up the physical
aspect of it as much as possible, but listen to what they themselves
had to say. Samuel Willard, minister of the Old South Church in the
latter part of the seventeenth century and author of the most complete textbook of Puritan divinity, more than once expressed his horror at "that Popish conceit of the Excellency of Virginity." Another
minister, John Cotton, wrote that

> Women are Creatures without which there is no comfortable
> Living for man: it is true of them what is wont to be said of
> Governments, *That bad ones are better than none*: They are a
> sort of Blasphemers then who dispise and decry them, and call
> them *a necessary Evil*, for they are *a necessary Good*.

These sentiments did not arise from an interpretation of marriage as
a spiritual partnership, in which sexual intercourse was a minor or
incidental matter. Cotton gave his opinion of "Platonic love" when
he recalled the case of

> one who immediately upon marriage, without ever approaching
> the *Nuptial Bed*, indented with the *Bride*, that by mutual con-
> sent they might both live such a life, and according did seques-
> tring themselves according to the custom of those times, from
> the rest of mankind, and afterwards from one another too, in
> their retired Cells, giving themselves up to a Contemplative life;
> and this is recorded as an instance of no little or ordinary Ver-
> tue; but I must be pardoned in it, if I can account it no other

than an effort of blind zeal, for they are the dictates of a blind
mind they follow therein, and not of that Holy Spirit, which
saith *It is not good that man should be alone.*

Here is as healthy an attitude as one could hope to find anywhere.
Cotton certainly cannot be accused of ignoring human nature. Nor
was he an isolated example among the Puritans. Another minister
stated plainly that "the Use of the Marriage Bed" is "founded in mans
Nature," and that consequently any withdrawal from sexual intercourse
upon the part of husband or wife "Denies all reliefe in Wedlock vnto
Human necessity: and sends it for supply vnto Beastiality when God
gives not the gift of Continency." In other words, sexual intercourse
was a human necessity and marriage the only proper supply for it.
These were the views of the New England clergy, the acknowledged
leaders of the community, the most Puritanical of the Puritans. As
proof that their congregations concurred with them, one may cite the
case in which the members of the First Church of Boston expelled
James Mattock because, among other offenses, "he denied Coniugall
fellowship vnto his wife for the space of 2 years together vpon pretense
of taking Revenge upon himself for his abusing of her before mar-
ryage." So strongly did the Puritans insist upon the sexual character
of marriage that one New Englander considered himself slandered
when it was reported, "that he Brock his deceased wife's hart with
Greife, that he would be absent from her 3 weeks together when he
was at home, and wold never come nere her, and such· Like."

There was just one limitation which the Puritans placed upon sexual relations in marriage: sex must not interfere with religion. Man's
chief end was to glorify God, and all earthly delights must promote
that end, not hinder it. Love for a wife was carried too far when it led
a man to neglect his God:

> . . . sometimes a man hath a good affection to Religion, but the
> love of his wife carries him away, a man may bee so transported
> to his wife, that hee dare not bee forward in Religion, lest hee
> displease his wife, and so the wife, lest shee displease her hus-
> band, and this is an inordinate love, when it exceeds measure.

Sexual pleasures, in this respect, were treated like other kinds of
pleasure. On a day of fast, when all comforts were supposed to be

foregone in behalf of religious contemplation, not only were tasty food and drink to be abandoned but sexual intercourse, too. On other occasions, when food, drink, and recreation were allowable, sexual intercourse was allowable too, though of course only between persons who were married to each other. The Puritans were not ascetics; they never wished to prevent the enjoyment of earthly delights. They merely demanded that the pleasures of the flesh be subordinated to the greater glory of God: husband and wife must not become "so transported with affection, that they look at no higher end than marriage it self." "Let such as have wives," said the ministers, "look at them not for their own ends, but to be fitted for Gods service, and bring them nearer to God."

Toward sexual intercourse outside marriage the Puritans were as frankly hostile as they were favorable to it in marriage. They passed laws to punish adultery with death, and fornication with whipping. Yet they had no misconceptions as to the capacity of human beings to obey such laws. Although the laws were commands of God, it was only natural—since the fall of Adam—for human beings to break them. Breaches must be punished lest the community suffer the wrath of God, but no offense, sexual or otherwise, could be occasion for surprise or for hushed tones of voice. How calmly the inhabitants of seventeenth-century New England could contemplate rape or attempted rape is evident in the following testimony offered before the Middlesex County Court of Massachusetts:

> The examination of Edward Wire taken the 7th of october and alsoe Zachery Johnson. who sayeth that Edward Wires mayd being sent into the towne about busenes meeting with a man that dogd hir from about Joseph Kettles house to goody marshes. She came into William Johnsones and desired Zachery Johnson to goe home with her for that the man dogd hir. accordingly he went with her and being then as far as Samuell Phips his house the man over tooke them. which man caled himselfe by the name of peter grant would have led the mayd but she oposed itt three times: and coming to Edward Wires house the said grant would have kist hir but she refused itt: wire being at prayer grant dragd the mayd between the said wiers and Nathanill frothinghams house. hee then flung the mayd downe in the streete and got atop hir; Johnson seeing it hee caled vppon the fellow to be sivill and not abuse the mayd then Edward wire came forth and ran to the said grant and took hold of him asking him what he did

to his mayd, the said grant asked whether she was his wife for
he did nothing to his wife: the said grant swearing he would
be the death of the said wire. when he came of the mayd; he
swore he would bring ten men to pul down his house and soe ran
away and they followed him as far as good[y] phipses house
where they mett with John Terry and George Chin with clubs in
there hands and soe they went away together. Zachy Johnson
going to Constable Heamans, and wire going home. there came
John Terry to his house to ask for beer and grant was in the
streete but afterward departed into the towne, both Johnson and
Wire both aferme that when grant was vppon the mayd she
cryed out severall times.

Deborah hadlocke being examined sayth that she mett with
the man that cals himselfe peeter grant about good prichards
that he dogd hir and followed hir to hir masters and there threw
hir downe and lay vppon hir but had not the use of hir body but
swore several othes that he would ly with hir and gett hir with
child before she got home.

Grant being present denys all saying he was drunk and did not
know what he did.

The Puritans became inured to sexual offenses, because there were
so many. The impression which one gets from reading the records of
seventeenth-century New England courts is that illicit sexual intercourse was fairly common. The testimony given in cases of fornication and adultery—by far the most numerous class of criminal cases in
the records—suggests that many of the early New Englanders possessed a high degree of virility and very few inhibitions. Besides the
case of Peter Grant, take the testimony of Elizabeth Knight about the
manner of Richard Nevars's advances toward her:

The last publique day of Thanksgiving (in the year 1674) in
the evening as I was milking Richard Nevars came to me, and
offered me abuse in putting his hand, under my coates, but I
turning aside with much adoe, saved my self, and when I was
settled to milking he agen took me by the shoulder and pulled
me backward almost, but I clapped one hand on the Ground and
held fast the Cows teatt with the other hand, and cryed out, and
then came to mee Jonathan Abbot one of my Masters Servants,
whome the said Never asked wherefore he came, the said Abbot
said to look after you, what you doe unto the Maid, but the said
Never bid Abbot goe about his businesse but I bade the lad to
stay.

One reason for the abundance of sexual offenses was the number of men in the colonies who were unable to gratify their sexual desires in marriage. Many of the first settlers had wives in England. They had come to the new world to make a fortune, expecting either to bring their families after them or to return to England with some of the riches of America. Although these men left their wives behind, they brought their sexual appetites with them; and in spite of laws which required them to return to their families, they continued to stay, and more continued to arrive, as indictments against them throughout the seventeenth century clearly indicate.

Servants formed another group of men, and of women too, who could not ordinarily find supply for human necessity within the bounds of marriage. Most servants lived in the homes of their masters and could not marry without their consent, a consent which was not likely to be given unless the prospective husband or wife also belonged to the master's household. This situation will be better understood if it is recalled that most servants at this time were engaged by contract for a stated period. They were, in the language of the time, "covenant servants," who had agreed to stay with their masters for a number of years in return for a specified recompense, such as transportation to New England or education in some trade (the latter, of course, were known more specifically as apprentices). Even hired servants who worked for wages were usually single, for as soon as a man had enough money to buy or build a house of his own and to get married, he would set up in farming or trade for himself. It must be emphasized, however, that anyone who was not in business for himself was necessarily a servant. The economic organization of seventeenth-century New England had no place for the independent proletarian workman with a family of his own. All production was carried on in the household by the master of the family and his servants, so that most men were either servants or masters of servants; and the former, of course, were more numerous than the latter. Probably most of the inhabitants of Puritan New England could remember a time when they had been servants.

Theoretically no servant had a right to a private life. His time, day or night, belonged to his master, and both religion and law required that he obey his master scrupulously. But neither religion nor law could restrain the sexual impulses of youth, and if those impulses could not be expressed in marriage, they had to be given vent outside marriage. Servants had little difficulty in finding the occasions. Though they might be kept at work all day, it was easy enough to slip away at night. Once out of the house, there were several ways of meeting with a maid. The simplest way was to go to her bedchamber, if she was so fortunate as to have a private one of her own. Thus Jock, Mr. Solomon Phipps's Negro man, confessed in court

> that on the sixteenth day of May 1682, in the morning, betweene 12 and one of the clock, he did force open the back doores of the House of Laurence Hammond in Charlestowne, and came in to the House, and went up into the garret to Marie the Negro.
>
> He doth likewise acknowledge that one night the last week he forced into the House the same way, and went up to the Negro Woman Marie and that the like he hath done at severall other times before.

Joshua Fletcher took a more romantic way of visiting his lady:

> Joshua Fletcher . . . doth confesse and acknowledge that three severall nights, after bedtime, he went into Mr Fiskes Dwelling house at Chelmsford, at an open window by a ladder that he brought with him the said windo opening into a chamber, whose was the lodging place of Gresill Juell servant to mr. Fiske. and there he kept company with the said mayd. she sometimes having her cloathes on, and one time he found her in her bed.

Sometimes a maidservant might entertain callers in the parlor while the family were sleeping upstairs. John Knight described what was perhaps a common experience for masters. The crying of his child awakened him in the middle of the night, and he called to his maid, one Sarah Crouch, who was supposed to be sleeping with the child. Receiving no answer, he arose and

> went downe the stayres, and at the stair foot, the latch of doore was pulled in. I called severall times and at the last said if shee would not open the dore, I would breake it open, and when she opened the doore shee was all undressed and Sarah Largin with her undressed, also the said Sarah went out of doores and Dropped some of her clothes as shee went out. I enquired of Sarah Crouch what men they were, which was with them. Shee made mee no answer for some space of time, but at last shee told me Peeter Brigs was with them, I asked her whether Thomas Jones was not there, but shee would give mee no answer.

In the temperate climate of New England it was not always necessary
to seek out a maid at her home. Rachel Smith was seduced in an open
field "about nine of the clock at night, being darke, neither moone nor
starrs shineing." She was walking through the field when she met a
man who

> asked her where shee lived, and what her name was and shee told
> him. and then shee asked his name, and he told her Saijing that
> he was old Good-man Shepards man. Also shee saith he gave her
> strong liquors, and told her that it was not the first time he had
> been with maydes after his master was in bed.

Sometimes, of course, it was not necessary for a servant to go outside his master's house in order to satisfy his sexual urges. Many cases
of fornication are on record between servants living in the same house.
Even where servants had no private bedroom, even where the whole
family slept in a single room, it was not impossible to make love. In
fact many love affairs must have had their consummation upon a bed
in which other people were sleeping. Take for example the case of
Sarah Lepingwell. When Sarah was brought into court for having an
illegitimate child, she related that one night when her master's brother,
Thomas Hawes, was visiting the family, she went to bed early. Later,
after Hawes had gone to bed, he called to her to get him a pipe of tobacco. After refusing for some time,

> at the last I arose and did lite his pipe and cam and lay doune
> one my one bead and smoaked about half the pip and siting vp
> in my bead to giue him his pip my bead being a trundell bead
> at the sid of his bead he reached beyond the pip and Cauth me
> by the wrist and pulled me on the side of his bead but I biding
> him let me goe he bid me hold my peas the folks wold here me
> and if it be replyed come why did you not call out I Ansar I was
> posesed with fear of my mastar least my mastar shold think I
> did it only to bring a scandall on his brothar and thinking thay
> wold all beare witnes agaynst me but the thing is true that he did
> then begete me with child at that tim and the Child is Thomas
> Hauses and noe mans but his.

In his defense Hawes offered the testimony of another man who was
sleeping "on the same side of the bed," but the jury nevertheless accepted Sarah's story.

The fact that Sarah was intimidated by her master's brother suggests that maidservants may have been subject to sexual abuse by their masters. The records show that sometimes masters did take advantage of their position to force unwanted attentions upon their female servants. The case of Elizabeth Dickerman is a good example. She complained to the Middlesex County Court,

> against her master John Harris senior for profiring abus to her by way of forsing her to be naught with him: . . . he has tould her that if she tould her dame: what cariag he did show to her shee had as good be hanged and shee replyed then shee would run away and he sayd run the way is befor you: . . . she says if she should liwe ther shee shall be in fear of her lif.

The court accepted Elizabeth's complaint and ordered her master to be whipped twenty stripes.

So numerous did cases of fornication and adultery become in seventeenth-century New England that the problem of caring for the children of extra-marital unions was a serious one. The Puritans solved it, but in such a way as to increase rather than decrease the temptation to sin. In 1668 the General Court of Massachusetts ordered:

> that where any man is legally convicted to be the Father of a Bastard childe, he shall be at the care and charge to maintain and bring up the same, by such assistance of the Mother as nature requireth, and as the Court from time to time (according to circumstances) shall see meet to Order: and in case the Father of a Bastard, by confession or other manifest proof, upon trial of the case, do not appear to the Courts satisfaction, then the Man charged by the Woman to be the Father, shee holding constant in it, (especially being put upon the real discovery of the truth of it in the time of her Travail) shall be the reputed Father, and accordingly be liable to the charge of maintenance as aforesaid (though not to other punishment) notwithstanding his denial, unless the circumstances of the case and pleas be such, on the behalf of the man charged, as that the Court that have the cognizance thereon shall see reason to acquit him, and otherwise dispose of the Childe and education thereof.

As a result of this law a girl could give way to temptation without the fear of having to care for an illegitimate child by herself. Furthermore, she could, by a little simple lying, spare her lover the expense of sup-

porting the child. When Elizabeth Wells bore a child, less than a year
after this statute was passed, she laid it to James Tufts, her master's
son. Goodman Tufts affirmed that Andrew Robinson, servant to Goodman Dexter, was the real father, and he brought the following testimony as evidence:

> Wee Elizabeth Jefts aged 15 ears and Mary tufts aged 14 ears
> doe testyfie that their being one at our hous sumtime the last
> winter who sayed that thear was a new law made concerning
> bastards that If aney man wear aqused with a bastard and the
> woman which had aqused him did stand vnto it in her labor that
> he should bee the reputed father of it and should mayntaine it
> Elizabeth Wells hearing of the sayd law she sayed vnto vs that
> If shee should bee with Child shee would bee sure to lay it vn to
> won who was rich enough abell to mayntayne it wheather it wear
> his or no and shee farder sayed Elizabeth Jefts would not you doe
> so likewise If it weare your case and I sayed no by no means for
> right must tacke place: and the sayd Elizabeth wells sayed If it
> wear my Caus I think I should doe so.

A tragic unsigned letter that somehow found its way into the files of
the Middlesex County Court gives more direct evidence of the practice which Elizabeth Wells professed:

> der loue i remember my loue to you hoping your welfar and i
> hop to imbras the but now i rit to you to let you nowe that i am
> a child by you and i wil ether kil it or lay it to an other and you
> shal have no blame at al for I haue had many children and none
> have none of them. . . . [*i.e.*, none of their fathers is support-
> ing any of them.]

In face of the wholesale violation of the sexual codes to which all
these cases give testimony, the Puritans could not maintain the severe penalties which their laws provided. Although cases of adultery
occurred every year, the death penalty is not known to have been
applied more than three times. The usual punishment was a whipping
or a fine, or both, and perhaps a branding, combined with a symbolical
execution in the form of standing on the gallows for an hour with a
rope about the neck. Fornication met with a lighter whipping or a
lighter fine, while rape was treated in the same way as adultery. Though
the Puritans established a code of laws which demanded perfection—

which demanded, in other words, strict obedience to the will of God, they nevertheless knew that frail human beings could never live up to the code. When fornication, adultery, rape, or even buggery and sodomy appeared, they were not surprised, nor were they so severe with the offenders as their codes of law would lead one to believe. Sodomy, to be sure, they usually punished with death; but rape, adultery, and fornication they regarded as pardonable human weaknesses, all the more likely to appear in a religious community, where the normal course of sin was stopped by wholesome laws. Governor Bradford, in recounting the details of an epidemic of sexual misdemeanors in Plymouth, wrote resignedly:

> it may be in this case as it is with waters when their streames are stopped or damned up, when they gett passage they flow with more violence, and make more noys and disturbance, then when they are suffered to rune quietly in their owne chanels. So wickednes being here more stopped by strict laws, and the same more nerly looked unto, so as it cannot rune in a comone road of liberty as it would, and is inclined, it searches every wher, and at last breaks out wher it getts vente.

The estimate of human capacities here expressed led the Puritans not only to deal leniently with sexual offenses but also to take every precaution to prevent such offenses, rather than wait for the necessity of punishment. One precaution was to see that children got married as soon as possible. The wrong way to promote virtue, the Puritans thought, was to "ensnare" children in vows of virginity, as the Catholics did. As a result of such vows, children, "not being able to contain," would be guilty of "unnatural pollutions, and other filthy practices in secret: and too oft of horrid Murthers of the fruit of their bodies," said Thomas Cobbett. The way to avoid fornication and perversion was for parents to provide suitable husbands and wives for their children:

> Lot was to blame that looked not out seasonably for some fit matches for his two daughters, which had formerly minded marriage (witness the contract between them and two men in *Sodom*, called therfore for his Sons in Law, which had married his daughters, Gen. 19. 14.) for they seeing no man like to come into them in a conjugall way . . . then they plotted that incestuous course, whereby their Father was so highly dishonoured. . . .

As marriage was the way to prevent fornication, successful marriage was the way to prevent adultery. The Puritans did not wait for adultery to appear; instead, they took every means possible to make husbands and wives live together and respect each other. If a husband deserted his wife and remained within the jurisdiction of a Puritan government, he was promptly sent back to her. Where the wife had been left in England, the offense did not always come to light until the wayward husband had committed fornication or bigamy, and of course there must have been many offenses which never came to light. But where both husband and wife lived in New England, neither had much chance of leaving the other without being returned by order of the county court at its next sitting. When John Smith of Medfield left his wife and went to live with Patience Rawlins, he was sent home poorer by ten pounds and richer by thirty stripes. Similarly Mary Drury, who deserted her husband on the pretense that he was impotent, failed to convince the court that he actually was so, and had to return to him as well as to pay a fine of five pounds. The wife of Phillip Pointing received lighter treatment: when the court thought that she had overstayed her leave in Boston, they simply ordered her "to depart the Towne and goe to Tanton to her husband." The courts, moreover, were not satisfied with mere cohabitation; they insisted that it be peaceful cohabitation. Husbands and wives were forbidden by law to strike one another, and the law was enforced on numerous occasions. But the courts did not stop there. Henry Flood was required to give bond for good behavior because he had abused his wife simply by "ill words calling her whore and cursing of her." The wife of Christopher Collins was presented for railing at her husband and calling him "Gurley gutted divill." Apparently in this case the court thought that Mistress Collins was right, for although the fact was proved by two witnesses, she was discharged. On another occasion the court favored the husband: Jacob Pudeator, fined for striking and kicking his wife, had the sentence moderated when the court was informed that she was a woman "of great provocation."

Wherever there was strong suspicion that an illicit relation might arise between two persons, the authorities removed the temptation by forbidding the two to come together. As early as November, 1630, the Court of Assistants of Massachusetts prohibited a Mr. Clark from "cohabitacion and frequent keepeing company with Mrs. Freeman, vnder

paine of such punishment as the Court shall thinke meete to inflict."
Mr. Clark and Mr. Freeman were both bound "in XX£ apeece that
Mr. Clearke shall make his personall appearance att the nexte Court
to be holden in March nexte, and in the meane tyme to carry himselfe
in good behaviour towards all people and espetially towards Mrs. Freeman, concerning whome there is stronge suspicion of incontinency."
Forty-five years later the Suffolk County Court took the same kind of
measure to protect the husbands of Dorchester from the temptations
offered by the daughter of Robert Spurr. Spurr was presented by the
grand jury

> for entertaining persons at his house at unseasonable times both
> by day and night to the greife of theire wives and Relations &c
> The Court having heard what was alleaged and testified against
> him do Sentence him to bee admonish't and to pay Fees of
> Court and charge him upon his perill not to entertain any mar-
> ried men to keepe company with his daughter especially James
> Minott and Joseph Belcher.

In like manner Walter Hickson was forbidden to keep company with
Mary Bedwell, "And if at any time hereafter hee bee taken in company of the saide Mary Bedwell without other company to bee forth-
with apprehended by the Constable and to be whip't with ten stripes."
Elizabeth Wheeler and Joanna Peirce were admonished "for theire
disorderly carriage in the house of Thomas Watts being married women
and founde sitting in other mens Laps with theire Armes about theire
Necks." How little confidence the Puritans had in human nature is
even more clearly displayed by another case, in which Edmond Mad-
dock and his wife were brought to court "to answere to all such matters
as shalbe objected against them concerning Haarkwoody and Ezekiell
Euerells being at their house at unseasonable tyme of the night and
her being up with them after her husband was gone to bed." Haarkwoody and Everell had been found "by the Constable Henry Bridg-
hame about tenn of the Clock at night sitting by the fyre at the house
of Edmond Maddocks with his wyfe a suspicious weoman her husband
being on sleepe [sic] on the bedd." A similar distrust of human ability
to resist temptation is evident in the following order of the Connecticut Particular Court:

> James Hallett is to returne from the Correction house to his master Barclyt, who is to keepe him to hard labor, and course dyet during the pleasure of the Court provided that Barclet is first to remove his daughter from his family, before the sayd James enter therein.

These precautions, as we have already seen, did not eliminate fornication, adultery, or other sexual offenses, but they doubtless reduced the number from what it would otherwise have been.

In sum, the Puritan attitude toward sex, though directed by a belief in absolute, God-given moral values, never neglected human nature. The rules of conduct which the Puritans regarded as divinely ordained had been formulated for men, not for angels and not for beasts. God had created mankind in two sexes; He had ordained marriage as desirable for all, and sexual intercourse as essential to marriage. On the other hand, He had forbidden sexual intercourse outside of marriage. These were the moral principles which the Puritans sought to enforce in New England. But in their enforcement they took cognizance of human nature. They knew well enough that human beings since the fall of Adam were incapable of obeying perfectly the laws of God. Consequently, in the endeavor to enforce those laws they treated offenders with patience and understanding, and concentrated their efforts on prevention more than on punishment. The result was not a society in which most of us would care to live, for the methods of prevention often caused serious interference with personal liberty. It must nevertheless be admitted that in matters of sex the Puritans showed none of the blind zeal or narrow-minded bigotry which is too often supposed to have been characteristic of them. The more one learns about these people, the less do they appear to have resembled the sad and sour portraits which their modern critics have drawn of them.

3

The White Indians of Colonial America

JAMES AXTELL

• Although the Indians encountered at Jamestown and at Plymouth and at a score of other sites along the East Coast were unlettered, unwashed, unclothed, and "uncivilized," the European settlers quickly discovered that they were also "of a tractable, free, and loving nature, without guile or treachery"—to quote a seventeenth-century eyewitness. These native peoples were especially open with their knowledge and experience. For example, after the first desperate winter at Plymouth, during which time half the Pilgrims died, the Indians gave the survivors food and taught them to grow corn under primitive conditions. The following November, after a bountiful harvest, the two groups jointly celebrated America's first Thanksgiving.

Initially, many of the colonists believed that the Indians were descendants of the lost tribes of Israel, and the Europeans made honest, if somewhat misguided, efforts to Christianize them. But red-white relations deteriorated rapidly during the seventeenth century. Pressed by increasing numbers and eager to provide more space for their expanding society, the white settlers pushed farther and farther inland, thus forcing the Indians to battle for their very existence. As the struggle took on more violent dimensions—King Philip's War (1675–1676) was particularly bloody—myths of the worthlessness and brutality of the Indians had to be fabricated to justify the slaughter that ensued. Past experiences contradicting the image of the Indian as a savage tended to be forgotten.

The following article by James Axtell, which suggests that the simplicity, harmony, and cooperative spirit of Indian life

From the *William and Mary Quarterly* 32 (January 1975): 55–88. Reprinted with permission from the author and the publisher.

had greater appeal to colonists than the benefits of "civilization" had to the Indians, should be read in the context of the
suspicion, fear, and contempt which the white society was beginning to feel toward the Indian. We often think of the appeal of native culture as a recent phenomenon; yet those few
European settlers who were intimately exposed to it often
chose to remain "white Indians."

The English, like their French rivals, began their colonizing ventures
in North America with a sincere interest in converting the Indians to
Christianity and civilization. Nearly all the colonial charters granted by
the English monarchs in the seventeenth century assigned the wish to
extend the Christian Church and to redeem savage souls as a principal,
if not the principal, motive for colonization. This desire was grounded
in a set of complementary beliefs about "savagism" and "civilization."
First, the English held that the Indians, however benighted, were capable of conversion. "It is not the nature of men," they believed, "but
the education of men, which make them barbarous and uncivill."
Moreover, the English were confident that the Indians would want to
be converted once they were exposed to the superior quality of English
life. The strength of these beliefs was reflected in Cotton Mather's astonishment as late as 1721 that

> Tho' they saw a People Arrive among them, who were Clothed in
> *Habits* of much more Comfort and Splendour, than what there
> was to be seen in the *Rough Skins* with which they hardly cov-
> ered themselves; and who had *Houses full of Good Things*, vastly
> out-shining their squalid and dark *Wigwams*; And they saw this
> People Replenishing their *Fields*, with *Trees* and with *Grains*,
> and useful *Animals*, which until now they had been wholly Stran-
> gers to; yet they did not seem touch'd in the least, with any *Am-
> bition* to come at such Desireable Circumstances, or with any
> *Curiosity* to enquire after the *Religion* that was attended with
> them.

The second article of the English faith followed from their fundamental belief in the superiority of civilization, namely, that no civilized
person in possession of his faculties or free from undue restraint would
choose to become an Indian. "For, easy and unconstrained as the sav-

age life is," wrote the Reverend William Smith of Philadelphia, "certainly it could never be put in competition with the blessings of improved life and the light of religion, by any persons who have had the happiness of enjoying, and the capacity of discerning, them."

And yet, by the close of the colonial period, very few if any Indians had been transformed into civilized Englishmen. Most of the Indians who were educated by the English—some contemporaries thought *all* of them—returned to Indian society at the first opportunity to resume their Indian identities. On the other hand, large numbers of Englishmen had chosen to become Indians—by running away from colonial society to join Indian society, by not trying to escape after being captured, or by electing to remain with their Indian captors when treaties of peace periodically afforded them the opportunity to return home.

Perhaps the first colonist to recognize the disparity between the English dream and the American reality was Cadwallader Colden, surveyor-general and member of the King's council of New York. In his *History of the Five Indian Nations of Canada*, published in London in 1747, Colden described the Albany peace treaty between the French and the Iroquois in 1699, when "few of [the French captives] could be persuaded to return" to Canada. Lest his readers attribute this unusual behavior to "the Hardships they had endured in their own Country, under a tyrannical Government and a barren Soil," he quickly added that "the *English* had as much Difficulty to persuade the People, that had been taken Prisoners by the *French Indians*, to leave the *Indian* Manner of living, though no People enjoy more Liberty, and live in greater Plenty, than the common Inhabitants of *New-York* do." Colden, clearly amazed, elaborated:

> No Arguments, no Intreaties, nor Tears of their Friends and Relations, could persuade many of them to leave their new *Indian* Friends and Acquaintance[s]; several of them that were by the Caressings of their Relations persuaded to come Home, in a little Time grew tired of our Manner of living, and run away again to the *Indians*, and ended their Days with them. On the other Hand, *Indian* Children have been carefully educated among the *English*, cloathed and taught, yet, I think, there is not one Instance, that any of these, after they had Liberty to go among their own People, and were come to Age, would remain with the *English*, but returned to their own Nations, and became as fond of the *Indian* Manner of Life as those that knew nothing of a

civilized Manner of living. What I now tell of Christian Prisoners among *Indians* [he concluded his history], relates not only to what happened at the Conclusion of this War, but has been found true on many other Occasions.

Colden was not alone. Six years later Benjamin Franklin wondered how it was that

> When an Indian Child has been brought up among us, taught our language and habituated to our Customs, yet if he goes to see his relations and makes one Indian Ramble with them, there is no perswading him ever to return. [But] when white persons of either sex have been taken prisoners young by the Indians, and lived a while among them, tho' ransomed by their Friends, and treated with all imaginable tenderness to prevail with them to stay among the English, yet in a Short time they become disgusted with our manner of life, and the care and pains that are necessary to support it, and take the first good Opportunity of escaping again into the Woods, from whence there is no reclaiming them.

In short, "thousands of Europeans are Indians," as Hector de Crèvecoeur put it, "and we have no examples of even one of those Aborigines having from choice become Europeans!"

The English captives who foiled their countrymen's civilized assumptions by becoming Indians differed little from the general colonial population when they were captured. They were ordinary men, women, and children of yeoman stock, Protestants by faith, a variety of nationalities by birth, English by law, different from their countrymen only in their willingness to risk personal insecurity for the economic opportunities of the frontier. There was no discernible characteristic or pattern of characteristics that differentiated them from their captive neighbors who eventually rejected Indian life—with one exception. Most of the colonists captured by the Indians and adopted into Indian families were children of both sexes and young women, often the mothers of the captive children. They were, as one captivity narrative observed, the "weak and defenceless."

The pattern of taking women and children for adoption was consistent throughout the colonial period, but during the first century and one-half of Indian-white conflict, primarily in New England, it coexisted with a larger pattern of captivity that included all white colonists, men as well as women and children. The Canadian Indians who raided New England tended to take captives more for their ransom value than for adoption. When Mrs. James Johnson gave birth to a daughter on the trail to Canada, for example, her captor looked into her makeshift lean-to and "clapped his hands with joy, crying two monies for me, two monies for me." Although the New England legislatures occasionally tried to forbid the use of public moneys for "the Ransoming of Captives," thereby prolonging the Indians' "diabolical kidnapping mode of warfare," ransoms were constantly paid from both public and private funds. These payments became larger as inflation and the Indians' savvy increased. Thus when John and Tamsen Tibbetts redeemed two of their children from the Canadian Indians in 1729, it cost them £105 10s. (1,270 livres). "Being verry Poore," many families in similar situations could ill afford to pay such high premiums even "if they should sell all they have in the world."

When the long peace in the Middle Atlantic colonies collapsed in 1753, the Indians of Pennsylvania, southern New York, and the Ohio country had no Quebec or Montreal in which to sell their human chattels to compassionate French families or anxious English relatives. For this and other reasons they captured English settlers largely to replace members of their own families who had died, often from English musketballs or imported diseases. Consequently, women and children—the "weak and defenceless"—were the prime targets of Indian raids.

According to the pattern of warfare in the Pennsylvania theater, the Indians usually stopped at a French fort with their prisoners before proceeding to their own villages. A young French soldier captured by the English reported that at Fort Duquesne there were "a great number of English Prisoners," the older of whom "they are constantly sending . . . away to Montreal" as prisoners of war, "but that the Indians keep many of the Prisoners amongst them, chiefly young People whom they adopt and bring up in their own way." His intelligence was corroborated by Barbara Leininger and Marie LeRoy, who had been members of a party of two adults and eight children captured in 1755 and taken to Fort Duquesne. There they saw "many other Women and Children, they think an hundred who were carried away from the several provinces of P[ennsylvania] M[aryland] and V[irginia]." When the girls escaped from captivity three years later, they wrote a narrative in German chiefly to acquaint "the inhabitants of this country . . .

with the names and circumstances of those prisoners whom we met, at the various places where we were, in the course of our captivity." Of the fifty-two prisoners they had seen, thirty-four were children and fourteen were women, including six mothers with children of their own.

The close of hostilities in Pennsylvania came in 1764 after Col. Henry Bouquet defeated the Indians near Bushy Run and imposed peace. By the articles of agreement reached in October, the Delawares, Shawnees, and Senecas were to deliver up "all the Prisoners in [their] Possession, without any Exception, Englishmen, Frenchmen, Women, and Children, whether adopted in your Tribes, married, or living amongst you, under any Denomination, or Pretence whatever." In the weeks that followed, Bouquet's troops, including "the Relations of [some of] the People [the Indians] have Massacred, or taken Prisoners," encamped on the Muskingum in the heart of the Ohio country to collect the captives. After as many as nine years with the Indians, during which time many children had grown up, 81 "men" and 126 "women and children" were returned. At the same time a list was prepared of 88 prisoners who still remained in Shawnee towns to the west: 70 were classified as "women and children." Six months later, 44 of these prisoners were delivered up to Fort Pitt. When they were captured, all but 4 had been less than sixteen years old, while 37 had been less than eleven years old.

The Indians obviously chose their captives carefully so as to maximize the chances of acculturating them to Indian life. To judge by the results, their methods were hard to fault. Even when the English held the upper hand militarily, they were often embarrassed by the Indians' educational power. On November 12, 1764, at his camp on the Muskingum, Bouquet lectured the Shawnees who had not delivered all their captives: "As you are now going to Collect all our *Flesh*, and *Blood*, . . . I desire that you will use them with Tenderness, and look upon them as Brothers, and no longer as Captives." The utter gratuitousness of his remark was reflected—no doubt purposely—in the Shawnee speech when the Indians delivered their captives the following spring at Fort Pitt. "Father—Here is your *Flesh*, and *Blood* . . . they have been all tied to us by Adoption, although we now deliver them up to you. We will always look upon them as Relations, whenever the *Great Spirit* is pleased that we may visit them . . . Father—we have taken as much Care of these Prisoners, as if they were [our] own Flesh, and blood; they are become unacquainted with your Customs, and manners, and therefore, Father we request you will use them tender, and kindly, which will be a means of inducing them to live contentedly with you."

The Indians spoke the truth and the English knew it. Three days after his speech to the Shawnees, Bouquet had advised Lt.-Gov. Francis Fauquier of Virginia that the returning captives "ought to be treated by their Relations with Tenderness and Humanity, till Time and Reason make them forget their unnatural Attachments, but unless they are closely watch'd," he admitted, "they will certainly return to the Barbarians." And indeed they would have, for during a half-century of conflict captives had been returned who, like many of the Ohio prisoners, responded only to Indian names, spoke only Indian dialects, felt comfortable only in Indian clothes, and in general regarded their white saviors as barbarians and their deliverance as captivity. Had they not been compelled to return to English society by militarily enforced peace treaties, the ranks of the white Indians would have been greatly enlarged.

From the moment the Indians surrendered their English prisoners, the colonists faced a series of difficult problems. The first was the problem of getting the prisoners to remain with the English. When Bouquet sent the first group of restored captives to Fort Pitt, he ordered his officers there that "they are to be closely watched and well Secured" because "most of them, particularly those who have been a long time among the Indians, will take the first Opportunity to run away." The young children especially were "so completely savage that they were brought to the camp tied hand and foot." Fourteen-year-old John McCullough, who had lived with the Indians for "eight years, four months, and sixteen days" (by his parents' reckoning), had his legs tied "under the horses belly" and his arms tied behind his back with his father's garters, but to no avail. He escaped under the cover of night and returned to his Indian family for a year before he was finally carried to Fort Pitt under "strong guard." "Having been accustomed to look upon the Indians as the only connections they had, having been tenderly treated by them, and speaking their language," explained the Reverend William Smith, the historian of Bouquet's expedition, "it is no wonder that [the children] considered their new state in the light of a captivity, and parted from the savages with tears."

Children were not the only reluctant freedmen. "Several women eloped in the night, and ran off to join their Indian friends." Among them undoubtedly were some of the English women who had married Indian men and borne them children, and then had been forced by the English victory either to return with their half-breed children to a country of strangers, full of prejudice against Indians, or to risk escaping under English guns to their husbands and adopted culture. For Bouquet had "reduced the Shawanese and Delawares etc. to the most Humiliating Terms of Peace," boasted Gen. Thomas Gage. "He has Obliged them to deliver up even their Own Children born of white women." But even the victorious soldier could understand the dilemma into which these women had been pushed. When Bouquet was informed that the English wife of an Indian chief had eloped in the night with her husband and children, he "requested that no pursuit should be made, as she was happier with her Chief than she would be if restored to her home."

Although most of the returned captives did not try to escape, the emotional torment caused by the separation from their adopted families deeply impressed the colonists. The Indians "delivered up their beloved captives with the utmost reluctance; shed torrents of tears over them, recommending them to the care and protection of the commanding officer." One young woman "cryed and roared when asked to come and begged to Stay a little longer." "Some, who could not make their escape, clung to their savage acquaintance at parting, and continued many days in bitter lamentations, even refusing sustenance." Children "cried as if they should die when they were presented to us." With only small exaggeration an observer on the Muskingum could report that "every captive left the Indians with regret."

Another problem encountered by the English was the difficulty of communicating with the returned captives, a great many of whom had replaced their knowledge of English with an Algonquian or Iroquoian dialect, and their baptismal names with Indian or hybrid ones. This immediately raised another problem—that of restoring the captives to their relatives. Sir William Johnson, the superintendent of Indian affairs, "thought it best to advertise them [in the newspapers] immediately, but I believe it will be very difficult to find the Friends of some of them, as they are ignorant of their own Names, or former places of abode, nay cant speak a word of any language but Indian." The only recourse the English had in such instances was to describe them "more particularly . . . as to their features, Complexion etc. That by the Publication of Such descriptions their Relations, parents or friends may hereafter know and Claim them."

But if several colonial observers were right, a description of the captives' physiognomy was of little help after they had been with the Indians for any length of time. Peter Kalm's foreign eye found it difficult to distinguish European captives from their captors, "except by their color, which is somewhat whiter than that of the Indians," but many colonists could see little or no difference. To his Maine neighbors twelve-year-old John Durell "ever after [his two-year captivity] appeared more like an Indian than a white man." So did John Tarbell. After thirty years among the Indians in Canada, he made a visit to his relatives in Groton "in his Indian dress and with his Indian complexion (for by means of grease and paints but little difference could be discerned)." When O. M. Spencer returned after only eight months with the Shawnees, he was greeted with a newspaper allusion "to [his] looks and manners, as slightly resembling the Indians" and by a gaggle of visitors who exclaimed "in an under tone, 'How much he looks like an Indian!' " Such evidence reinforced the environmentalism of the time, which held that white men "who have incorporated themselves with any of [the Indian] tribes" soon acquire "a great resemblance to the savages, not only in their manners, but in their colour and the expression of the countenance."

The final English problem was perhaps the most embarrassing in its manifestations, and certainly was so in its implications. For many Indians who had adopted white captives, the return of their "own Flesh, and Blood" to the English was unendurable. At the earliest opportunity, after bitter memories of the wars had faded on both sides, they journeyed through the English settlements to visit their estranged children, just as the Shawnee speaker had promised Bouquet they would. Jonathan Hoyt's Indian father visited him so often in Deerfield, sometimes bringing his captive sister, that Hoyt had to petition the Massachusetts General Court for reimbursement for their support. In 1760 Sir William Johnson reported that a Canadian Indian "has been since down to Schenectady to visit one Newkirk of that place, who was some years a Prisoner in his House, and sent home about a year ago with this Indians Sister, who came with her Brother now purely to see Said Newkirk whom she calls her Son and is verry fond of."

Obviously the feelings were mutual. Elizabeth Gilbert, adopted at the age of twelve, "always retained an affection toward John Huston, her Indian father (as she called him), for she remembered his kindness to her when in captivity." Even an adult who had spent less than six months with the Indians honored the chief who had adopted him. In 1799, eleven years after Thomas Ridout's release, his friend and father, Kakinathucca, "accompanied by three more Shawanese chiefs, came to pay me a visit at my house in York town (Toronto). He regarded myself and family with peculiar pleasure, and my wife and children contemplated with great satisfaction the noble and good qualities of this worthy Indian." The bond of affection that had grown in the Indian villages was clearly not an attachment that the English could dismiss as "unnatural."

Children who had been raised by Indian parents from infancy could be excused perhaps for their unwillingness to return, but the adults who displayed a similar reluctance, especially the women who had married Indian men and borne them children, drew another reaction. "For the honour of humanity," wrote Smith, "we would suppose those persons to have been of the lowest rank, either bred up in ignorance and distressing penury, or who had lived so long with the Indians as to forget all their former connections. For, easy and unconstrained as the savage life is, certainly it could never be put in competition with the blessings of improved life and the light of religion, by any persons who have had the happiness of enjoying, and the capacity of discerning, them." If Smith was struck by the contrast between the visible impact of Indian education and his own cultural assumptions, he never said so.

To find a satisfactory explanation for the extraordinary drawing power of Indian culture, we should begin where the colonists themselves first came under its sway—on the trail to Indian country. For although the Indians were known for their patience, they wasted no time in beginning the educational process that would transform their hostile or fearful white captives into affectionate Indian relatives.

Perhaps the first transaction after the Indians had selected their prisoners and hurried them into cover was to replace their hard-heeled

shoes with the footwear of the forest—moccasins. These were universally approved by the prisoners, who admitted that they traveled
with "abundant more ease" than before. And on more than one occasion the knee-deep snows of northern New England forced the Indians
to make snowshoes for their prisoners in order to maintain their pace
of twenty-five to thirty miles a day. Such an introduction to the su-
perbly adapted technology of the Indians alone would not convert the
English, but it was a beginning.

The lack of substantial food supplies forced the captives to accom-
modate their stomachs as best they could to Indian trail fare, which
ranged from nuts, berries, roots, and parched corn to beaver guts, horse-
flank, and semi-raw venison and moose, eaten without the customary
English accompaniments of bread or salt. When there was nothing to
eat, the Indians would "gird up their loins with a string," a technique
that at least one captive found "very useful" when applied to himself.
Although their food was often "unsavory" and in short supply, the Indians always shared it equally with the captives, who, being hungry,
"relished [it] very well."

Sometimes the lessons learned from the Indians were unexpectedly
vital. When Stephen Williams, an eleven-year-old captive from Deerfield, found himself separated from his party on the way to Canada,
he "Hellowed" for his Indian master. When the boy was found, the
Indian threatened to kill him because, as Williams remembered five
years later, "the Indians will never allow anybody to Hollow in the
woods. Their manner is to make a noise like wolves or any other wild
creatures, when they call to one another." The reason, of course, was
that they did not wish to be discovered by their enemies. To the young
neophyte Indian this was a lesson in survival not soon forgotten.

Two other lessons were equally unexpected but instrumental in preparing the captives for even greater surprises when they reached the
Indian settlements. Both served to undermine the English horror of
the Indians as bloodthirsty fiends who defile "any Woman they take
alive" before "putting her to Death." Many redeemed prisoners made
a point of insisting that, although they had been completely powerless
in captivity, "the Indians are very civil towards their captive women,
not offering any incivility by any indecent carriage." Thomas Ridout
testified that "during the whole of the time I was with the Indians I
never once witnessed an indecent or improper action amongst any of

the Indians, whether young or old." Even Smith admitted that "from every enquiry that has been made, it appears—that no woman thus saved is preserved from base motives, or need fear the violation of her honour." If there had been the least exception, we can be sure that this champion of civilization would have made the most of it.

One reason for the Indians' lack of sexual interest in their female captives was perhaps aesthetic, for the New England Indians, at least, esteemed black the color of beauty. A more fundamental reason derived from the main purpose of taking captives, which was to secure new members for their families and clans. Under the Indians' strong incest taboos, no warrior would attempt to violate his future sister or cousin. "Were he to indulge himself with a captive taken in war, and much more were he to offer violence in order to gratify his lust, he would incur indelible disgrace." Indeed, the taboo seems to have extended to the whole tribe. As George Croghan testified after long acquaintance with the Indians, "they have No [J]uri[s]diction or Laws butt that of Nature yett I have known more than onest thire Councils, order men to be putt to Death for Committing Rapes, wh[ich] is a Crime they Despise." Since murder was a crime to be revenged by the victim's family in its own way and time, rape was the only capital offense punished by the tribe as a whole.

Captive testimony also chipped away at the stereotype of the Indians' cruelty. When Mrs. Isabella M'Coy was taken from Epsom, New Hampshire, in 1747, her neighbors later remembered that "she did indeed find the journey [to Canada] fatiguing, and her fare scanty and precarious. But in her treatment from the Indians, she experienced a very agreeable disappointment. The kindness she received from them was far greater than she had expected from those who were so often distinguished for their cruelties." More frequent still was recognition of the Indians' kindness to children. Thomas Hutchinson told a common story of how "some of the children who were taken at Deerfield, they drew upon slays; at other times they have been known to carry them in their arms or upon their backs to Canada. This tenderness," he noted, "has occasioned the beginning of an affection, which in a few years has been so rivetted, that the parents of the children, who have gone to Canada to seek them, could by no means prevail upon them to leave the Indians and return home." The affections of a four-year-old Pennsylvania boy, who became Old White Chief among the

Iroquois, seem to have taken even less time to become "rivetted." "The last I remember of my mother," he recalled in 1836, "she was running, carrying me in her arms. Suddenly she fell to the ground on her face, and I was taken from her. Overwhelmed with fright, I knew nothing more until I opened my eyes to find myself in the lap of an Indian woman. Looking kindly down into my face she smiled on me, and gave me some dried deer's meat and maple sugar. From that hour I believe she loved me as a mother. I am sure I returned to her the affection of a son."

When the returning war parties approached the first Indian village, the educational process took on a new complexion. As one captive explained, "Whenever the warriors return from an excursion against an enemy, their return to the tribe or village must be designated by warlike ceremonial; the captives or spoils, which may happen to crown their valor, must be conducted in a triumphant form, and decorated to every possible advantage." Accordingly, the cheek, chin, and forehead of every captive were painted with traditional dashes of vermilion mixed with bear's grease. Belts of wampum were hung around their necks, Indian clothes were substituted for English, and the men and boys had their hair plucked or shaved in Indian fashion. The physical transformation was so effective, said a twenty-six-year-old soldier, "that I began to think I was an Indian." Younger captives were less aware of the small distance between role-playing and real acceptance of the Indian lifestyle. When her captor dressed Frances Slocum, not yet five years old, in "beautiful wampum beads," she remembered at the end of a long and happy life as an Indian that he "made me look, as I thought, very fine. I was much pleased with the beautiful wampum."

The prisoners were then introduced to a "new school" of song and dance. "Little did we expect," remarked an English woman, "that the accomplishment of dancing would ever be taught us, by the savages. But the war dance must now be held; and every prisoner that could move must take its awkward steps. The figure consisted of circular motion round the fire; each sang his own music, and the best dancer was the one most violent in motion." To prepare for the event each captive had rehearsed a short Indian song on the trail. Mrs. Johnson recalled many years later that her song was "danna witchee natchepung; my son's was nar wiscumpton." Nehemiah How could not master the Indian pronunciation, so he was allowed to sing in English "I don't know where I go." In view of the Indians' strong sense of ceremonial propriety, it is small wonder that one captive thought that they "Seem[e]d to be Very much a mind I Should git it perfect."

Upon entering the village the Indians let forth with some distinctive music of their own. "When we came near the main Body of the Enemy," wrote Thomas Brown, a captive soldier from Fort William Henry, "the *Indians* made a Live-Shout, as they call it when they bring in a Prisoner alive (different from the Shout they make when they bring in Scalps, which they call a Dead-Shout)." According to another soldier, "their Voices are so sharp, shrill, loud and deep, that when they join together after one has made his Cry, it makes a most dreadful and horrible Noise, that stupifies the very Senses," a noise that naturally frightened many captives until they learned that it was not their death knell.

They had good reason to think that their end was near when the whole village turned out to form a gauntlet from the entrance to the center of the village and their captors ordered them to run through it. With ax handles, tomahawks, hoop poles, clubs, and switches the Indians flogged the racing captives as if to beat the whiteness out of them. In most villages, significantly, "it was only the more elderly People both Male and Female wh[ic]h rece[iv]ed this Useage—the young prisoners of Both Sexes Escaped without it" or were rescued from any serious harm by one or more villagers, perhaps indicating the Indian perception of the captives' various educability. When ten-year-old John Brickell was knocked down by the blows of his Seneca captors, "a very big Indian came up, and threw the company off me, and took me by the arm, and led me along through the lines with such rapidity that I scarcely touched the ground, and was not once struck after he took me."

The purpose of the gauntlet was the subject of some difference of opinion. A French soldier who had spent several years among the northeastern Indians believed that a prisoner "so unfortunate as to fall in the course of the bastonnade must get up quickly and keep on, or he will be beaten to death on the spot." On the other hand, Pierre de Charlevoix, the learned traveler and historian of Canada, wrote that "even when they seem to strike at random, and to be actuated only by fury, they take care never to touch any part where a blow might prove mortal." Both Frenchmen were primarily describing the Indians' treatment of other Indians and white men. Leininger and LeRoy drew a somewhat different conclusion from their own treatment. Their welcome at the Indian village of Kittanning, they said, "consisted of three blows each, on the back. They were, however, administered with great mercy. Indeed, we concluded that we were beaten merely in order to keep up an ancient usage, and not with the intention of injuring us."

William Walton came closest to revealing the Indians' intentions in his account of the Gilbert family's captivity. The Indians usually beat the captives with "great Severity," he said, "by way of Revenge for their Relations who have been slain." Since the object of taking captives was to satisfy the Indian families who had lost relatives, the gauntlet served as the first of three initiation rites into Indian society, a purgative ceremony by which the bereaved Indians could exorcise their anger and anguish, and the captives could begin their cultural transformation.

If the first rite tried to beat the whiteness out of the captives, the second tried to wash it out. James Smith's experience was typical.

> The old chief, holding me by the hand, made a long speech, very loud, and when he had done he handed me to three squaws, who led me by the hand down the bank into the river until the water was up to our middle. The squaws then made signs to me to plunge myself into the water, but I did not understand them. I thought that the result of the council was that I should be drowned, and that these young ladies were to be the executioners. They all laid violent hold of me, and I for some time opposed them with all my might, which occasioned loud laughter by the multitude that were on the bank of the river. At length one of the squaws made out to speak a little English (for I believe they began to be afraid of me) and said, 'No hurt you.' On this I gave myself up to their ladyships, who were as good as their word; for though they plunged me under water and washed and rubbed me severely, yet I could not say they hurt me much.

More than one captive had to receive similar assurance, but their worst fears were being laid to rest.

Symbolically purged of their whiteness by their Indian baptism, the initiates were dressed in new Indian clothes and decorated with feathers, jewelry, and paint. Then, with great solemnity, the village gathered around the council fire, where after a "profound silence" one of the chiefs spoke. Even a hostile captive, Zadock Steele, had to admit that although he could not understand the language spoken, he could "plainly discover a great share of native eloquence." The chief's speech, he said, was "of considerable length, and its effect obviously manifested weight of argument, solemnity of thought, and at least human sensibility." But even this the twenty-two-year-old New Englander could not appreciate on its own terms, for in the next breath he denigrated the ceremony as "an assemblage of barbarism, assuming the appearance of civilization."

A more charitable account was given by James Smith, who through an interpreter was addressed in the following words:

> My son, you are now flesh of our flesh and bone of our bone. By the ceremony that was performed this day, every drop of white blood was washed out of your veins. You are taken into the Caughnewaga nation and initiated into a war-like tribe. You are adopted into a great family and now received with great seriousness and solemnity in the room and place of a great man. After what has passed this day you are now one of us by an old strong law and custom. My son, you have now nothing to fear. We are now under the same obligations to love, support and defend you that we are to love and to defend one another. Therefore you are to consider yourself as one of our people.

"At this time," admitted the eighteen-year-old Smith, "I did not believe this fine speech, especially that of the white blood being washed out of me; but since that time I have found that there was much sincerity in said speech; for from that day I never knew them to make any distinction between me and themselves in any respect whatever until I left them . . . we all shared one fate." It is a chord that sounds through nearly every captivity narrative: "They treated me . . . in every way as one of themselves."

When the adoption ceremony had ended, the captive was taken to the wigwam of his new family, who greeted him with a "most dismal howling, crying bitterly, and wringing their hands in all the agonies of grief for a deceased relative." "The higher in favour the adopted Prisoners [were] to be placed, the greater Lamentation [was] made over them." After a threnodic memorial to the lost member, which may have "added to the Terror of the Captives," who "imagined it to be no other than a Prelude to inevitable Destruction," the mood suddenly shifted. "I never saw . . . such hug[g]ing and kissing from the women and crying for joy," exclaimed one young recipient. Then an interpreter introduced each member of the new family—in one case "from brother

to seventh cousins"—and "they came to me one after another," said
another captive, "and shook me by the hand, in token that they considered me to stand in the same relationship to them as the one in
whose stead I was placed."

Most young captives assumed the place of Indian sons and daughters,
but occasionally the match was not exact. Mary Jemison replaced a
brother who had been killed in "Washington's war," while twenty-six-
year-old Titus King assumed the unlikely role of a grandfather. Although their sex and age may not always have corresponded, the
adopted captives succeeded to all the deceased's rights and obligations—
the same dignities, honors, and often the same names. "But the one
adopted," reported a French soldier, "must be prudent and wise in his
conduct, if he wants to make himself as well liked as the man he is
replacing. This seldom fails to occur, because he is continually reminded of the dead man's conduct and good deeds."

So literal could the replacement become at times that no amount of
exemplary conduct could alter the captive's reception. Thomas Peart, a
twenty-three-year-old Pennsylvanian, was adopted as an uncle in an
Iroquois family, but "the old Man, whose Place [he] was to fill, had
never been considered by his Family as possessed of any Merit." Accordingly, Peart's dress, although in the Indian style, was "in a meaner
Manner, as they did not hold him high in Esteem after his Adoption."
Since his heart was not in becoming an Indian anyway, and "observing
that they treated him just as they had done the old worthless Indian
. . . he therefore concluded he would only fill his Predecessor's Station, and used no Endeavours to please them."

When the prisoners had been introduced to all their new relatives
and neighbors, the Indians proceeded to shower them with gifts. Luke
Swetland, taken from Pennsylvania during the Revolution, was unusually feted with "three hats, five blankets, near twenty pipes, six
razors, six knives, several spoons, gun and ammunition, fireworks, several Indian pockets [pouches], one Indian razor, awls, needles, goose
quills, paper and many other things of small value"—enough to make
him the complete Indian warrior. Most captives, however, settled for a
new shirt or dress, a pair of decorated moccasins, and abundant promises of future kindness, which later prompted the captives to acknowledge once again that the Indians were "a[s] good as their word." "All
the family was as kind to me," related Thomas Gist, "as if I had really

been the nearest of relation they had in the world." The two women who adopted Jemison were no less loving. "I was ever considered and treated by them as a real sister," she said near the end of a long life with them, "the same as though I had been born of their mother."

Treatment such as this—and it was almost universal—left an indelible mark on every captive, whether or not they eventually returned to English society. Although captives like Mrs. Johnson found their adoption an "unnatural situation," they had to defend the humanity of the practice. "Those who have profited by refinement and education," she argued, "ought to abate part of the prejudice, which prompts them to look with an eye of censure on this untutored race. . . . Do they ever adopt an enemy," she asked, "and salute him by the tender name of brother?" It is not difficult to imagine what effect such feelings must have had in younger people less habituated to English culture, especially those who had lost their own parents.

The formalities, purgations, and initiations were now completed. Only one thing remained for the Indians: by their daily example and instruction to "make an Indian of you," as the Delawares told Brickell. This required a steady union of two things: the willingness and gratitude of the captives, and the consistent love and trust of the Indians. By the extraordinary ceremonies through which they had passed, most captives had had their worst fears allayed. From a state of apprehension or even terror they had suddenly emerged with their persons intact and a solemn invitation to begin a new life, as full of love, challenge, and satisfaction as any they had known. For "when they [the Indians] once determine to give life, they give every thing with it, which, in their apprehension, belongs to it." The sudden release from anxiety into a realm of affirmative possibility must have disposed many captives to accept the Indian way of life.

According to the adopted colonists who recounted the stories of their new lives, Indian life was more than capable of claiming their respect and allegiance, even if they eventually returned to English society. The first indication that the Indians were serious in their professions of equality came when the adopted captives were given freedom of movement within and without the Indian villages. Naturally the degree of freedom and its timing depended on the captive's willingness to enter into the spirit of Indian life.

Despite his adult years, Ridout had earned his captor's trust by the

third night of their march to the Shawnee villages. Having tied his prisoner with a rope to himself the first two nights, the Indian "never afterwards used this precaution, leaving me at perfect liberty, and frequently
during the nights that were frosty and cold," Ridout recalled, "I found
his hand over me to examine whether or not I was covered." As soon
as seventeen-year-old John Leeth, an Indian trader's clerk, reached his
new family's village, "my father gave me and his two [Indian] sons our
freedom, with a rifle, two pounds of powder, four pounds of lead, a
blanket, shirt, match-coat, pair of leggings, etc. to each, as our freedom
dues; and told us to shift for ourselves." Eleven-year-old Benjamin-
Gilbert, "considered as the [Indian] King's Successor," was of course
"entirely freed from Restraint, so that he even began to be delighted
with his Manner of Life." Even Steele, a somewhat reluctant Indian at
twenty-two, was "allowed the privilege of visiting any part of the village, in the day time, and was received with marks of fraternal affection,
and treated with all the civility an Indian is capable to bestow."

The presence of other white prisoners complicated the trust relationship somewhat. Captives who were previously known to each other,
especially from the same family, were not always allowed to converse
"much together, as [the Indians] imagined they would remember their
former Situation, and become less contented with their present Manner of Life." Benjamin Peart, for example, was allowed the frequent
company of "Two white Men who had been taken Prisoners, the one
from Susquehanna, the other from Minisinks, both in Pennsylvania,"
even though he was a Pennsylvanian himself. But when he met his
captive wife and infant son by chance at Fort Niagara, the Indians
"separated them again the same Day, and took [his] Wife about Four
Miles Distance."

Captives who were strangers were permitted not only to visit frequently but occasionally to live together. When Gist suddenly moved
from his adopted aunt's house back to her brother's, she "imajined I
was affronted," he wrote, and "came and asked me the reason why I
had left her, or what injury she or any of the family had done me that
I should leave her without so much as leting her know of it. I told her
it was the company of my fellow prisoners that drew me to the town.
She said that it was not so far but I mite have walked to see them every
two or three days, and ask some of them to come and see me those days
that I did not chuse to go abroad, and that all such persons as I thought

proper to bring to the house should be as welcom[e] as one of the family, and made many promises how kind she would be if I would return. However," boasted the twenty-four-year-old Gist, "I was obstinate and would not." It is not surprising that captives who enjoyed such autonomy were also trusted under the same roof. John Brickell remarked that three white prisoners, "Patton, Johnston, and Mrs. Baker [of Kentucky] had all lived with me in the same house among the Indians, and we were as intimate as brothers and sisters."

Once the captives had earned the basic trust of their Indian families, nothing in Indian life was denied them. When they reached the appropriate age, the Indians offered to find them suitable marriage partners. Understandably, some of the older captives balked at this, sensing that it was calculated to bind them with marital ties to a culture they were otherwise hesitant to accept. When Joseph Gilbert, a forty-one-year-old father and husband, was adopted into a leading family, his new relatives informed him that "if he would marry amongst them, he should enjoy the Privileges which they enjoyed; but this Proposal he was not disposed to comply with, . . . as he was not over anxious to conceal his Dislike to them." Elizabeth Peart, his twenty-year-old married sister, was equally reluctant. During her adoption ceremony "they obliged her to sit down with a young Man an Indian, and the eldest Chieftain of the Family repeating a Jargon of Words to her unintelligible, but which she considered as some form amongst them of Marriage," she was visited with "the most violent agitations, as she was determined, at all events, to oppose any step of this Nature." Marie LeRoy's honor was even more dearly bought. When "it was at length determined by the [Indians] that [she] should marry one of the natives, who had been selected for her," she told a fellow captive that "she would sooner be shot than have him for her husband." Whether her revulsion was directed toward the act itself or toward the particular suitor was not said.

The distinction is pertinent because the weight of evidence suggests that marriage was not compulsory for the captives, and common sense tells us that any form of compulsion would have defeated the Indians' purpose in trying to persuade the captives to adopt their way of life. Mary Jemison, at the time a captive for two years, was unusual in implying that she was forced to marry an Indian. "Not long after the Delawares came to live with us, at Wiisho," she recalled, "my sisters told me that I must go and live with one of them, whose name was

She-nin-jee. Not daring to cross them, or disobey their commands, with a great degree of reluctance I went; and Sheninjee and I were married according to Indian custom." Considering the tenderness and kindness with which most captives reported they were treated, it is likely that she was less compelled in reality than in her perception and memory of it.

For even hostile witnesses could not bring themselves to charge that force was ever used to promote marriages. The Puritan minister John Williams said only that "great *essays* [were] made to get [captives] married" among the Canadian Indians by whom he was captured. Elizabeth Hanson and her husband "could by no means obtain from their hands" their sixteen-year-old daughter, "for the squaw, to whom she was given, had a son whom she intended my daughter should in time *be prevailed with to marry*." Mrs. Hanson was probably less concerned that her daughter would be forced to marry an Indian than that she might "in time" want to, for as she acknowledged from her personal experience, "the Indians are very civil towards their captive women, not offering any incivility by any indecent carriage." An observer of the return of the white prisoners to Bouquet spoke for his contemporaries when he reported—with an almost audible sigh of relief—that "there had not been a solitary instance among them of any woman having her delicacy injured by being compelled to marry. They had been left liberty of choice, and those who chose to remain single were not sufferers on that account."

Not only were younger captives and consenting adults under no compulsion, either actual or perceived, to marry, but they enjoyed as wide a latitude of choice as any Indian. When Gist returned to his Indian aunt's lodge, she was so happy that she "dress'd me as fine as she could, and . . . told me if I wanted a wife she would get a pretty young girl for me." It was in the same spirit of exuberant generosity that Spencer's adopted mother rewarded his first hunting exploit. "She heard all the particulars of the affair with great satisfaction," he remembered, "and frequently saying, 'Enee, wessah' (that is right, that is good), said I would one day become a great hunter, and placing her forefingers together (by which sign the Indians represent marriage) and then pointing to Sotonegoo" (a thirteen-year-old girl whom Spencer described as "rather homely, but cheerful and good natured, with bright, laughing eyes") "told me that when I should become a man I should have her for a wife." Sotonegoo cannot have been averse to the idea, for when Spencer was redeemed shortly afterward she "sobbed loudly as [he] took her hand, and for the moment deeply affected, bade her farewell."

So free from compulsion were the captives that several married fellow white prisoners. In 1715 the priest of the Jesuit mission at Sault-au-Recollect "married Ignace shoetak8anni [Joseph Rising, aged twenty-one] and Elizabeth T8atog8ach [Abigail Nims, aged fifteen], both English, who wish to remain with the Christian Indians, not only renouncing their nation, but even wishing to live *en sauvages*." But from the Indians' standpoint, and perhaps from their own, captives such as John Leeth and Thomas Armstrong may have had the best of all possible marriages. After some years with the Indians, Leeth "was married to a young woman, seventeen or eighteen years of age; also a prisoner to the Indians; who had been taken by them when about twenty months old." Armstrong, an adopted Seneca, also married a "full blooded white woman, who like himself had been a captive among the Indians, from infancy, who unlike him, had not acquired a knowledge of one word of the English language, being essentially Indian in all save blood." Their commitment to each other deepened their commitment to the Indian culture of which they had become equal members.

The captives' social equality was also demonstrated by their being asked to share in the affairs of war and peace, matters of supreme importance to Indian society. When the Senecas who had adopted Thomas Peart decided to "make a War Excursion," they asked him to go with them. But since he was in no mood—and no physical condition —to play the Indian, "he determinately refused them, and was therefore left at Home with the Family." The young Englishman who became Old White Chief was far more eager to defend his new culture, but his origins somewhat limited his military activity. "When I grew to manhood," he recalled, "I went with them [his Iroquois kinsmen] on the warpath against the neighboring tribes, but never against the white settlers, lest by some unlucky accident I might be recognized and claimed by former friends." Other captives—many of them famous renegades—were less cautious. Charlevoix noticed in his travels in Canada that adopted captives "frequently enter into the spirit of the nation, of which they are become members, in such a manner, that they make no difficulty of going to war against their own countrymen." It was behavior such as this that prompted Sir William Johnson to praise Bouquet after his expedition to the Ohio for compelling the Indians to give up every white person, even the "Children born of White Women. That mixed Race," he wrote, referring to first-generation captives as well, "forgetting their Ancestry on one side are found to be the most Inveterate of any, and would greatly Augment their numbers."

It is ironic that the most famous renegade of all should have introduced ten-year-old Spencer to the ultimate opportunity for an adopted captive. When he had been a captive for less than three weeks, Spencer met Simon Girty, "the very picture of a villain," at a Shawnee village below his own. After various boasts and enquiries, wrote Spencer, "he ended by telling me that I would never see home; but if I should 'turn out to be a good hunter and a brave warrior I might one day be a chief.'" Girty's prediction may not have been meant to tease a small boy with impossible delusions of grandeur, for the Indians of the Northeast readily admitted white captives to their highest councils and offices.

Just after Ridout was captured on the Ohio, he was surprised to meet an English-speaking "white man, about twenty-two years of age, who had been taken prisoner when a lad and had been adopted, and now was a chief among the Shawanese." He need not have been surprised, for there were many more like him. John Tarbell, the man who visited his Groton relatives in Indian dress, was not only "one of the wealthiest" of the Caughnawagas but "the eldest chief and chief speaker of the tribe." Timothy Rice, formerly of Westborough, Massachusetts, was also made one of the clan chiefs of Caughnawaga [Québec], partly by inheritance from his Indian father but largely for "his own Super[io]r Talents" and "warlike Spirit for which he was much celebrated."

Perhaps the most telling evidence of the Indians' receptivity to adopted white leadership comes from Old White Chief, an adopted Iroquois.

> I was made a chief at an early age [he recalled in 1836] and as my sons grew to manhood they also were made chiefs. . . . After my youngest son was made chief I could see, as I thought, that some of the Indians were jealous of the distinction I enjoyed and it gave me uneasiness. This was the first time I ever entertained the thought of leaving my Indian friends. I felt sure that it was displeasing to the Indians to have three of my sons, as well as myself, promoted to the office of chief. My wife was well pleased to leave with me, and my sons said, "Father, we will go wherever you will lead us."

I then broke the subject to some of my Indian relatives, who were very much disturbed at my decision. They immediately called the chiefs and warriors together and laid the plan before them. They gravely deliberated upon the subject for some hours, and then a large majority decided that they would not consent to our leaving. They said, "We cannot give up our son and brother" (meaning myself) "nor our nephews" (meaning my children). "They have lived on our game and grown strong and powerful among us. They are good and true men. We cannot do without them. We cannot give them to the pale faces. We shall grow weak if they leave us. We will give them the best we have left. Let them choose where they will live. No one shall disturb them. We need their wisdom and their strength to help us. If they are in high places, let them be there. We know they will honor us."

"We yielded to their importunity," said the old chief, and "I have never had any reason to regret my decision." In public office as in every sphere of Indian life, the English captives found that the color of their skin was unimportant; only their talent and their inclination of heart mattered.

Understandably, neither their skill nor their loyalty was left to chance. From the moment the captives, especially the young ones, came under their charge, the Indians made a concerted effort to inculcate in them Indian habits of mind and body. If the captives could be taught to think, act, and react like Indians, they would effectively cease to be English and would assume an Indian identity. This was the Indians' goal, toward which they bent every effort in the weeks and months that followed their formal adoption of the white captives.

The educational character of Indian society was recognized by even the most inveterately English captives. Titus King, a twenty-six-year-old New England soldier, spent a year with the Canadian Indians at St. Francis trying—unsuccessfully—to undo their education of "Eight or tin young [English] Children." What "an awfull School this [is] for Children," he wrote. "When We See how Quick they will Fall in with the Indians ways, nothing Seems to be more takeing in Six months time they Forsake Father and mother Forgit thir own Land Refuess to Speak there own toungue and Seemin[g]ly be Holley Swollowed up with the Indians." The older the person, of course, the longer it took to become fully Indianized. Mary Jemison, captured at the age of twelve, took three or four years to forget her natural parents and the home she had once loved. "If I had been taken in infancy," she said, "I should have been contented in my situation." Some captives, commonly those over fifteen or sixteen years old, never made the transition from English to Indian. Twenty-four-year-old Gist, soldier and son of a famous scout and Indian agent, accommodated himself to his adoption and Indian life for just one year and then made plans to escape. "All curiosity with regard to acting the part of an Indian," he related, "which I could do very well, being througherly [thoroughly] satisfied, I was determined to be what I really was."

Children, however, took little time to "fall in with the Indians ways." Titus King mentioned six months. The Reverend John Williams witnessed the effects of eight or nine months when he stopped at St. Francis in February 1704. There, he said, "we found several poor children, who had been taken from the eastward [Maine] the summer before; a sight very affecting, they being in habit very much like Indians, and in manners very much symbolizing with them." When young Joseph Noble visited his captive sister in Montreal, "he still belonged to the St. François tribe of Indians, and was dressed remarkably fine, having forty or fifty broaches in his shirt, clasps on his arm, and a great variety of knots and bells about his clothing. He brought his little sister . . . a young fawn, a basket of cranberries, and a lump of sap sugar." Sometime later he was purchased from the Indians by a French gentleman who promptly "dressed him in the French style; but he never appeared so bold and majestic, so spirited and vivacious, as when arrayed in his Indian habit and associating with his Indian friends."

The key to any culture is its language, and the young captives were quick to learn the Indian dialects of their new families. Their retentive memories and flair for imitation made them ready students, while the Indian languages, at once oral, concrete, and mythopoeic, lightened the task. In less than six months ten-year-old Spencer had "acquired a sufficient knowledge of the Shawnee tongue to understand all ordinary conversation and, indeed, the greater part of all that I heard (accompanied, as their conversation and speeches were, with the most significant gestures)," which enabled him to listen "with much pleasure and sometimes with deep interest" to his Indian mother tell of battles, heroes, and history in the long winter evenings. When Jemima Howe was allowed to visit her four-year-old son at a neighboring Indian village in Canada, he greeted her "in the Indian tongue" with "Mother, are you come?" He too had been a captive for only six months.

The early weeks of captivity could be disquieting if there were no English-speaking Indians or prisoners in the village to lend the comfort of a familiar language while the captives struggled to acquire a strange one. If a captive's family left for their winter hunting camp before he could learn their language, he might find himself, like Gist, "without any com[p]any that could unders[t]and one word that I spake." "Thus I continued, near five months," he wrote, "sometimes reading, other times singing, never melancholy but when alone. . . . About the first of April (1759) I prevailed on the family to return to town, and by the last of the month all the Indians and prisoners returned, when I once more had the pleasure to talk to people that understood what I said."

Younger captives probably missed the familiarity of English less than the adult Gist. Certainly they never lacked eager teachers. Mary Jemison recalled that her Seneca sisters were "diligent in teaching me their language; and to their great satisfaction I soon learned so that I could understand it readily, and speak it fluently." Even Gist was the recipient of enthusiastic, if informal, instruction from a native speaker. One of his adopted cousins, who was about five or six years old and his "favorite in the family," was always "chattering some thing" with him. "From him," said Gist affectionately, "I learn'd more than from all the rest, and he learn'd English as fast as [I] did Indian."

As in any school, language was only one of many subjects of instruction. Since the Indians generally assumed that whites were physically inferior to themselves, captive boys were often prepared for the hardy life of hunters and warriors by a rigorous program of physical training. John McCullough, aged eight, was put through the traditional Indian course by his adoptive uncle. "In the beginning of winter," McCullough recalled, "he used to raise me by day light every morning, and make me sit down in the creek up to my chin in the cold water, in order to make me hardy as he said, whilst he would sit on the bank smoking his pipe until he thought I had been long enough in the water, he would then bid me to dive. After I came out of the water he would order me not to go near the fire until I would be dry. I was kept at that till the water was frozen over, he would then break the ice for me and send me in as before." As shocking as it may have been to his system, such treatment did nothing to turn him against Indian life. Indeed, he was transparently proud that he had borne up under the strenuous regimen "with the firmness of an Indian." Becoming an Indian was as much a challenge and an adventure for the young colonists as it was a "sore trial," and many of them responded to it with alacrity and zest. Of children their age we should not expect any less.

The captives were taught not only to speak and to endure as Indians but to act as Indians in the daily social and economic life of the community. Naturally, boys were taught the part of men and girls the part of women, and according to most colonial sources—written, it should be noted, predominantly by men—the boys enjoyed the better fate. An Ohio pioneer remembered that the prisoners from his party were "put into different families, the women to hard drudging and the boys to run wild with the young Indians, to amuse themselves with bow and arrow, dabble in the water, or obey any other notion their wild natures might dictate." William Walton, the author of the Gilbert family captivity narrative, also felt that the "Labour and Drudgery" in an Indian family fell to "the Share of the Women." He described fourteen-year-old Abner Gilbert as living a "dronish Indian life, idle and poor, having no other Employ than the gathering of Hickory-Nuts; and although young," Walton insisted, "his Situation was very irksome." Just how irksome the boy found his freedom from colonial farm chores was revealed when the ingenuous Walton related that "Abner, having no useful Employ, amused himself with catching fish in the Lake. . . . Not being of an impatient Disposition," said Walton soberly, "he bore his Captivity without repining."

While most captive boys had "nothing to do, but cut a little wood for the fire," draw water for cooking and drinking, and "shoot Blackbirds that came to eat up the corn," they enjoyed "some leisure" for "hunting and other innocent devertions in the woods." Women and girls, on the other hand, shared the burdens—onerous ones in English eyes—of their Indian counterparts. But Jemison, who had been taught English ways for twelve years before becoming an Indian, felt that the Indian women's labor "was not severe," their tasks "probably not harder than that [sic] of white women," and their cares "certainly . . . not half as numerous, nor as great." The work of one year was "exactly similar, in almost every respect, to that of the others, without that endless variety that is to be observed in the common labor of the white people. . . . In the summer season, we planted, tended and harvested our corn, and generally had all our children with us; but had no master to oversee or drive us, so that we could work as leisurely as we pleased. . . . In the season of hunting, it was our business, in addition to our cooking, to bring home the game that was taken by the [men], dress it, and carefully preserve the eatable meat, and prepare or dress the skins." "Spinning, weaving, sewing, stocking knitting," and like domestic tasks of colonial women were generally unknown. Unless Jemison was correct, it would be virtually impossible to understand why so many women and girls chose to become Indians. A life of unremitting drudgery, as the English saw it, could certainly hold no attraction for civilized women fresh from frontier farms and villages.

The final and most difficult step in the captives' transition from English to Indian was to acquire the ability to think as Indians, to share unconsciously the values, beliefs, and standards of Indian culture. From an English perspective, this should have been nearly an impossible task for civilized people because they perceived Indian culture as immoral and irreligious and totally antithetical to the civilized life they had known, however briefly. "Certainly," William Smith assumed, "it could never be put in competition with the blessings of improved life and the light of religion." But many captives soon discovered that the English had no monopoly on virtue and that in many ways the Indians were morally superior to the English, more Christian than the Christians.

As early as 1643 Roger Williams had written a book to suggest such a thing, but he could be dismissed as a misguided visionary who let the Narragansetts go to his head. It was more difficult to dismiss someone like Brickell, who had lived with the Indians for four and one-half years and had no ax to grind with established religion. "The Delawares are the best people to train up children I ever was with," he wrote. "Their leisure hours are, in a great measure, spent in training up their children to observe what they believe to be right. . . . [A]s a nation they may be considered fit examples for many of us Christians to follow. They certainly follow what they are taught to believe right more closely, and I might say more honestly, in general, than we Christians do the divine precepts of our Redeemer. . . . I know I am influenced to good, even at this day," he concluded, "more from what I learned among them,

than what I learned among people of my own color." After many decades with them, Jemison insisted that "the moral character of the Indians was . . . uncontaminated. Their fidelity was perfect, and became
proverbial; they were strictly honest; they despised deception and falsehood; and chastity was held in high veneration." Even the tory historian Peter Oliver, who was no friend to the Indians, admitted that
"they have a Religion of their own, which, to the eternal Disgrace of
many Nations who boast of Politeness, is more influential on their Conduct than that of those who hold them in so great Contempt." To the
acute discomfort of the colonists, more than one captive maintained
that the Indians were a "far more moral race than the whites."

In the principled school of Indian life the captives experienced a
decisive shift in their cultural and personal identities, a shift that often
fostered a considerable degree of what might be called "conversion
zeal." A French officer reported that "those Prisoners whom the Indians
keep with them . . . are often more brutish, boisterous in their Behaviour and loose in their Manners than the Indians," and thought that
"they affect that kind of Behaviour thro' Fear of and to recommend
themselves to the Indians." Matthew Bunn, a nineteen-year-old soldier,
was the object of such behavior when he was enslaved—not adopted—
by the Maumee in 1791. "After I had eaten," he related, "they brought
me a little prisoner boy, that had been taken about two years before, on
the river called Monongahela, though he delighted more in the ways of
the savages than in the ways of Christians; he used me worse than any
of the Indians, for he would tell me to do this, that, and the other, and
if I did not do it, or made any resistance, the Indians would threaten to
kill me, and he would kick and cuff me about in such a manner, that
I hardly dared to say my soul was my own." What Bunn experienced
was the attempt of the new converts to pattern their behavior after
their young Indian counterparts, who, a Puritan minister observed, "are
as much to be dreaded by captives as those of maturer years, and in
many cases much more so; for, unlike cultivated people, they have no
restraints upon their mischievous and savage propensities, which they
indulge in cruelties."

Although fear undoubtedly accounted for some of the converts' initial
behavior, desire to win the approval of their new relatives also played
a part. "I had lived in my new habitation about a week," recalled
Spencer, "and having given up all hope of escaping . . . began to re-

gard it as my future home. . . . I strove to be cheerful, and by my ready obedience to ingratiate myself with Cooh-coo-cheeh [his Indian mistress], for whose kindness I felt grateful." A year after James Smith had been adopted, a number of prisoners were brought in by his new kinsmen and a gauntlet formed to welcome them. Smith "went and told them how they were to act" and then "fell into one of the ranks with the Indians, shouting and yelling like them." One middle-aged man's turn came, and "as they were not very severe on him," confessed the new Indian, "as he passed me I hit him with a piece of pumpkin— which pleased the Indians much." If their zeal to emulate the Indians sometimes exceeded their mercy, the captives had nonetheless fulfilled their new families' expectations: they had begun to act as Indians in spirit as well as body. Only time would be necessary to transform their conscious efforts into unconscious habits and complete their cultural conversion.

"By what power does it come to pass," asked Crèvecoeur, "that children who have been adopted when young among these people, . . . and even grown persons . . . can never be prevailed on to re-adopt European manners?" Given the malleability of youth, we should not be surprised that children underwent a rather sudden and permanent transition from English to Indian—although we might be pressed to explain why so few Indian children made the transition in the opposite direction. But the adult colonists who became Indians cannot be explained as easily, for the simple reason that they, unlike many of the children, were fully conscious of their cultural identities while they were being subjected to the Indians' assiduous attempts to convert them. Consequently, their cultural metamorphosis involved a large degree of personal choice.

The great majority of white Indians left no explanations for their choice. Forgetting their original language and their past, they simply disappeared into their adopted society. But those captives who returned to write narratives of their experiences left several clues to the motives of those who chose to stay behind. They stayed because they found Indian life to possess a strong sense of community, abundant love, and uncommon integrity—values that the English colonists also honored, if less successfully. But Indian life was attractive for other values—for social equality, mobility, adventure, and, as two adult converts acknowledged, "the most perfect freedom, the ease of living, [and] the absence of those cares and corroding solicitudes which so often prevail with us." As we have learned recently, these were values that were not being realized in the older, increasingly crowded, fragmented, and contentious communities of the Atlantic seaboard, or even in the newer frontier settlements. By contrast, as Crèvecoeur said, there must have been in the Indians' "social bond something singularly captivating." Whatever it was, its power had no better measure than the large number of English colonists who became, contrary to the civilized assumptions of their countrymen, white Indians.

4

Benjamin Franklin As Experimental Philosopher

SAMUEL DEVONS

• Benjamin Franklin will be remembered and revered by Americans as long as we seek to know how full and varied human existence can be. As a resident of Philadelphia, he did more than any person in the eighteenth century to make cities livable and urbane. As an author, he offered practical hints on how to improve thrift and productivity. As a diplomat in European capitals, he made the intellectual transition from defender of empire to signer of the Declaration of Independence. As a man, he led a dazzling romantic life and even after the age of seventy was the intimate companion of some of the most elegant ladies of Paris.

It was as a scientist, however, that Benjamin Franklin best revealed his true nature, and it was as a scientist that he learned a method of inquiry that would serve him well in other fields. We are inclined to think of Benjamin Franklin the experimenter with some amusement, perhaps because of his crude equipment or because of the oft-told tale of the kite and electricity. But Samuel Devons reminds us that Franklin's research put him at the cutting edge of knowledge in his time. In 1753, for example, the Royal Society recognized him with its highest scientific honor, the Copley Medal.

The essay below illustrates that Franklin's genius lay in his ability to find a simple uniform principle in a bewildering array of detail. Always curious, always aware of his own fallibility, and always willing to be instructed by observation and experience, Franklin summed up his philosophy during de-

This article was originally published in the *American Journal of Physics* (*Am. Journ. of Phys.* 45, 1148 [1977]). Permission to reprint this article has been granted by the *American Journal of Physics* and the American Association of Physics Teachers.

AUTHOR'S NOTE: I am happy to record my indebtedness to Professor I. B. Cohen for his comments on the present paper.

bate at the Constitutional Convention of 1787, when he
urged members to vote for an imperfect document. "Having
lived long," he said, "I have experienced many Instances of
being obliged, by better Information, or fuller Consideration,
to change Opinions even on Important Subjects, which I
once thought right, but found to be otherwise." Each member, he urged, should "doubt a little of his own Infallibility."

In 1751, when Dr. William Watson, rich apothecary and amateur of
science, and for a brief time Franklin's rival, presented to the Royal
Society of London Franklin's newly published electrical discoveries, he
felt compelled to excuse his inadequacy: "To give even the shortest
account of all the experiments contained in Mr. Franklin's book," he
sighed, "would exceed greatly the time allowed for these purposes by
the Royal Society."

One can sympathize with Dr. Watson. He was reviewing Franklin's first scientific publication, a slim volume of but a few dozen
pages, relating the outcome of the early Philadelphia experiments of
1747–50 (before the famous lightning experiments), but written with
Franklin's unfeigned candor and unadorned lucidity, and with no
words wasted. It was impossible to condense or to summarize or to
improve upon. And how many times since has it seemed that what
has been written about Franklin is no match for what he himself
wrote?

And how indeed can one summarize, as our celebrations here demand, one aspect of a life so brimful of activity of every conceivable
variety? "The most versatile genius that ever lived" is an encomium
that has been applied to Franklin with some justification. A man of
innumerable parts, but the parts are not separable. There is an essential integrity in all that he did: not so much that he applied experience gained in one sphere to activity in another, but rather that he
expressed his whole incomparable self in every sphere. To present
Benjamin Franklin as an "Experimental Philosopher," and more particularly as an explorer of electricity where his scientific genius found
its fullest expression, is not so much to depict a particular part of
Franklin, as to portray in a particular light the unique whole.

Franklin's electricity, like all Franklin's science, is so much in character with Franklin himself. It exemplifies his superb common sense—developed to a highly uncommon degree and expressed alike in practice and principle, in purpose and procedure. Its hallmarks are native wit coupled to a keen eye and skilled hands; leavened by wisdom born of experience and enriched by philosophical enlightenment, but never overburdened by a surfeit of sophistry or scholarship.

Franklin's science epitomizes Franklin, and Franklin his era in science: the age of the amateur—pursuing science to satisfy curiosity, for amusement, for enlightenment, possibly for benefit, but as a passion more than a profession. Electricity in the mid-18th century might have been made for Franklin and Franklin for electricity: their meeting, however accidental historically, seemed preordained!

Born in Boston, in 1706, "of humble stock" as the phrase goes—his father an emigrant soap-boiler and candle-maker—the sixth, youngest son of ten children, his "formal" school education began at eight and was completed at age ten. From then on he was not only self-taught in the practical, worldly sense; he diligently and systematically educated himself. He read widely—both classical and contemporary writings—and taught himself French, Italian, Spanish, and Latin. At twelve, he is an apprenticed printer; at fifteen he is not only reading, but writing, and publishing (with his brother) a "radical" newspaper. At eighteen, he is a seasoned journalist and printer; at twenty, having gained wide experience and traveled afar, he establishes his own printing-publishing business. He is now, and remains for the rest of his life, his own master, a citizen of his new home, Philadelphia.

Printing and publishing provide Franklin not only with a good living, but the opportunity to disseminate his ideas and ideals. Matching his skill as an artisan, his diligence in trade, and his acumen in business, is his powerful gift as a writer: equally able to inform, instruct, and to enlighten, to entertain and to influence.

And Franklin is never at a loss for subject matter. His curiosity is aroused, his mind stirred and pen moved by everything and everybody he encounters: from smokeless chimneys to the grand architecture of nature; from the cultivation of silkworms to the management of civic affairs. Thoughts, deeds, works, and words—all were ineluctably linked. Within a few years he had written articles on *Liberty and Necessity; Pleasure and Pain; On the Need for Paper Money;* and *On Pleasant Dreams;* he was publishing two newspapers, had started up that endless stream of advice, wit, and homespun philosophy—*Poor Richard's Almanac*—and had argued for the defense of the Colony in a pamphlet entitled *Plain Truth!* Concurrently he had organized the first lending library, was Grandmaster of the Freemasons, had established the first fire brigade, and was clerk to the Pennsylvania Assembly and a member of the City Council. He reorganized the mails, helped raise troops and erect blockhouses, and founded a moral-philosophical debating society—the Junto Club, the forerunner of the American Philosophical Society. With no exaggeration it was said of him that "he gave the impulse to nearly every measure or project for the welfare and prosperity of Philadelphia undertaken in his day."

It is impossible to conceive of Benjamin Franklin, more than 40 years old, prosperous citizen, husband and father, deeply immersed in business and civic affairs of every variety, devoting his whole attention or all his boundless energies to any one subject. Yet for a few years, from about 1747 to 1750, one subject—electricity—seems to have fully capitivated, if not captured, him. Early in 1747, he wrote his friend Collison in London: "I never was engaged in a study [electricity] that so totally engrossed my time as this has lately done."

Of course there had to be time off to attend to defending the colony from attacks by the Indians (or was it really the French?). Convincing Quakers of the need for a militia must have taxed even Franklin's energies and powers of persuasion! Nonetheless, it was his contributions to electrical science during those few years that earned for Franklin his immense reputation, in his day, as a natural philosopher and ensured his place, for all time, in the history of science.

Electricity in the mid-18th century, a favorite hunting ground for amateurs, was viewed with more than circumspection by the scientifically learned, particularly many of the great mathematical savants. The renowned Leonhard Euler, for example, in his celebrated letters to a German princess, writes: "The subject [electricity] . . . almost terrifies me. The variety it presents is immense, and the enumeration of its parts serves rather to confound than to inform—almost every day [there is] discovered some new phenomenon . . . the fatigue of wading through diffuse, long, tedious detail."

But this "tedious detail" did not daunt the amateurs—and Franklin was an amateur in the best and literal sense of the word. In the 18th century it was not unusual for a gentleman with sufficient leisure and money to dabble in science; but how many of the dilettantes could claim Franklin's distinction of having acquired his opportunities entirely by the efforts of his own hands and brain? Here Benjamin Franklin was, if not unique, certainly outstanding. Years as an artisan and entrepreneur had gained for him intimate practical insight into the vagaries of men and materials, and he knew how to coax the most out of both. And Nature, whether majestic or miniscule, was for him always fascinating; intriguing, perplexing, capricious, sometimes trying, perhaps. But tedious? Never!

How Benjamin Franklin became so absorbed with electricity at this particular time need not detain us: the story (or some story) has been told and retold. In any event, there was at this time a great surge of interest—both scientific and popular—in the subject, whose immediate climax was to be the discovery of the Leyden jar. Franklin was following, albeit at a distance, the main lines of scientific development in Europe and he must have already noticed the increasing prominence of electrical investigations. When the moment arrived, he set about the business with characteristic directness and dispatch. He did not wait to build grand apparatus: a simple glass tube from his friend Collison and common artifacts—personal, domestic, and from his trade—wine glasses, bottles, salt-cellars, gun-barrels, gilt-paper book-bindings, etc., were pressed into service. His "team" of co-workers was likewise spontaneous and opportune. It included: a local judge, a silversmith, and an "unemployed" Baptist minister.

With such naive paraphernalia, with such an odd group of collaborators, in a remote colony, far from the European centers of science and enlightenment, how could an unsophisticated tinkerer—as Franklin has often been dubbed—possibly probe the profundities of the new electrical science? Indeed, his contemporary and great opponent—the learned Abbé Nollet in Paris—was (at first!) convinced that no such *American* philosopher could possibly exist. He was a fiction fabricated by his enemies to torment him!

More persistent has been the assessment of Franklin's experiments in electricity as crude and qualitative, lacking proper instruments and therefore quantitative significance, successful only because of the simplicity of the phenomena he examined. What lack of appreciation of history and misunderstanding of the true nature of scientific discovery this betrays! The simplicity was not in the phenomena: these were attended by all the baffling complexities, all the capriciousness of real phenomena. It was the art of the experimenter that extracted from them the "simple" principles and made the experiments seem simple—afterwards! Simplicity was the antithesis of *confusion*, not of subtlety!

To find a simple uniform principle underlying and buried in the bewildering variety of detail was precisely Franklin's great achievement. It was the sort of principle which Franklin could recognize and appreciate *a priori*; and one whose role and significance in electricity he could demonstrate. His view of Nature, influenced no doubt by the current fashionable expositions of a simplified philosophical Newtonianism, included notions of permanent immutable "elements," the work of the great Architect and Lawgiver; and of endless variety and change in the actual world which only disguised, but did not destroy, the underlying permanence and order. In any event, he seems from the outset to have introduced this notion—of something *conserved*—into his interpretations. Very soon he made it the basic axiom of his electrical theory. The famous "single fluid" hypothesis—the subject of more than a century of controversy—is really a side issue. Conservation of two (or more) fluids could also have worked (as many later appreciated), but this would not only have complicated matters unnecessarily; it would also have made the significance of the essential feature—*conservation*—harder to perceive and therefore harder to demonstrate. One fluid was enough; a second would have been not so much wrong as superfluous.

A basic experimental language—with its own grammar and idiom—was essential both to demonstrate the principle and to pursue its implications. Stripped of some of its more archaic terminology—the electric "fires" and "atmospheres," the "pores" and the "effluvia," Franklin's basic grammar ran thus: ordinary "unelectrified" objects which produced no spark, shock, or attraction and repulsion were identified as bodies in which the electricity was in "equilibrium." Electrification consisted, then, in disturbing the equilibrium—not by *creating* electricity but by transferring it from one body to another, thereby producing a deficit $(-)$ in one and an excess $(+)$ in the other. Conversely, electricity is never destroyed; rather, equilibrium may be restored by the passage of electricity from the region of excess to that of deficit, and this may be signaled by the familiar spark or shock. It could be facilitated by the particular technique of discharge to or from sharp points.

This is Franklin's basic grammar. His experiments are models of clear conception, keen observation, and cogent analysis. For a century or so, since the experiments of Burgomeister von Guericke, glass, and many other materials, had been rubbed and the sparks and shocks witnessed. The new and decisive feature which Franklin introduces and exploits is the electrical isolation of both producer of electricity (silk, glass, and all) and its recipient. Here for the first time are deliberately arranged, clearly recognized and exploited "closed" electrical systems. For the rest, the experimental technique is ludicrously simple: one person standing on wax rubs the tube; another, similarly isolated, "draws the fire." A third, standing on the floor (unisolated), acts simply to register the extent of electrification of each of the other two, by taking a spark with his knuckle.

This procedure of "isolation" is soon skillfully exploited in Franklin's masterly elucidation of the new sensation: the Leyden jar. Born out of attempts to *store* (or literally to bottle!) electricity, and conceived of as such, its extraordinary powers were, and would have remained, a mystery. It was Franklin who perceived, clearly demonstrated, and emphatically asserted that there was *no* net charge of electricity in the Leyden jar—just the close proximity of a surplus on one side and a deficiency on the other! Wherein lay the particular merit of such a proximate combination? After all, *all* unelectrified bodies contain immense quantities of such surpluses and deficits in close proximity. This was a more subtle matter for which Franklin invented his own peculiar detailed theory (which later experiments compelled him to modify) based on the mystique of glass. Franklin's studies of the Leyden jar, so central in the development of his ideas, provided a splendid illustration of both the power and the limitations of his experimental procedures and electrical principles.

In experiments with the original, hand-held, water-filled Leyden jar, he showed by decanting the water from a "charged" jar that the electricity did not reside in the water, but rather that the electrification was, seemingly, associated with, and retained by, the glass separating the water from his hand outside. "Thus, the whole force of the bottle, and power of giving a shock, is in the *glass itself*; the non-electrics [i.e., conductors] in contact with the two surfaces, serving only to *give* and *receive* to and from the several parts of the glass; that is, to give on one side and take away from the other."

But how could he be sure that the form of the glass, or indeed the nature of the conductors—the water, hand, etc.—did not play a significant role?

> To find, then, whether glass had this property merely as glass, or whether the form contributed anything to it, we took a pane of sash-glass, and, laying it on the hand, placed a plate of lead on its upper surface; then electrified that plate, and bringing a finger to it there was a spark and shock. We then took two plates of lead of equal dimensions, but less than the glass by two inches every way, and electrified the glass between them, by electrifying the uppermost lead; then separated the glass from the lead, in doing which that little fire might be in the lead was taken out, and the glass being touched in the electrified parts with a finger, afforded only very small pricking sparks, but a great number of them might be taken from different places. Then dexterously placing it again between the leaden plates, and completing a circle between the two surfaces, a violent shock ensued. Which demonstrates the power to reside in glass as glass.

Franklin's detecting instrument—his finger taking the spark and shock—was certainly rudimentary. Even his most sensitive detector—his suspended cork-balls—were capable of responding only to strongly charged objects (corresponding to potential differences of several kilovolts). Surely more sensitive and precise instruments would have enhanced his experiments, endowed them with more quantitative significance? Let us see then what might have ensued had Franklin performed this Leyden jar experiment using a more sensitive electrometer or gold-leaf electroscope, which proved such valuable tools a few decades later.

Here I use a demountable Leyden jar, similar to Franklin's glass and lead plate, but for convenience, cup-shaped, rather than plane. (It is a contemporary product made, I believe, to demonstrate Franklin's experiments, and assuming perhaps that their outcome is known!) We have a pair of such Leyden jars. Each comprises an outer metal cup (grounded), an insulating lining, and an inner metal cup. We charge the first, strongly, sufficient to give a shock, or to show on this crude detector—a suspended cork-ball, à-la-Franklin. The other jar is uncharged. Now we remove the inner metal cups from both jars and replace each by that from the other jar. We find—just as in Franklin's experiment—that the electrification does *not* follow the "charged" conductor, but remains with the insulator. Now we repeat the experiment, but with a much smaller charge, one which gives a barely perceptible shock but is readily detected by this gold-leaf electroscope. Now, in contrast, the electrification seems to follow not the insulator, but the conductors!

Perhaps Franklin was not completely and blissfully ignorant of the qualitative differences that could result from experimenting at widely different levels of electrification. (We notice how he seemed content to treat "what little fire might be in the lead" as insignificant!) Yet he does arrive at a simple, definite, and essentially quantitative conclusion. This he does not by accumulating a mass of detailed (and possibly meaningless) numerical data, but rather by multiplying the variety of experiments which can guide his perceptions towards what is significant. He neither pursues nor claims a numerical precision, one that could be illusory where the particular circumstances are little understood. As for enhanced sensitivity, the perceptions of the experimenter, like those of the nervous system, can suffer by being too indiscriminantly sensitive.

At the level of electrification which he employed, Franklin could find a certain uniformity which was, to him, significant. To relate his experiments to his general principles, he characteristically clothed the abstractions of the latter in picturesque detail. To be sure, this led him to an untenable, one might even say naive, view of the role of the glass (insulator) in the Leyden jar; but was not this a small price to pay for the discovery of the conservation of electric charge?

Franklin's discoveries and speculations greatly impressed the cognoscenti of the Royal Society in 1750, but the full impact of Franklin's electricity—on both the philosophical and lay world—came a year or two later, when the precise procedures he had laid down (based on a bold extrapolation of his experiments and his own principles, of course) for demonstrating the identity of lightning and electricity were successfully exploited; first by Dalibard at Paris. Franklin's fame spread rapidly; "Franklinism" and the "Philadelphia Experiments" became household terms.

In 1753, the Royal Society awarded him its highest scientific honor, the Copley Medal.

The law of conservation of charge, the principle of the Leyden jar (condenser), and the invention of the lightning conductor epitomize Franklin's lasting contributions to science. But for Franklin himself, in his own time and in his own wide circle of friends, electricity was but one part of his boundless interest in matters scientific. On the basis of theoretical principles and practical experiments, he designed and made fuel-saving fireplaces; devised cures for smoking chimneys and draughty rooms; proposed improved techniques of navigation; studied the resistance to motion of boats in canals, the cultivation of grass, and the husbandry of hedges; and he was actively involved in the promotion of silk production in America. His inventions ranged from a novel musical instrument, his "Armonica," to bifocal spectacles; his enquiries from the generation of cold by evaporation, and the causes of the common cold. His eminently sensible views on the heating and circulation of the blood, on gallstones, on lead poisoning, and atmospheric pollution, etc., earned the widespread respect of professional physicians.

Nothing, at any time or place, that caught Franklin's keen eye—and little escaped it—failed to stir his mind and as often as not move him to experiment.

And what matter if his boundless curiosity and endless speculation often outstripped his ability to resolve the innumerable problems which he energetically pursued? Posing questions seemed to give him as much satisfaction as answering them; and the answers he does essay are so often, as he readily acknowledges "but conjectures and suppositions, which ought always to give place when careful observation militates against them." Although Franklin can, and does, propound what he believes to be true with forceful eloquence, there is no trace of stubbornness in his defense of a belief simply because it is his own. Indeed, he makes a virtue of his errors and limitations: "A frank acknowledgement of one's ignorance is not only the easiest way to get rid of a difficulty, but the likeliest way to obtain information, and I therefore practice it."

With this complete unconcern about discovering, or disclosing his own ignorance, he can embark on a long trail of enquiry, seeking to learn from every circumstance and opportunity and listening to all who can proffer information, with little apparent concern about reaching the final destination of a definite conclusion.

A fascinating example of such a roving enquiry is one prompted by a chance observation on board ship between England and America. He describes the incident in a letter to his London friend, Dr. John Pringle:

> During our passage to Madeira, the weather being warm and the cabin windows constantly open for the benefit of air, the candles at night flared and run very much, which was an inconvenience. At Madeira, we got oil to burn, and with a common glass tumbler or beaker, slung in wire, and suspended to the ceiling of the cabin, and a little wire hoop for the wick, furnished with corks to float on the oil, I made an Italian lamp, that gave us very good light all over the table. The glass at bottom contained water to about one third of its height; another third was taken up with oil; the rest was left empty that the sides of the glass might protect the flame from the wind. There is nothing remarkable in all this; but what follows is particular. At supper, looking on the lamp, I remarked, that though the surface of the oil was perfectly tranquil, and duly preserved its position and distance with regard to the brim of the glass, the water under the oil was in great commotion, rising and falling in irregular waves, which continued during the whole evening. The lamp was kept burning as a watch-light all night, till the oil was spent, and the water only remained. In the morning I observed, that though the motion of the ship continued the same, the water was now quiet, and its surface as tranquil as that of the oil had been the evening before. At night again, when oil was put upon it, the water resumed its irregular motions, rising in high waves almost to the surfaces of the oil, but without disturbing the smooth level of that surface. And this was repeated every day during the voyage.

Franklin can scarcely believe his eyes; but what he cannot understand he does not forget. At home, on dry land, he soon reproduces the effect. It is indeed striking, as you can see by a reproduction of his experiments. Ten years later, Franklin is still puzzling over what he recalls as the "wonderful quietness of oil on agitated waters." But in the meantime, he has enquired far and wide about what may be similar oil-on-water phenomena, and some earlier observations and recollections of his own have been evoked. He recalls Pliny's mention of divers stilling water by oil; and his earlier experience at sea, in 1757, when he noticed that the wakes of some among a large fleet of ships were remarkably smooth. On enquiring, the captain told him that "the cooks have, I suppose, been just emptying greasy water through the scuppers." Another "old captain" informs him that the fishermen in Bermuda, and in Lisbon, practice calming ruffled water with oil, and confirms Pliny's account of the same practice by Mediterranean divers. From "a gentleman from Rhode Island" he learns that "the harbour of Newport was ever smooth while any whaling vessels were in it; which probably arose from hence, that the blubber which they sometimes bring loose in the hold, or the leakage of their barrels, might afford some oil, to mix with that water, which from time to time they pump out to keep their vessel free."

All this leads, inevitably, to experiment—performed on a pond on Clapham Common, London—which not only confirms the reality of the phenomenon, but leads to a new surprise—the remarkable spreading power of oil. A mere teaspoonful covers some half-an-acre of water!

Thereafter, Franklin tells us, whenever he went into the country he took with him "a little oil in the upper hollow of [his] bamboo cane" so that he can share the surprise and the pleasure of the experiment with others. The phenomenon of the swinging lamp which started all this train of enquiry remained unforgotten but unexplained; or Franklin remains skeptical of the proffered explanations:

> I have shown this experiment to a number of ingenious persons. Those who are but slightly acquainted with the principles of hydrostatics, and are apt to fancy immediately that they understand it, and readily attempt to explain it; but their explanations have been different, and to me not very intelligible. Others, more deeply skilled in those principles, seem to wonder at it, and promise to consider it.

Franklin made no pretensions of deep learning in fluid mechanics or of the mathematical subtleties involved. Of his theory of storms he confessed: "If my hypothesis is not the truth, it is at least as naked. For I have not, with some of our learned moderns, disguised my nonsense in Greek, cloyed it in algebra, or adorned it in fluxions."

But he was not unappreciative of the power of mathematics. When young, he had invented a mathematics of his own: a "moral or prudential algebra" in which, as in his electricity, an accounting could be made of good (positive) and bad (negative), and by their mutual cancellation, the net result estimated. And in later years, he displays, in his reply to Madame Brillon's accusations of inconstancy, a mellow sense of mathematical nicety. It is "as plain as Euclid that who ever was constant to several persons was more constant than he who was only constant to one."

Remarkably, this irrepressible interest in science continued unabated even as Franklin became ever more engrossed and burdened by affairs of state. From oil on troubled water, he could turn readily to political diplomacy; from the nature of atmospheric storms to warnings and prognostications of impending political disaster. Experimental science and practical politics, natural philosophy and political philosophy seemed barely separate.

Benjamin Franklin was the supreme amateur. Balzac could sum him up as the inventor of the lightning rod, the political hoax ("canard"), and the republic! His only profession—as he described himself in his own epitaph—was that of "printer." For the rest, he did what interested him, and what he believed necessary and good. He wrote and spoke as he felt, and what he felt to be true. Not a professional—either in science or letters or politics—he had no professional reputation to establish or to defend. He probably held more public offices than anyone before him, or since, and yet he could justly claim: "I never did, directly or indirectly, solicit any man's vote." His preeminence as a statesman was unquestioned, and yet it was through anonymous satire that he delivered some of his most influential political thrusts.

His electrical discoveries and ideas had immense influence; his theories were, for decades, exploited and developed by many who followed him; yet he could honestly assert: "I have never entered into any controversy in defense of my philosophical opinions. If they are right, trial and experience will support them; if wrong they ought to be refuted and rejected. . . . I have no private interest in the reception of my inventions, having never made, nor proposed to make, the least profit of them."

This willingness to let deeds speak for themselves, and to use words to convey ideas rather than to solicit acquiescence, is the more remarkable in one so gifted in the powers of persuasion. Franklin possessed this power to the highest degree—yet he never abused it. In all his writing, whether he is explaining some simple matter to the young Mary Stevenson, or to the sophisticated Madame Helvetius, whether expounding his views to the savants of his day, or denouncing the policies of King George's haughty ministers, or musing in his own autobiography, it is always the same voice: Franklin expressing lucidly, forcibly, but with natural ease, what he thinks and believes.

No pleading, no pretensions, no puffery. His experimental philosophy—his dialogue with Nature—has the same essential character. He does not try to teach Nature, to impose his views on it, but to converse with and learn from it. He has no illusions about the difference between a dialogue with Nature and a political debate. Yet in his approach to both, it is the same Franklin. It is not that he brings to his politics the standards of impartial truth he has learned from science. Rather he brings to both—science and politics—his own incomparable blend of honesty, insight, and imagination. He would have agreed with Bacon that "Nature to be commanded must first be obeyed."

A like motto would serve him in government, as a public servant: a people to be governed must first be served. In science one must assume that Nature already knows what we are trying to learn: in politics he would advise a similar stance. He would take his cue from Pope's lines: "Men must be taught as if you taught them not, / And things unknown, proposed as things forgot."

Franklin lived his philosophy; and his philosophy was a practical one. If truth was his goal, honesty was his constant guide that might with good fortune lead him there. Honest, practical utility prompts alike much of his scientific enterprise and his industrious diplomacy, but the ideals of scientific truth and social justice are never far absent. And if truth and justice are unattainable ideals, there remains the more modest task of combating error and injustice; in Michael Faraday's more solemn expression, "the high and pure philosophic desire to remove error as well as discover truth."

Franklin was no idealist, yet stirred by ideals: no pragmatist, though all he did was stamped with purpose. The truth was for him a natural by-product of honesty as the ideal was of the practical. He allegorizes his philosophy in a parable of a hard-working, prosperous farmer imparting his final advice to his heir: "My son, I gave thee now a valuable parcel of land; I assure you I have found a considerable quantity of gold by digging there. Thee mayest do the same: but thee must carefully observe this, *Never dig more than plough deep.*"

Finally, there is Franklin's own brand of humor and humility! The scale of his achievements rendered modesty unfitting and cynicism implausible. Yet he was quite aware of the world's and his own limitations. Poor Richard warns that "in a corrupt age, that putting the world in order would breed confusion." Truth (and justice) must remain unattainable ideals; but there was no monopoly of honesty (or honest purpose). Never did Franklin assume that office, rank, or reputation entitled his views to more respect than did their intrinsic merit. In the presumption of omnipotence he saw evil only compounded by the added conceit of omniscience. Nor did Franklin confuse the right to speak freely with the demand to be heard.

Minister Turgot portrays him, with Latin verve: "He snatched fire from the Heavens and the Sceptre from the Tyrant's hand." His Scottish admirer, Lord Kames, pays tribute in more sombre words: "A man who makes a great figure in the learned world, and one who would make a still greater figure, were virtue as much regarded in this declining age as knowledge." For Franklin himself, the search for knowledge was also the path to virtue. And just as at times we err in judgment so also we stray from the path of true virtue. Franklin was certainly no saint!

Franklin's style of experimental exploration, its spontaneity, its unsophisticated light-heartedness, its gaiety and its deceptive simplicity, even naivete, all seem to belong to a bygone age. His effluvia, electric fire, and atmospheres, his sparks and shocks—all are now historical curiosities. But his law of conservation of electricity—whether in its simple Franklinian form, or embodied in some highly sophisticated abstraction—remains: challenged from time to time, but still part of the bedrock of basic principles. But that is not the whole—or perhaps even the major part of Franklin's philosophical legacy. The apparent paradox of Franklin, at once the pragmatist and the idealist, the man of the world and the workshop, equally at home and at ease with printers, politicians, and philosophers, lies deep in Franklin's philosophy. If in the probing of Nature, truth remains undiscovered, if in the affairs of nations the final tasks remain unresolved, then this at least—or at best?—we may learn: the truth about ourselves!

So, of science he could write: "If there is no other Use discovered for Electricity, this, however, is something considerable: *that it may help make a vain man humble*." And of politics: "The first mistake in public business is the going into it."

From innumerable finite accomplishments—practical, political, and philosophical—derive his assurance and authority; from the awareness of boundless unattained ideals—his humility. "Knowledge is proud that it has learnt so much / Wisdom is humble that it knows no more." Franklin's younger contemporary, William Cowper, might have written the lines for him!

But it is with his own clear voice that we should part company with Benjamin Franklin. His deeds were numberless, but his ideals he could sum up in three words: Truth, Sincerity, and Integrity.

5

Land of the Unfree: Legal Limitations on Liberty in Pre-Revolutionary America

LINDA GRANT DE PAUW

● In 1776, representatives of thirteen British colonies in North America boldly affixed their signatures to the Declaration of Independence. Arguing that all men were endowed by their creator with certain "inalienable" rights, they gave liberty as the purpose of the new United States. Based on the theory of natural rights, which had been espoused earlier by John Locke and Jean Jacques Rousseau, the Declaration of Independence is the most important of all American historical documents.

Actually, the notion of freedom was rather new in 1776. Until the twentieth century, in many parts of the world serfs were bound to the land, meaning that they lacked the freedom to come and go as they pleased without undue restraint. Freedom of religion, the right to worship with groups of one's own choosing, was unknown before the Protestant Reformation. The right to vote and to hold office was practically nonexistent before the nineteenth century, as was freedom of speech and of the press. Prior to the Habeas Corpus Act (1679) in England and for centuries thereafter in most countries, a person could be seized or kept in prison indefinitely without trial or hearing.

Even in the United States, long known as "the Land of the Free," the concept of liberty has expanded only gradually. The idea of equality, for example, has come only slowly to be associated with the idea of freedom. And for specific minorities, women and blacks being notable examples, many liberties are seen only as operative for white men. But whatever its shortcomings, the United States has usually come closer to

Reprinted by permission from *Maryland Historical Magazine* 68 (Winter 1973): 355-368.

the ideals and spirit of the universal symbol of freedom, the
Statue of Liberty, than have other nations of the world.

The fortune that Thomas Jefferson pledged with his life and sacred
honor in support of the declaration that all men are created equal and
endowed with inalienable rights to life, liberty, and the pursuit of happiness included, in the summer of 1776, almost two hundred slaves.
The incongruity of a slave-owning people basing their Revolution on
such exalted doctrines did not escape remark by contemporaries any
more than it has escaped notice by historians. "How is it" sneered
Samuel Johnson, "that we hear the loudest *yelps* for liberty among
the drivers of negroes?" The Loyalist Thomas Hutchinson dryly observed that there seemed to be some discrepancy between the declaration that all men were equal and a practice that deprived "more
than a hundred thousand Africans of their rights to liberty."
    Even those Englishmen who sympathized with the American cause
were repelled by the paradox. "If there be an object truly ridiculous
in nature," Thomas Day commented, "it is an American patriot signing resolutions of independence with the one hand, and with the
other brandishing a whip over his affrighted slaves." And the patriots
themselves were not insensitive to it. "I have sometimes been ready
to think," Abigail Adams wrote to her husband, "that the passion for
liberty cannot be equally strong in the breasts of those who have been
accustomed to deprive their fellow creatures of theirs." Patrick Henry
confessed amazement that men as sincerely "fond of liberty" and gen-
uinely religious as himself tolerated slavery. "Would anyone believe,"
he asked, "I am the master of slaves of my own purchase!"
    Historians writing about the age of the American Revolution have
tended to ignore the paradox more frequently than they have attempted to resolve it, but in recent years serious attention has been
given to the enslaved blacks, and such New Left historians as Jesse
Lemish and Staughton Lynd have pointed out the limitations on the
rights of such groups as merchant seamen and urban workers. Yet the
full magnitude of the paradox is still unmeasured, for it appears that
the contradiction between Lockean ideals and social practice in the
year 1776 was not only more pronounced than contemporaries and
traditional historians described but even exceeds the dimensions sug-

gested by recent historians of the New Left. Had Lockean dicta been applied to all the human beings in British North America on the eve of the Revolution, and had all been permitted to enjoy the natural and legal rights of freemen, it would have been necessary to alter the status of more than 85 percent of the population. In law and in fact no more than 15 percent of the Revolutionary generation was free to enjoy life, liberty, and the pursuit of happiness unhampered by any restraints except those to which they had given their consent.

The unfree of Revolutionary America may be conveniently considered in five categories: Negroes, white servants, women, minors, and propertyless adult white males. These categories overlap and the proportion of the total population falling into each of the categories differed from one part of the country to another. Thus there were proportionately more women in New England than in backcountry North Carolina, many more blacks, proportionally, in Virginia than in New Jersey, and a larger proportion of disfranchised adult white males in South Carolina than in Massachusetts.

It is also true that legal limitations on liberty do not necessarily coincide either with a psychological sense of freedom or with social practices. The unfree were rarely, in fact, exploited to the full limit allowed by law. Nor has there been any attempt in this brief essay to present a precise description of legal status based on the myriad of local traditions, statutes, and common law interpretation. The following summaries claim to be correct in outline, not to have exhausted the complexities of the subject, which are vast and largely unstudied. It is clear, however, that for each of the unfree groups the law placed definite theoretical limits on the rights Locke viewed as inalienable.

The black slaves, the most visible of the colonial unfree, comprised approximately 20 percent of the colonial population, a proportion twice as great as that formed by the black population of the United States today. These slaves were legally chattel property. The law saw no self-evident right to liberty attached to the person of the dark-skinned laborer from Africa, and, indeed, the law had little concern for his right to life. The deliberate murder of a slave was not necessarily a felony in Virginia before the Revolution, for the law assumed that no one would intentionally destroy his own estate. Slaves had no right to hold property of their own and enjoyed the use of no more than the master allowed. As for the third right in Jefferson's trinity, pursuing happiness, if that took the form of taking time off from the master's work, it was a punishable offense.

There were a small number of free blacks in Revolutionary America, most of them in the North. Their status was superior to that of the slave, but they were still limited politically, socially, and economically in all of the colonies. For most legal purposes there was no distinction made between free and enslaved Negroes. They might have some time they could call their own for pursuing happiness, but they were forbidden to pursue it in a tavern. In Rhode Island a free black man could not even purchase a quart of cider.

White servants in colonial America comprised a class perhaps half as large as the slave force but unbalanced in age and sex distribution in favor of young adult males. Their status was superior to that of Negroes but still substantially below that of freemen. In many ways the servant was merely a slave with prospects of eventual freedom and whose entry into his lowly station had been more or less voluntary. When, in November 1775, Lord Dunmore attempted to lure blacks into the British army by offering them freedom as a bounty, the same offer was extended to white servants.

The servant's labor belonged to his master twenty-four hours a day, seven days a week. Like the black slave, he was a chattel. He had no property himself but what his master allowed. He could not marry without his master's permission and, like a black man, he could not drink liquor in a tavern. Running away and disobedience were severely punished, and stories of inhuman cruelty to white servants are common. Like a slave, a white servant could be sold against his will away from his wife and family or seized to satisfy his master's debts. There seems little to recommend the legislation governing servants over that governing blacks—with one exception. White servants, unlike slaves, had personal rights to life and contract rights to a minimum standard of living. They could bring suit to enforce these rights and the courts would enforce them even to the extent of freeing the servant outright.

The legal status of colonial women was determined by the tradition of the British common law with certain modifications forced by pioneer American conditions, most of which were made before the end of the seventeenth century. Blackstone's *Commentaries*, which began to circulate as an admired authority among colonial lawyers in the decade before the Revolution, described a theoretical position for English females that varied substantially from that held by free English men. Under common law, Blackstone taught, a woman ceased to exist if she married, for she and her spouse became one flesh and the flesh was his. She was no longer responsible for her debts or even for all of her personal actions. She had no legal control over any property either inherited or earned. And if her husband judged her disobedient or saucy he could chastise her as he did his children and servants. This was considered proper as he might be held responsible for her misbehavior in cases short of murder and high treason. Although divorce laws were relatively liberal for a time in the seventeenth century, a reaction in the Revolutionary era made divorce, regardless of cause, practically impossible for a woman to obtain.

The status of unmarried women, both widows and spinsters, was considerably better. By a law of 1419 known as "couverte de Baron" an unattached woman, the "Feme Sole," was entitled to engage in business enterprises on her own account. A widow was entitled to one-third of the family estate and might be willed even more. So long as she did not remarry she could invest or dispose of this property as she wished. There was, however, great social pressure on women to marry. Although women made up almost half of the total population when all age groups are included, the sex ratio of men to women in the marriageable age group (i.e., between sixteen and sixty) was extremely high—160.8 men to every 100 women. Consequently spinsters were few and they were generally propertyless dependents in the home of a male relative. Widows commonly remarried before their husbands had been buried a year—unless they were remarkably unattractive, elderly, or poor. Those in the last category, who could not support themselves on one-third of their deceased husband's estate, would be subject to the poor laws unless a male relative could be found to take them in. The poor law prescribed compulsory labor for the poor so that impoverished widows might be bound out to serve as domestics. In Wareham, Massachusetts (admittedly an exceptional case) there was an annual auction of indigent widows.

Americans under the age of twenty-one, a clear majority of the population in 1776, were legal infants, and the right to liberty of such persons was far from self-evident to the founding fathers, although they were aware that it seemed to follow, at least for older children, from the Lockean premises. It would be a mistake to confuse the class of legal minors in Revolutionary America with modern adolescents. Blackstone declared a boy of twelve fit to take an oath of allegiance and a girl of seven ready to be given in marriage. The age of discretion for most purposes fell between seven and fourteen and all children above this age group were subject to capital punishment for felonies and bore most of the responsibilities if not the privileges of adults. Children entered the labor force well before they entered their teens, and they developed a degree of maturity and experience in the world that would be considered unhealthily precocious today. The large number of men in their early twenties who served competently as field officers in the Revolutionary armies and sat in the Continental Congresses could only have appeared in a society that considered teenage boys adults even though it deprived them of full legal rights. Male children of the age of sixteen were taxable and liable for militia duty. And since the population of colonial America was generally young, sixteen being the median age, unfree males between sixteen and twenty-one comprised one quarter of the total taxable male population. In an age when the mortality rates among infants and children were high and when a youth of sixteen had less than an even chance of surviving to the age of thirty, the loss of even a few years of liberty was a significant grievance.

Furthermore, theories of child nurture in colonial days were distinctly grim, based on the still formidable patriarchical traditions that had prescribed death for a "rebellious and incorrigible son." Obedience to parents was a duty imposed by divine as well as human law to be enforced by corporal punishment if necessary. Minors were expected to work for their parents as soon as they could walk, but they had no personal property rights before they came of legal age. Authority over children above ten or fourteen was frequently transferred from the natural parents to a master. The institution of apprenticeship was still viable at the time of the Revolution and was the usual path for a young man who did not intend to become a farmer but wished to learn a trade. Girls might also become apprenticed. Apprenticeship articles were drawn to standards set by colonial legislatures and generally required the consent of the child as well as of his parents. But children of poor or otherwise incompetent parents might be sold against their will to masters who promised, sometimes deceitfully, to provide for them adequately and teach them a trade before they came of age.

Once apprenticed, a child's labor belonged to the master as fully as did that of any servant. Even visits to his own parents could be forbidden and the free-time conduct of apprentices was subject to the same sort of restrictions that applied to adult servants or slaves. Disobedience to a master as to a father could be punished with the whip. If a child came to detest the trade his father apprenticed him to, or if the master failed to make him proficient in the craft, his entire future would be warped, for once of age and free it would be too late to begin again to acquire the skills needed to make a living.

These four groups—Negroes, servants, women, and minors—together comprised approximately 80 percent of the two and a half million Americans in the year 1776. The legal doctrine applied to these classes excluded them from the category of persons who should enjoy the "inalienable rights" of which the Declaration speaks. But perhaps the most significant mark of their unfreedom was their usual lack of a right to vote, for the privilege of consenting to the laws was the essential right of a free man in Lockean theory. Indeed, the very word "enfranchise" was defined in the eighteenth century as the equivalent of the word "emancipate"; it meant "to make free."

Interestingly enough, the prohibition on the suffrage does not appear to have been absolute either in law or in fact for any of the unfree groups. Colonial suffrage legislation tended to be vague. Only Virginia, South Carolina, and Georgia specifically confined the franchise to white voters and there are recorded cases of Negroes, mulattoes, and Indians actually casting ballots. When in 1778 a provision excluding blacks from the suffrage was inserted in the proposed Massachusetts constitution, a citizen observed in the *Independent Chronicle* that "a black, tawny or reddish skin is not so unfavorable in hue to the genuine son of liberty, as a tory complection." Rare instances of bond servants casting votes are known and enough servants presumed to exercise the franchise in Albany, New York, to necessitate their specific exclusion from participation in city elections in 1773.

Only Pennsylvania, Delaware, South Carolina, and Georgia specifically disfranchised females who otherwise qualified as property holders. When Hannah Lee Corbin protested to her brother Richard Henry

Lee in 1778 that Virginia women ought not to be taxed if they had
not the right to vote, he replied that "women were already possessed
of that right," and, apparently, some women did vote for a time in
Virginia as well as in New England and the middle colonies. But
these cases were rare and it is significant that Mrs. Corbin did not
know she had the franchise until her brother so informed her.

Only six states explicitly stated that voters must be twenty-one
years of age (Pennsylvania, South Carolina, Virginia, Connecticut,
New York, and North Carolina), and there are recorded cases of
young men under legal age occasionally registering their votes.

In all likelihood, however, the liberality of colonial suffrage legislation was due to careless draftsmanship rather than to any desire to
permit members of the unfree classes to vote. The intention was to
limit the franchise to free, adult, white males and others who voted
slipped through by accident as a result of laxity among election inspectors. Indeed, we know of such cases chiefly because they served as
grounds for complaint in disputed elections.

A fifth group of colonial Americans, adult white males with little
or no property, was deprived of the vote in colonial elections and so
fell short of full liberty in the Lockean sense. But they were privileged
above the other unfree groups since they were legally entitled to acquire property and were protected from physical abuse except such as
was administered by public authority after trial as punishment for offenses against the state. Some of these disfranchised males were idiots,
invalids, or residents of workhouses. Others were simply too poor to
qualify under the arbitrary property requirements of the various elec-
toral laws. Statistically they are the least significant of the unfree, although they have had more than their share of attention from critics
of consensus history. They made up between 5 and 10 percent of the
total population. If they are added to the 80 percent of the population in the other unfree categories, which were limited not merely in
their political rights but in their rights to personal liberty and property as well, then only 10 to 15 percent of the American population
remain to qualify as "freemen" in the fullest sense.

It is curious that this startling statistic has somehow escaped comment by historians. While the enslavement of Negroes and disfranchisement of some adult white males may be noted in passing as
undemocratic elements in pre-Revolutionary America, the disfran-

chisement and worse of the other unfree classes is accepted without remark even in our enlightened age. Thus, Elisha P. Douglass defines democracy in his *Rebels and Democrats* as "a political system in which all adult males enjoyed equal political rights." Robert Brown writes in *Middle-Class Democracy and the Revolution in Massachusetts*, "The only valid approach . . . is to find out how many adult men could vote out of the total adult male population," and he concludes that "if anything with the appearance of a man could vote there was little problem of a restricted electorate." And finally, the author of this paper casually observed in *The Eleventh Pillar*, "The important ratio is that of qualified voters to adult white males."

Today almost 65 percent of the total population is enfranchised and in law, at least, virtually all of the people are secured in property rights and protected from physical abuse by private parties. Yet even our age finds it self-evident that women and young people should have been excluded from colonial political life. Since this is the case, we should not find it difficult to understand how the men of two centuries ago could accept the contradiction between their Lockean principles and their discriminatory practice without too much discomfort.

It would be both uncharitable and simplistic to dismiss the founding fathers as hypocrites because they tolerated this inconsistency. Some conflict between ideal principles and social practice is inevitable if the ideals are at all noble and the society composed of human beings rather than angels. Nor is such contradiction undesirable. Quite the opposite, since it induces men, who will always fall short of perfection in their day to day experience, to consider the possibility of alternative social arrangements superior to their own. Thus John Adams was vastly amused when his Abigail presumed to apply the Revolutionary slogans to the condition of married ladies. But after puzzling over her remarks for a month he realized that, indeed, he could discover no moral foundation for government that would justify the exclusion of any class of people from full participation. Of course it was "impossible," he wrote to James Sullivan, that the principle of consent should ever be carried so far. But the logic was undeniable and if it were followed to its conclusion "women will demand a vote; lads from twelve to twenty-one will think their rights not enough attended to; and every man who has not a farthing, will demand an equal voice with any other, in all acts of state." Adams seems to have predicted the long range impact of the Revolutionary doctrine accurately enough.

Again, Patrick Henry, facing up to the contrast between his words and his practice of keeping slaves, wrote, "I will not, I cannot justify it. However culpable my conduct, I will so far pay my devoir to virtue, as to own the excellence and rectitude of her precepts, and lament my want of conformity to them."

In the final analysis, however, the contradiction was tolerable to Americans because they compared the extent of liberty in their society not with the Lockean ideal but with the extent of liberty in other contemporary or historically known societies. From this perspective there was no doubt that the Americans of 1776 were remarkably free. Even the slaves, servants, women, and children of America enjoyed positions superior to those held by similar classes in other lands and other times. And surely a land in which more than 10 percent of the population owned property and had a voice in the government was a wonder in an age when the civilized world was ruled by hereditary monarchs and property ownership was a prerogative of aristocrats. Even in England, where the political liberty of the early eighteenth century had made her people the envy of Europe, no more than 25 percent of "the active male population" had voted in even the freest parts of the kingdom—and after the first third of the century even this electorate had dwindled. Yet, to quote J. H. Plumb, "This was England's vast singularity, a unique situation amongst the major powers of the world."

Surely the gap that separated American society from the Lockean ideal was no more impressive than that which separated colonial American society from the societies of Europe. If freedom had a home anywhere in the world in the year 1776 it was in the new United States of America. But if "democracy" implies government by consent of the governed or at least by consent of a majority of those governed and not merely of an adult white male elite, then those historians from Bancroft to Brown who have described American society of the mid-eighteenth century as "democratic" are simply wrong. The opinion of Carl Becker and many others that colonial governments "did in a rough and ready way, conform to the kind of government for which Locke furnished a reasoned foundation" is vastly overstated. And the attempts of the New Left history to view the American Revolution "from the bottom up" will be superficial so long as "the bottom" is conceived in a way that still excludes the majority of the population.

6

Why Men Fought in the American Revolution

ROBERT MIDDLEKAUFF

• War has always been a dirty business. Although there have been many occasions when the outbreak of hostilities between nations has been greeted with celebrations, with brass bands, and with finely attired ladies blowing kisses to handsomely uniformed young soldiers, more common has been the experience of human tragedy, of husbands and fathers left to rest forever under faraway fields, of others whose broken bodies could never be healed. The study of battle is therefore always a study of fear, and usually of courage. It is also a study of solidarity and often of disintegration, for it is toward disintegration of human groups that warfare is directed.

Most studies of modern war focus on grand strategy and on generals. Rather less has been said about the human being in the thick of danger, of the role of compulsion and of ideology in getting men to risk life and love. Since the Civil War, when the draft was first instituted on a state basis, Americans have not often had the possibility of opting out of battle. When the nation called they were obliged to go, and only in the Vietnam War did a vocal fraction resist the patriotic appeal.

The American Revolution was different. The central government was weak, and in any event it was actively supported only by a minority of the population. Military service in the Continental Army, as in all armies, promised separation from home and from loved ones. Pay was meager and logistical support minimal. To be wounded was to court terrible pain and primitive medical treatment; to be captured often meant slow starvation aboard the infamous prison ships in New

From the *Huntington Library Quarterly* 43 (Spring 1980). Published with the permission of the *Huntington Library Quarterly*.

York Harbor. And the opponent was the world's foremost military power.

"Why Men Fought in the American Revolution" deals with a question that is central to the human experience. Whether the draft is reinstituted or not in the United States, the society will no doubt have to face again the agonizing question of whether to fight. As the fear of war in the Middle East and in Europe rises in the 1980s, Robert Middlekauff's analysis of decisions reached more than two centuries ago is disturbingly relevant to our own circumstances.

In the Battle of Eutaw Springs, South Carolina, the last major action of the Revolutionary War before Cornwallis surrendered at Yorktown, over 500 Americans were killed and wounded. Nathanael Greene had led some 2200 men into the Springs; his casualties thus equaled almost one fourth of his army. More men would die in battles in the next two years, and others would suffer terrible wounds. Although the statistics are notoriously unreliable, they show that the Revolution killed a higher percentage of those who served on the American side than any war in our history, always excepting the Civil War.

Why did these men—those who survived and those who died—fight? Why did they hold their ground, endure the strain of battle, with men dying about them and danger to themselves so obvious? Undoubtedly the reasons varied from battle to battle, but just as undoubtedly there was some experience common to all these battles—and fairly uniform reasons for the actions of the men who fought despite their deepest impulses, which must have been to run from the field in order to escape the danger.

Some men did run, throwing down their muskets and packs in order to speed their flight. American units broke in large actions and small, at Brooklyn, Kip's Bay, White Plains, Brandywine, Germantown, Camden, and Hobkirk's Hill, to cite the most important instances. Yet many men did not break and run even in the disasters to American arms. They held their ground until they were killed, and they fought tenaciously while pulling back.

In most actions the Continentals, the regulars, fought more bravely than the militia. We need to know why these men fought and why the American regulars performed better than the militia. The answers surely will help us to understand the Revolution, especially if we can discover whether what made men fight reflected what they believed—and felt—about the Revolution.

Several explanations of the willingness to fight and die, if necessary, may be dismissed at once. One is that soldiers on both sides fought out of fear of their officers, fearing them more than they did battle. Frederick the Great had described this condition as ideal, but it did not exist in ideal or practice in either the American or British army. The British soldier usually possessed a more professional spirit than the American, an attitude compounded from confidence in his skill and pride in belonging to an old established institution. British regiments carried proud names—the Royal Welsh Fusiliers, the Black Watch, the King's Own—whose officers usually behaved extraordinarily bravely in battle and expected their men to follow their examples. British officers disciplined their men more harshly than American officers did and generally trained them more effectively in the movements of battle. But neither they nor American officers instilled the fear that Frederick found so desirable. Spirit, bravery, a reliance on the bayonet were all expected of professional soldiers, but professionals acted out of pride—not fear of their officers.

Still, coercion and force were never absent from the life of either army. There were, however, limits on their use and their effectiveness. The fear of flogging might prevent a soldier from deserting from camp, but it could not guarantee that he would remain steady under fire. Fear of ridicule may have aided in keeping some troops in place, however. Eighteenth-century infantry went into combat in fairly close lines and officers could keep an eye on many of their men. If the formation was tight enough officers might strike laggards and even order "skulkers," Washington's term for those who turned tail, shot down. Just before the move to Dorchester Heights in March 1776, the word went out that any American who ran from the action would be "fired down upon the spot." The troops themselves approved of this threat, according to one of the chaplains.

Washington repeated the threat just before the Battle of Brooklyn later that year, though he seems not to have posted men behind the lines to carry it out. Daniel Morgan urged Nathanael Greene to place sharpshooters behind the militia, and Greene may have done so at Guilford Court House. No one thought that an entire army could be held in place against its will, and these threats to shoot soldiers who retired without orders were never widely issued.

A tactic that surely would have appealed to many soldiers would have been to send them into battle drunk. Undoubtedly some—on both sides—did enter combat with their senses deadened by rum. Both armies commonly issued an additional ration of rum on the eve of some extraordinary action—a long, difficult march, for example, or a battle, were two of the usual reasons. A common order on such occasions ran: "The troops should have an extraordinary allowance of rum," usually a gill, four ounces of unknown alcoholic content, which if taken down at the propitious moment might dull fears and summon courage. At Camden no supply of rum existed; Gates or his staff substituted molasses to no good effect, according to Otho Williams. The British fought brilliantly at Guilford Court House unaided by anything stronger than their own large spirits. In most actions soldiers went into battle with very little more than themselves and their comrades to lean upon.

Belief in the Holy Spirit surely sustained some in the American army, perhaps more than in the enemy's. There are a good many references to the divine or to Providence in the letters and diaries of ordinary soldiers. Often, however, these expressions are in the form of thanks to the Lord for permitting these soldiers to survive. There is little that suggests soldiers believed that faith rendered them invulnerable to the enemy's bullets. Many did consider the glorious cause to be sacred; their war, as the ministers who sent them off to kill never tired of reminding them, was just and providential.

Others clearly saw more immediate advantages in the fight: the plunder of the enemy's dead. At Monmouth Court House, where Clinton withdrew after dark leaving the field strewn with British corpses, the plundering carried American soldiers into the houses of civilians who had fled to save themselves. The soldiers' actions were so blatant and so unrestrained that Washington ordered their packs searched. And at Eutaw Springs, the Americans virtually gave up victory to the opportunity of ransacking British tents. Some died in their greed, shot down by an enemy given time to regroup while his camp was torn apart by men looking for something to carry off. But even these men probably fought for something besides plunder. When it beckoned they collapsed, but it had not drawn them to the field; nor had it kept them there in a savage struggle.

Inspired leadership helped soldiers face death, but they sometimes fought bravely even when their leaders let them down. Yet officers' courage and the example of officers throwing off wounds to remain in the fight undoubtedly helped their men stick. Charles Stedman remarked on Captain Maitland, who at Guilford Court House was hit, dropped behind for a few minutes to get his wound dressed, then returned to the battle. Cornwallis obviously filled Sergeant Lamb with pride, struggling forward to press into the struggle after his horse was killed. Washington's presence meant much at Princeton, though his exposure to enemy fire may also have made his troops uneasy. His quiet exhortation as he passed among the men who were about to assault Trenton—"Soldiers, keep by your officers"—remained in the mind of a Connecticut soldier until he died fifty years later. There was only one Washington, one Cornwallis, and their influence on men in battle, few of whom could have seen them, was of course slight. Junior and noncommissioned officers carried the burden of tactical direction; they had to show their troops what must be done and somehow persuade, cajole, or force them to do it. The praise ordinary soldiers lavished on sergeants and junior officers suggests that these leaders played important parts in their troops' willingness to fight. Still, important as it was, their part does not really explain why men fought.

In suggesting this conclusion about military leadership, I do not wish to be understood as agreeing with Tolstoy's scornful verdict on generals—that despite all their plans and orders they do not affect the results of battles at all. Tolstoy did not reserve all his scorn for generals—historians are also derided in War and Peace for finding a rational order in battles where only chaos existed. "The activity of a commander in chief does not at all resemble the activity we imagine to ourselves when we sit at ease in our studies examining some campaign on the map, with a certain number of troops on this and that side in a certain known locality, and begin our plans from some given moment. A commander in chief is never dealing with the beginning of any event—the position from which we always contemplate it. The commander in chief is always in the midst of a series of shifting events and so he never can at any moment consider the whole import of an event that is occurring."

The full import of battle will as surely escape historians as participants. But we have to begin somewhere in trying to explain why men fought rather than ran from revolutionary battlefields. The battlefield may indeed be the place to begin, since we have dismissed leadership, fear of officers, religious belief, the power of drink, and other possible explanations of why men fought and died.

The eighteenth-century battlefield was, compared to that of the twentieth, an intimate theater, especially intimate in the engagements of the Revolution, which were usually small even by the standards of the day. The killing range of the musket—eighty to one hundred yards—enforced intimacy, as did the reliance on the bayonet and the general ineffectiveness of artillery. Soldiers had to come to close quarters to kill; this fact reduced the mystery of battle, though perhaps not its terrors. But at least the battlefield lost some of its impersonality. In fact, in contrast to twentieth-century combat, in which the enemy usually remains unseen and the source of incoming fire unknown, in eighteenth-century battles the foe could be seen and sometimes even touched. Seeing one's enemy may have aroused a singular intensity of feeling uncommon in modern battles. The assault with the bayonet—the most desired objective of infantry tactics—seems indeed to have evoked an emotional climax. Before it occurred tension and anxiety built up as the troops marched from their column into a line of attack. The purpose of their movements was well understood by themselves and their enemies, who must have watched with feelings of dread and fascination. When the order came sending them forward, rage, even madness, replaced the attacker's anxiety, while terror and desperation sometimes filled those receiving the charge. Surely it is revealing that the Americans who ran from battle did so most often at the moment they understood that their enemy had started forward with the bayonet. This happened to several units at Brandywine and to the militia at Camden and Guilford Court House. The loneliness, the sense of isolation reported by modern soldiers, was probably missing at such moments. All was clear—especially that glittering line of advancing steel.

Whether this awful clarity was harder to bear than losing sight of the enemy is problematical. American troops ran at Germantown after grappling with the British and then finding the field of battle covered by fog. At that time groping blindly, they and their enemy struggled over ground resembling a scene of modern combat. The enemy was hidden at a critical moment, and American fears were generated by not knowing what was happening—or about to happen. They could not see the enemy, and they could not see one another, an especially important fact. For, as S. L. A. Marshall, the twentieth-century historian, has suggested in his book *Men Against Fire*, what sustains men in the extraordinary circumstances of battle may be their relationships with their comrades.

These men found that sustaining such relationships was possible in the intimacy of the American battlefield—and not just because the limited arena robbed battle of some of its mystery. More importantly it permitted the troops to give one another moral or psychological support. The enemy could be seen, but so could one's comrades; they could be seen and communicated with.

Eighteenth-century infantry tactics called for men to move and fire from tight formations which permitted them to talk and to give one another information—and reassurance and comfort. If properly done, marching and firing found infantrymen compressed into files in which their shoulders touched. In battle physical contact with one's comrades on either side must have helped men control their fears. Firing the musket from three compact lines, the English practice, also involved physical contact. The men of the front rank crouched on their right knees; the men of the center rank placed their left feet inside the right feet of the front; the rear rank did the same thing behind the center. This stance was called—in a revealing term—"locking." The very density of this formation sometimes aroused criticism from officers who complained that it led to inaccurate fire. The front rank, conscious of the closeness of the center, might fire too low; the rear rank tended to "throw" its shots into the air, as firing too high was called; only the center rank took careful aim, according to the critics. Whatever the truth of these charges about accuracy of fire, men in these dense formations compiled a fine record of holding their ground. And it is worth noting that the inaccuracy of men in the rear rank bespoke their concern for their fellows in front of them.

British and American soldiers in the Revolution often spoke of fighting with "spirit" and "behaving well" under fire. Sometimes these phrases referred to daring exploits under great danger, but more often they seem to have meant holding together, giving one another support, reforming the lines when they were broken or fell into disorder, disorder such as overtook the Americans at Greenspring, Virginia, early in July 1781 when Cornwallis lured Anthony Wayne into crossing the James with a heavily outnumbered force. Wayne saw his mistake and decided to make the best of it, not by a hasty retreat from the ambush, but by attacking. The odds against the Americans were formidable, but as an ordinary soldier who was there saw it, the inspired conduct of the infantry saved them—"our troops behaved well, fighting with great spirit and bravery. The infantry were oft broke; but just as oft rallied and formed at a word."

These troops had been spread out when the British surprised them, but they formed as quickly as possible. Here was a test of men's spirits, a test they passed in part because of their disciplined formation. In contrast at Camden, where the militia collapsed as soon as the battle began, an open alignment may have contributed to their fear. Gates placed the Virginians on the far left apparently expecting them to cover more ground than their numbers allowed. At any rate they went into the battle in a single line with at least five feet between each man and the next, a distance which intensified a feeling of isolation in the heat and noise of the firing. And to make such feelings worse, these men were especially exposed, stretched out at one end of the line with no supporters behind them.

Troops in tight lines consciously reassured one another in several ways. British troops usually talked and cheered—"huzzaing" whether standing their ground, running forward, or firing. The Americans may have done less talking and cheering, though there is evidence that they learned to imitate the enemy. Giving a cheer at the end of a successful engagement was standard practice. The British cheered at Lexington and then marched off to be shot down on the road running from Concord. The Americans shouted their joy at Harlem Heights, an understandable action and one which for most of 1776 they rarely had opportunity to perform.

The most deplorable failures to stand and fight usually occurred among the American militia. Yet there were militia companies that performed with great success, remaining whole units under the most deadly volleys. The New England companies at Bunker Hill held out under a fire that veteran British officers compared to the worst they had experienced in Europe. Lord Rawdon remarked on how unusual it was for defenders to stick to their posts even after the assaulting troops had entered the ditch around a redoubt. The New Englanders did it. They also held steady at Princeton—"They were the first who regularly formed" and stood up under the balls "which whistled their thousand different notes around our heads," according to Charles Willson Peale, whose Philadelphia militia also proved their steadiness.

What was different about these companies? Why did they fight when others around them ran? The answer may lie in the relationships among their men. Men in the New England companies, in the Philadelphia militia, and in the other units that held together, were neighbors. They knew one another; they had something to prove to one another; they had their "honor" to protect. Their active service in the Revolution may have been short, but they had been together in one way or another for a fairly long time—for several years, in most cases. Their companies, after all, had been formed from towns and villages. Some clearly had known one another all their lives.

Elsewhere, especially in the thinly settled southern colonies, companies were usually composed of men—farmers, farmers' sons, farm laborers, artisans, and new immigrants—who did not know one another. They were, to use a term much used in a later war, companies of "stragglers" without common attachments, with almost no knowledge of their fellows. For them, even bunched tightly in line, the battlefield was an empty, lonely place. Absence of personal bonds and their own parochialism, coupled to inadequate training and imperfect discipline, often led to disintegration under fire.

According to conventional wisdom, the nearer the American militia were to home the better they fought, fighting for their homes and no one else's. Proximity to home, however, may have been a distraction which weakened resolve; for the irony of going into battle and perhaps to their deaths when home and safety lay close down the road could not have escaped many. Almost every senior American general commented on the propensity of the militia to desert—and if they were not deserting they seemed perpetually in transit between home and camp, usually without authorization.

Paradoxically, of all the Americans who fought, the militiamen best exemplified in themselves and in their behavior the ideals and purposes of the Revolution. They had enjoyed independence, or at least personal liberty, long before it was proclaimed in the Declaration. They instinctively felt their equality with others and in many places insisted upon demonstrating it by choosing their own officers. Their sense of their liberty permitted, even compelled, them to serve only for short enlistments, to leave camp when they liked, to scorn the orders of others—and especially those orders to fight when they preferred to flee. Their integration into their society drove them to resist military discipline; and their ethos of personal freedom stimulated hatred of the machine that served as the model for the army. They were not pieces of machine, and they would serve it only reluctantly and skeptically. At their best—at Cowpens, for example—they fought well; at their worst, at Camden, they fought not at all. There they were, as Greene said, "ungovernable." What was lacking in the militia was a set of professional standards, requirements and rules which might regulate their conduct in battle. What was lacking was professional pride. Coming and going to camp as they liked, shooting their guns for the pleasure of the sound, the militia annoyed the Continentals, who soon learned that most of them could not be trusted.

The British regulars were at the opposite pole. They had been pulled out of society, carefully segregated from it, tightly disciplined, and highly trained. Their values were the values of the army, for the most part, no more and no less. The officers, to be sure, were in certain respects very different from the men. They embodied the style and standards of gentlemen who believed in service to their king and who fought for honor and glory.

With these ideals and a mission of service to the king defining their calling, British officers held themselves as aloof as possible from the peculiar horrors of war. Not that they did not fight; they sought combat and danger, but by the conventions which shaped their understanding of battle they insulated themselves as much as possible from the ghastly business of killing and dying. Thus the results of battle might be long lists of dead and wounded, but the results were also "honourable and glorious," as Charles Stedman described Guilford Court House, or reflected "dishonour upon British arms," as he described Cowpens. Actions and gunfire were "smart" and "brisk" and

sometimes "hot," and occasionally a "difficult piece of work." They
might also be described lightly—Harlem Heights was "this silly business" to Lord Rawdon. To their men, British officers spoke a clean,
no-nonsense language. Howe's terse "look to your bayonets" summed
up a tough professional's expectations.

For all the distance between British officers and men, they gave remarkable support to one another in battle. They usually deployed
carefully, keeping up their spirits with drum and fife. They talked and
shouted and cheered, and coming on with their bayonets at the ready
"huzzaing," or coming on "firing and huzzaing," they must have sustained a sense of shared experience. Their ranks might be thinned by
an American volley, but on they came, exhorting one another to "push
on! push on!" as at Bunker Hill and the battles that followed. Although terrible losses naturally dispirited them, they almost always
maintained the integrity of their regiments as fighting units, and when
they were defeated, or nearly so as at Guilford Court House, they re-
covered their pride and fought well thereafter. And there was no hint
at Yorktown that the ranks wanted to surrender, even though they had
suffered dreadfully.

The Continentals, the American regulars, lacked the polish of their
British counterparts but, at least from Monmouth on, they showed a
steadiness under fire almost as impressive as their enemy's. And they
demonstrated a brave endurance: defeated, they retired, pulled themselves together, and came back to try again.

These qualities—patience and endurance—endeared them to many.
For example, John Laurens, on Washington's staff in 1778, wanted
desperately to command them. In what amounted to a plea for command, Laurens wrote: "I would cherish those dear, ragged Continentals, whose patience will be the admiration of future ages, and glory in
bleeding with them." This statement was all the more extraordinary
coming from Laurens, a South Carolinian aristocrat. The soldiers he
admired were anything but aristocratic. As the war dragged on, they
came more and more from the poor and the propertyless. Most probably entered the army as substitutes for men who had rather pay than
serve, or as the recipients of bounties and the promise of land. In
time some, perhaps many, assimilated the ideals of the Revolution. As
Baron Steuben observed in training them, they differed from European troops in at least one regard: they wanted to know why they

were told to do certain things. Unlike European soldiers who did what they were told, the Continentals asked why.

Continental officers aped the style of their British counterparts. They aspired to gentility and often, failing to achieve it, betrayed their anxiety by an excessive concern for their honor. Not surprisingly, like their British peers, they also used the vocabularies of gentlemen in describing battle.

Their troops, innocent of such polish, spoke with words from their immediate experience of physical combat. They found few euphemisms for the horrors of battle. Thus Private David How, September 1776, in New York noted in his diary: "Isaac Fowls had his head shot off with a cannon ball this morning." And Sergeant Thomas McCarty reported an engagement between a British foraging party and American infantry near New Brunswick in February 1777: "We attacked the body, and bullets flew like hail. We stayed about 15 minutes and then retreated with loss." After the battle inspection of the field revealed that the British had killed the American wounded— "The men that was wounded in the thigh or leg, they dashed out their brains with their muskets and run them through with their bayonets, made them like sieves. This was barbarity to the utmost." The pain of seeing his comrades mutilated by shot and shell at White Plains remained with Elisha Bostwick, a Connecticut soldier, all his life: A cannon ball "cut down Lt. Youngs Platoon which was next to that of mine[;] the ball first took off the head of Smith, a Stout heavy man and dashed it open, then took Taylor across the Bowels, it then Struck Sergeant Garret of our Company on the hip [and] took off the point of the hip bone[.] Smith and Taylor were left on the spot. Sergeant Garret was carried but died the Same day now to think, oh! what a sight that was to see within a distance of six rods those men with their legs and arms and guns and packs all in a heap[.]"

The Continentals occupied the psychological and moral ground somewhere between the militia and the British professionals. From 1777 on their enlistments were for three years or the duration of the war. This long service allowed them to learn more of their craft and to become seasoned. That does not mean that on the battlefield they lost their fear. Experience in combat almost never leaves one indifferent to danger, unless after prolonged and extreme fatigue one comes to consider oneself already dead. Seasoned troops simply learn to deal with their fear more effectively than raw troops do, in part because they have come to realize that everyone feels it and that they can rely on their fellows.

By winter 1779–1780, the Continentals were beginning to believe that they had no one save themselves to lean on. Their soldierly qualifications so widely admired in America—their "habit of subordination," their patience under fatigue, their ability to stand sufferings and privations of every kind may in fact have led to a bitter resignation that saw them through a good deal of fighting. At Morristown during this winter, they felt abandoned in their cold and hunger. They knew that food and clothing existed in America to keep them healthy and comfortable, and yet little of either came to the army. Understandably their dissatisfaction increased as they realized that once again suffering had been left to them. Dissatisfaction in these months slowly turned into a feeling of martyrdom. They felt themselves to be martyrs to the "glorious cause." They would fulfill the ideals of the Revolution and see things through to independence because the civilian population would not.

Thus the Continentals in the last four years of the active war, though less articulate and less independent than the militia, assimilated one part of the "cause" more fully. They had advanced further in making American purposes in the Revolution their own. They had in their sense of isolation and neglect probably come to be more nationalistic than the militia—though surely no more American.

Although these sources of the Continentals' feeling seem curious, they served to reinforce the tough professional ethic these men also came to absorb. Set apart from the militia by the length of their service, by their officers' esteem for them, and by their own contempt for part-time soldiers, the Continentals slowly developed resilience and pride. Their country might ignore them in camp, might allow their bellies to shrivel and their backs to freeze, might allow them to wear rags, but in battle they would not be ignored. And in battle they would support one another in the knowledge that their own moral and professional resources remained sure.

The meaning of these complex attitudes is not what it seems to be. At first sight the performance of militia and Continentals seems to suggest that the great principles of the Revolution made little difference on the battlefield. Or if principles did make a difference, say especially to the militia saturated with natural rights and a deep and persistent distrust of standing armies, they served not to strengthen the will to combat but to disable it. And the Continentals, recruited increasingly from the poor and dispossessed, apparently fought better as they came to resemble their professional and apolitical enemy, the British infantry.

These conclusions are in part askew. To be sure, there is truth—and paradox—in the fact that some Americans' commitments to revolutionary principles made them unreliable on the battlefield. Still, their devotion to their principles helped bring them there. George Washington, their commander-in-chief, never tired of reminding them that their cause arrayed free men against mercenaries. They were fighting for the "blessings of liberty," he told them in 1776, and should they not acquit themselves like men, slavery would replace their freedom. The challenge to behave like men was not an empty one. Courage, honor, gallantry in the service of liberty, all those words calculated to bring a blush of embarrassment to jaded twentieth-century men, defined manhood for the eighteenth century. In battle those words gained an extraordinary resonance as they were embodied in the actions of brave men. Indeed it is likely that many Americans who developed a narrow professional spirit found battle broadly educative, forcing them to consider the purposes of their professional skill.

On one level those purposes had to be understood as having a remarkable importance if men were to fight—and die. For battle forced American soldiers into a situation which nothing in their usual experience had prepared them for. They were to kill other men in the expectation that even if they did they might be killed themselves. However defined, especially by a Revolution in the name of life, liberty, and the pursuit of happiness, this situation was unnatural.

On another level, one which, perhaps, made the strain of battle endurable, the situation of American soldiers, though unusual, was not really foreign to them. For what battle presented in stark form was one of the classic problems free men face: choosing between the rival claims of public responsibility and private wishes, or in eighteenth-century terms, choosing between virtue—devotion to the public trust—and personal liberty. In battle, virtue demanded that men give up their liberties and perhaps even their lives for others. Each time they fought they had in effect to weigh the claims of society and liberty. Should they fight or run? They knew that the choice might mean life or death. For those American soldiers who were servants, apprentices, poor men substituting for men with money to hire them, the choice might not have seemed to involve moral decision. After all they had never enjoyed much personal liberty. But not even in that contrivance of eighteenth-century authoritarianism in which they now found themselves, the professional army, could they avoid a moral decision. Compressed into dense formations, they were reminded by their nearness to their comrades that they too had an opportunity to uphold virtue. By standing firm they served their fellows and honor; by running, they served only themselves.

Thus battle tested the inner qualities of men, tried their souls, as Thomas Paine said. Many men died in the test that battle made of their spirits. Some soldiers called this trial cruel; others called it "glorious." Perhaps this difference in perception suggests how difficult it was in the Revolution to be both a soldier and an American. Nor has it ever been easy since.

7

Watermelon Armies and Whiskey Boys

GERALD CARSON

• Although Americans hold ambivalent views about alcoholic beverages, it cannot be denied that whiskey has played an important role in our culture from its very inception. The Pilgrims carried liquor with them on the Mayflower, and Congress itself voted to provide supplies of spirits to the American army during Revolutionary times. During the 1700s whiskey was said to be vital to the workers in the Southern states because of the hot climate.

To the Scotch-Irish of Pennsylvania, whiskey was not only an economic commodity but as necessary to their lives as Bibles and plows. Thus, when Alexander Hamilton proposed an internal revenue tax on distilled liquors, rumblings of dissatisfaction arose from the western Pennsylvania frontier. Because they based their livelihood on distilling grain rather than transporting the crop across the mountains, the farmers regarded the tax as discriminatory and leveled their shotguns at the revenue agents who came to collect. Public protests erupted, thousands marched on Pittsburgh, and there was talk of secession from the United States. Ultimately, President George Washington sent in federal troops.

Alexander Hamilton thought that the use of the army would illustrate the power of the newly created government to enforce the law. As you read Carson's witty and colorful account of the Whiskey Rebellion of 1794, consider the question of the use of federal troops to force compliance with a locally unpopular national policy. Does the use of military force, as Hamilton suggested, increase the citizen's respect for and adherence to the national laws? What similarities, if any, do you find between the quelling of the Whiskey Rebellion of 1794 and the use of the military to enforce integrated education in Little Rock, Arkansas, in 1957 and to dispel youth-

*ful protesters at the Democratic National Convention in
Chicago in August 1968?*

When one recalls that the President of the United States, the Secretary of War, the Secretary of the Treasury and the governors of four states once mobilized against the farmers of western Pennsylvania almost as large an army as ever took the field in the Revolutionary War, the event appears at first glance as one of the more improbable episodes in the annals of this country. Thirteen thousand grenadiers, dragoons, foot soldiers and pioneers, a train of artillery with six-pounders, mortars and several "grasshoppers," equipped with mountains of ammunition, forage, baggage and a bountiful stock of tax-paid whiskey, paraded over the mountains to Pittsburgh against a gaggle of homespun rebels who had already dispersed.

Yet the march had a rationale. President George Washington and his Secretary of the Treasury, Alexander Hamilton, moved to counter civil commotion with overwhelming force because they well understood that the viability of the United States Constitution was involved. Soon after he assumed his post at the Treasury, Hamilton had proposed, to the astonishment of the country, that the United States should meet fully and promptly its financial obligations, including the assumption of the debts contracted by the states in the struggle for independence. The money was partly to be raised by laying an excise tax upon distilled spirits. The tax, which was universally detested in the West—"odious" was the word most commonly used to describe it—became law on March 3, 1791.

The news of the passage of the measure was greeted with a roar of indignation in the back country settlements. The duty was laid uniformly upon all the states, as the Constitution provided. If the West had to pay more, Secretary Hamilton explained, it was only because it used more whiskey. The East could, if it so desired, forgo beverage spirits and fall back on cider and beer. The South could not. It had neither orchards nor breweries. To Virginia and Maryland the excise tax appeared to be as unjust and oppressive as the well-remembered Molasses Act and the tea duties of George III. "The time will come," predicted fiery James Jackson of Georgia in the House of Representatives, "when a shirt shall not be washed without an excise."

Kentucky, then thinly settled, but already producing its characteristic hand-made, whole-souled liquor from planished copper stills, was of the opinion that the law was unconstitutional. Deputy revenue collectors throughout the Bluegrass region were assaulted, their papers stolen, their horses' ears cropped and their saddles cut to pieces. On one wild night the people of Lexington dragged a stuffed dummy through the streets and hanged in effigy Colonel Thomas Marshall, the chief collector for the district.

Yet in no other place did popular fury rise so high, spread so rapidly, involve a whole population so completely, express so many assorted grievances, as in the Pennsylvania frontier counties of Fayette, Allegheny, Westmoreland and Washington. In these counties, around 1791, a light plume of wood smoke rose from the chimneys of no less than five thousand log stillhouses. The rates went into effect on July first. The whiskey-maker could choose whether he would pay a yearly levy on his still capacity or a gallonage tax ranging from nine to eleven cents on his actual production.

Before the month was out, "committees of correspondence," in the old Revolutionary phrase, were speeding horsemen over the ridges and through the valleys to arouse the people to arm and assemble. The majority, but not all, of the men who made the whiskey decided to "forbear" from paying the tax. The revenue officers were thoroughly worked over. Robert Johnson, for example, collector for Washington and Allegheny counties, was waylaid near Pigeon Creek by a mob disguised in women's clothing. They cut off his hair, gave him a coat of tar and feathers and stole his horse.

The Pennsylvania troubles were rooted in the economic importance and impregnable social position of mellow old Monongahela rye whiskey. In 1825, for instance, when the Philadelphia Society for Promoting Agriculture offered a gold medal to the person in Pennsylvania who carried on large-scale farming operations without providing ardent spirits for his farm workers, the medal could not be awarded. There were no entries for the uncoveted honor.

The frontier people had been reared from childhood on the family jug of farmer whiskey. They found the taste pleasant, the effect agreeable. Whiskey was usually involved when there was kissing or fighting. It beatified the rituals of birth and death. The doctor kept a bottle in his office for his own use under the deceptive label "Arsenic

—Deadly poison." The lawyer produced the bottle when the papers were signed. Whiskey was available in the prothonotary's office when the trial-list was made up. Jurors got their dram, and the constable drew his ration for his services on election day. The hospitable barrel and the tin cup were the mark of the successful political candidate. The United States Army issued a gill to a man every day. Ministers of the gospel were paid in rye whiskey, for they were shepherds of a devout flock, Scotch Presbyterians mostly, who took their Bible straight, especially where it said: "Give strong drink unto him that is ready to perish, and wine unto those that be of heavy hearts."

With grain the most abundant commodity west of the mountains, the farmers could eat it or drink it, but they couldn't sell it in distant markets unless it was reduced in bulk and enhanced in value. A Pennsylvania farmer's "best holt," then, was whiskey. A pack-horse could move only four bushels of grain. But it could carry twenty-four bushels if it was condensed into two kegs of whiskey slung across its back, while the price of the goods would double when they reached the eastern markets. So whiskey became the remittance of the fringe settlements for salt, sugar, nails, bar iron, pewter plates, powder and shot. Along the Western rivers where men saw few shilling pieces, a gallon of good, sound rye whiskey was a stable measure of value.

The bitter resistance of the Western men to the whiskey tax involved both practical considerations and principles. First, the excise payment was due and must be paid in hard money as soon as the water-white distillate flowed from the condensing coil. The principle concerned the whole repulsive idea of an internal revenue levy. The settlers of western Pennsylvania were a bold, hardy, emigrant race who brought with them bitter memories of oppression under the excise laws in Scotland and Ireland, involving invasion of their homes, confiscation of their property and a system of paid informers. Revenue collectors were social outcasts in a society which warmly seconded Doctor Samuel Johnson's definition of excise: "a hateful tax levied upon commodities, and adjudged not by the common judges of property, but wretches hired by those to whom excise is paid."

The whiskey boys of Pennsylvania saw it as simply a matter of sound Whig doctrine to resist the exciseman as he made his rounds with Dicas' hydrometer to measure the proof of the whiskey and his marking iron to brand the casks with his findings. Earlier, Pennsylvania had taxed spirits. But whiskey produced for purely private use was exempt. William Findley of Westmoreland County, a member of Congress at the time and a sympathetic interpreter of the Western point of view, looked into this angle. To his astonishment, he learned that all of the whiskey distilled in the West was for purely personal use. So far as the state's excise tax was concerned, or any other tax, for that matter, the sturdy Celtic peoples of the Monongahela region had cheerfully returned to nature: they just didn't pay. About every sixth man made whiskey. But all were involved in the problem, since the other five took their grain to the stillhouse where the maste. distiller turned it into liquid form.

The state had been lenient. But now matters had taken a more serious turn. The new federal government in Philadelphia was dividing the whole country up into "districts" for the purpose of collecting the money. And the districts were subdivided into smaller "surveys." The transmontane Pennsylvanians found themselves in the grip of something known as the fourth survey, with General John Neville, hitherto a popular citizen and leader, getting ready to enforce the law, with a reward paid to informers and a percentage to the collectors, who appeared to be a rapacious set.

The first meeting of public protest against the 1791 federal tax was held at Redstone Old Fort, now Brownsville. The proceedings were moderate on that occasion, and scarcely went beyond the right of petition. Another meeting in August, more characteristic of others which were to follow, was radical in tone, disorderly, threatening. It passed resolves to the effect that any person taking office under the revenue law was an enemy of society.

When warrants were issued in the affair of Robert Johnson, the process server was robbed, beaten, tarred and feathered and left tied to a tree in the forest. As the inspectors' offices were established, they were systematically raided. Liberty poles reappeared as whiskey poles. The stills of operators who paid the tax were riddled with bullets in attacks sardonically known as "mending" the still. This led to a popular description of the Whiskey Boys as "Tom the Tinker's Men," an ironical reference to the familiar, itinerant repairer of pots and kettles. Notices proposing measures for thwarting the law, or aimed at coercing the distillers, were posted on trees or published in the *Pittsburgh Gazette* over the signature, "Tom the Tinker," nom de plume of the insurgent John Holcroft and other anti-tax agitators. Findley, who tried to build a bridge of understanding between the backwoodsmen and the central government, described the outbreak as not the result of any concerted plan, but rather as a flame, "an infatuation almost incredible."

An additional grievance grew out of the circumstance that offenders were required to appear in the federal court at Philadelphia, three hundred miles away. The whiskey-makers saw this distant government as being no less oppressive than one seated in London, and often drew the parallel. The Scotch-Irish of western Pennsylvania were, in sum, anti-federalist, anti-tax, and it may be added, anti-Indian. West of Pittsburgh lay Indian country. The men of the west held to a simple concept of how to solve the Indian problem: extermination. The Indians had the same program, in reverse, and were getting better results. The bungling campaigns which generals Hamar and St. Clair had conducted in the early 1790's made the people of the fringe settlements despair of the ability of the Union to protect them.

Congress amended the excise tax law in 1792 and again in 1794 to lighten the burden on country distillers. A further conciliatory step was taken. To ease the hardships of the judicial process, Congress gave to the state courts jurisdiction in excise offenses so that accused persons might be tried in their own vicinity. But some fifty or sixty writs already issued and returnable at Philadelphia resulted in men being carried away from their fields during harvest time. This convinced the insurgents that the federalist East was seeking a pretext to discipline the democratic West.

One day in July, while the papers were being served, William Miller, a delinquent farmer-distiller, and political supporter of General Neville, saw the General riding up his lane accompanied by a stranger who turned out to be a United States marshal from Philadelphia. The marshal unlimbered an official paper and began to read a summons. It ordered said Miller peremptorily to "set aside all manner of business and excuses" and appear in his "proper person" before a Philadelphia judge. Miller had been planning to sell his property and remove to Kentucky. The cost of the trip to Philadelphia and the fine for which he was liable would eat up the value of his land and betterments. The farm was as good as gone.

"I felt my blood boil at seeing General Neville along to pilot the sheriff to my very door," Miller said afterward. "I felt myself mad with passion."

As Neville and the marshal rode away, a party from the county militia which was mustered at Mingo Creek fired upon them, but there were no casualties. When the General reached Bower Hill, his country home above the Chartiers Valley, another party under the command of John Holcroft awaited him there and demanded his commission and official papers. The demand was refused and both sides began to shoot. As the rebels closed in on the main house, a flanking fire came from the Negro cabins on the plantation. The Whiskey Boys were driven off with one killed and four wounded.

The next day, Major James McFarlane, a veteran of the Revolution, led an attack in force upon Neville's painted and wall-papered mansion, furnished with such marvels as carpets, mirrors, pictures and prints and an eight-day clock. The house was now defended by a dozen soldiers from Fort Fayette at Pittsburgh. A fire-fight followed during which a soldier was shot and McFarlane was killed—by treachery, the rebels said, when a white flag was displayed. The soldiers surrendered and were either released or allowed to escape. Neville was not found, but his cabins, barns, outbuildings and finally the residence were all burned to the ground. Stocks of grain were destroyed, all fences leveled, as the victors broke up the furniture, liberated the mirrors and clock, and distributed Neville's supply of liquor to the mob.

The funeral of McFarlane caused great excitement. Among those present were Hugh Henry Brackenridge, author, lawyer and one of the western moderates, and David Bradford, prosecuting attorney for Washington County. The former wished to find ways to reduce the tension; the latter to increase it. Bradford was a rash, impetuous Marylander, ambitious for power and position. Some thought him a second-rate lawyer. Others disagreed. They said he was third-rate. But he had a gift for rough mob eloquence. Bradford had already robbed the United States mails to find out what information was being sent east against the conspirators. He had already called for the people to make a choice of "submission or opposition . . . with *head, heart, hand* and *voice*."

At Major McFarlane's funeral service Bradford worked powerfully upon the feelings of his sympathizers as he described "the murder of McFarlane." Brackenridge also spoke, using wit and drollery to let down the pressure and to make palatable his warning to the insurgents that they were flirting with the possibility of being hanged. But the temper of the throng was for Bradford, clearly revealed in the epitaph which was set over McFarlane's grave. It said "He fell . . . by the hands of an unprincipled villain in the support of what he supposed to be the rights of his country."

The high-water mark of the insurrection was the occupation of Pittsburgh. After the fight and the funeral, Bradford called out the militia regiments of the four disaffected counties. They were commanded to rendezvous at Braddock's Field, near Pittsburgh, with arms, full equipment and four days' rations. At the field there was a great beating of drums, much marching and counter-marching, almost a holiday spirit. Men in hunting shirts practiced shooting at the mark until a dense pall of smoke hung over the plain, as there had been thirty-nine years before at the time of General Braddock's disaster. There were between five and seven thousand men on the field, many meditating in an ugly mood upon their enemies holed up in the town, talking of storming Fort Fayette and burning Pittsburgh as "a second Sodom."

Bradford's dream was the establishment of an independent state with himself cast as a sort of Washington of the West. Elected by acclaim as Major General, he dashed about the field on a superb horse in a fancy uniform, his sword flashing, plumes floating out from his hat. As he harangued the multitude, Bradford received applications for commissions in the service of—what? No one quite knew.

Marching in good order, strung out over two and a half miles of road, the rebels advanced on August first toward Pittsburgh in what was hopefully interpreted as a "visit," though the temper of the whiskey soldiers was perhaps nearer to that of one man who twirled his hat on the muzzle of his rifle and shouted, "I have a bad hat now, but I expect to have a better one soon." While the panic-stricken burghers buried the silver and locked up the girls, the mob marched in on what is now Fourth Avenue to the vicinity of the present Balti-more and Ohio Railroad station. A reception committee extended nervous hospitality in the form of hams, poultry, dried venison, bear meat, water and whiskey. They agreed to banish certain citizens ob-noxious to the insurrectionists. One building on a suburban farm was burned. Another attempt at arson failed to come off. The day cost Brackenridge four barrels of prime Monongahela. It was better, he reflected, "to be employed in extinguishing the fire of their thirst than of my house." Pittsburgh was fortunate in getting the main body in and then out again without a battle or a burning.

All through the month of August armed bands continued to patrol the roads as a "scrub Congress," in the phrase of one scoffer, met at Parkinson's Ferry, now Monongahela, to debate, pass resolutions and move somewhat uncertainly toward separation from the United States. Wild and ignorant rumors won belief. It was said that Congress was extending the excise levy to plows at a dollar each, that every wagon entering Philadelphia would be forced to pay a dollar, that a tax was soon to be established at Pittsburgh of fifteen shillings for the birth of every boy baby, and ten for each girl.

With the terrorizing of Pittsburgh, it was evident that the crisis had arrived. The President requisitioned 15,000 militia from Pennsyl-vania, New Jersey, Virginia and Maryland, of whom about 13,000 actually marched. Would the citizens of one state invade another to compel obedience to federal law? Here one gets a glimpse of the larger importance of the affair. Both the national government and the state of Pennsylvania sent commissioners to the West with offers of pardon upon satisfactory assurances that the people would obey the laws. Albert Gallatin, William Findley, Brackenridge and others made a desperate effort to win the people to compliance, though their motives were often questioned by both the rebels and the federal authorities. The response to the offer of amnesty was judged not to be sufficiently positive. Pressed by Hamilton to have federal power show its teeth, Washington announced that the troops would march.

The army was aroused. In particular, the New Jersey militia were ready for lynch law because they had been derided in a western news-paper as a "Water-mellon Army" and an uncomplimentary estimate was made of their military capabilities. The piece was written as a take-off on the kind of negotiations which preceded an Indian treaty.

Possibly the idea was suggested by the fact that the Whiskey Boys
were often called "White Indians." At any rate, in the satire the Indians admonished the great council in Philadelphia: ". . . Brothers,
we have that powerful monarch, Capt. Whiskey, to command us. By
the power of his influence, and a love to *his person* we are compelled
to every great and heroic act. . . . We, the Six United Nations of
White Indians . . . have all imbibed his principles and passions—
that is a love of whiskey. . . . Brothers, you must not think to
frighten us with . . . infantry, cavalry and artillery, composed of
your water-mellon armies from the Jersey shores; they would cut a
much better figure in warring with the crabs and oysters about the
Capes of Delaware."

Captain Whiskey was answered hotly by "A Jersey Blue." He
pointed out that "the water-melon army of New Jersey" was going
to march westward shortly with "ten-inch howitzers for throwing a
species of mellon very useful for curing a *gravel occasioned by whiskey!*" The expedition was tagged thereafter as the "Watermelon
Army."

The troops moved in two columns under the command of General
Henry (Light Horse Harry) Lee, Governor of Virginia. Old Dan
Morgan was there and young Meriwether Lewis, five nephews of
President Washington, the governors of Pennsylvania and New
Jersey, too, and many a veteran blooded in Revolutionary fighting,
including the extraordinary German, Captain John Fries of the Bucks
County militia, and his remarkable dog to which the Captain gave the
name of a beverage he occasionally enjoyed—Whiskey.

The left wing marched west during October, 1794, over General
Braddock's old route from Virginia and Maryland to Cumberland
on the Potomac, then northwest into Pennsylvania, to join forces with
the right wing at Union Town. The Pennsylvania and New Jersey
corps proceeded via Norristown and Reading to Harrisburg and
Carlisle. There, on October 4th, President Washington arrived, accompanied by Colonel Hamilton. The representatives of the disaffected counties told the President at Carlisle that the army was
not needed but Hamilton convinced him that it was. Washington
proceeded with the troops as far as Bedford, then returned to Philadelphia for the meeting of Congress. Hamilton ordered a roundup
of many of the rebels and personally interrogated the most important

ones. Brackenridge, incidentally, came off well in his encounter with Hamilton, who declared that he was satisfied with Brackenridge's conduct.

By the time the expedition had crossed the mountains, the uprising was already coming apart at the seams. David Bradford, who had been excluded from the offer of amnesty, fled to Spanish Louisiana. About two thousand of the best riflemen in the West also left the country, including many a distiller, who loaded his pot still on a pack horse or a keel boat and sought asylum in Kentucky where, hopefully, a man could make "the creature" without giving the public debt a lift.

The punitive army moved forward in glorious autumn weather, raiding chicken coops, consuming prodigious quantities of the commodity which lay at the heart of the controversy. Richard Howell, governor of New Jersey and commander of the right wing, revived the spirits of the Jersey troops by composing a marching song, "Dash to the Mountains, Jersey Blue":

> To arms once more, our hero cries,
> Sedition lives and order dies;
> To peace and ease then did adieu
> And dash to the mountains, Jersey Blue.

Faded diaries, old letters and orderly books preserve something of the gala atmosphere of the expedition. At Trenton a Miss Forman and a Miss Milnor were most amiable. Newtown, Pennsylvania, was ticketed as a poor place for hay. At Potts Grove a captain of the cavalry troop got kicked in the shin by his horse. Among the Virginians, Meriwether Lewis enjoyed the martial excitement, wrote to his mother in high spirits of the "mountains of beef and oceans of Whiskey"; sent regards "to all the girls" and announced that he would bring "an Insergiant Girl to se them next fall bearing the title of Mrs. Lewis." If there was such a girl, he soon forgot her.

Yet where there is an army in being there are bound to be unpleasant occurrences. Men were lashed. Quartermasters stole government property. A soldier was ordered to put a Scotch-Irish rebel under guard. In execution of the order, he ran said insurgent through with his bayonet, of which the prisoner died. At Carlisle a dragoon's pistol went off and hit a countryman in the groin; he too died. On November 13, long remembered in many a cabin and stump-clearing as "the dismal night," the Jersey horse captured various citizens whom they described grimly as "the whiskey pole gentry," dragging them out of bed, tying them back to back. The troopers held their prisoners in a damp cellar for twenty-four hours without food or water, before marching them off at gun point to a collection center at Washington, Pennsylvania.

In late November, finding no one to fight, the army turned east again, leaving a volunteer force under General Morgan to conciliate and consolidate the position during the winter. Twenty "Yahoos" were carried back to Philadelphia and were paraded by the Philadelphia Horse through the streets of the city with placards marked "Insurrection" attached to their hats, in an odd federalist version of a Roman triumph. The cavalry was composed, as an admirer said, of "young men of the first property of the city," with beautiful mounts, uniforms of the finest blue broadcloth. They held their swords elevated in the right hand while the light flashed from their silver stirrups, martingales and jingling bridles. Stretched over half a mile they came, first two troopers abreast, then a pair of Yahoos, walking; then two more mounted men, and so on.

The army, meditating upon their fatigues and hardships, called for a substantial number of hangings. Samuel Hodgson, Commissary-general of the army, wrote to a Pittsburgh confidant, "We all lament that so few of the insurgents fell—such disorders can only be cured by copious bleedings. . . ." Philip Freneau, friend and literary colleague of Brackenridge, suggested in retrospect—ironically, of course—the benefits which would have accrued to the country "if Washington had drawn and quartered thirty or forty of the whiskey boys." Most of the captives escaped any punishment other than that of being held in jail without a trial for ten or twelve months. One died. Two were finally tried and sentenced to death. Eventually both were let off.

Gradually the bitterness receded. In August, 1794, General Anthony Wayne had crushed the Indians at the Battle of Fallen Timbers. A treaty was concluded with Spain in October, 1795, clearing the Mississippi for Western trade. The movement of the army into the Pennsylvania hinterland, meanwhile, brought with it a flood of cash which furnished the distillers with currency for paying their taxes. These events served to produce a better feeling toward the Union.

If the rising was a failure, so was the liquor tax. The military adventure alone, without ordinary costs of collection, ran up a bill of $1,500,000, or about one third of all the money that was realized during the life of the revenue act. The excise was quietly repealed during Jefferson's administration. Yet the watermelon armies and the Whiskey Boys made a not inconsiderable contribution to our constitutional history. Through them, the year 1794 completed what 1787 had begun; for it established the reality of a federal union whose law was not a suggestion but a command.

8

The Great Jefferson Taboo

FAWN M. BRODIE

• One of the most talented individuals ever to sit in the White House, Thomas Jefferson is the only American President who may be honestly classified as a Renaissance man. Exceptionally gifted in a wide spectrum of activities, he not only authored the Declaration of Independence and the classic Notes on the State of Virginia but also mastered Greek and Latin, conversed in French and Italian, designed his own estate at Monticello, became an accomplished horticulturist and violinist, founded the University of Virginia, and still made time to participate dramatically in the politics of his era. He distinguished himself as Governor of Virginia, as Ambassador to France, as George Washington's first Secretary of State, as a founder of the Democratic-Republican party, as a spokesman for individual freedom in the Kentucky Resolutions of 1798, and of course as President of the United States. In his inaugural address of 1801, he proclaimed: "We are all Republicans, we are all Federalists." But in his performance as President he displayed a unique talent for mobilizing the members of his party into a cohesive unit.

Jefferson's private life was almost as fascinating as his public career. He was tall and slender with a sunny disposition and excellent health. At the age of thirty-nine, he was widowed by the death of his wife Martha, for whom he felt a deep and lasting affection. The question posed in the following essay by the late professor Fawn Brodie is whether Jefferson then took as a mistress a beautiful slave girl by the name of Sally Hemings. According to Brodie, they did in fact have an affair, and their lovemaking resulted in as many as seven children. Other respected scholars, most notably biog-

Reprinted by permission from *American Heritage* (June 1972). © 1972 American Heritage Publishing Company, Inc.

rapher Dumas Malone, have strongly disputed Brodie's conclusion and insisted that Jefferson was incapable of such immoral behavior. The long and bitter argument on this taboo
subject is likely to continue.

Thomas Jefferson spent his earliest years on a plantation in Tuckahoe,
Virginia, where the blacks outnumbered the whites ten to one. Here
he learned about the hierarchies of power and saw early that a white
child could tyrannize over a black adult. Here his basic sympathy with
emancipation, which we see in him as a young man, had its roots in
what he called, in his *Notes on the State of Virginia,* the "daily exercise in tyranny." But along with a pervasive anger at slavery, there also
developed in Jefferson at some period a conviction he could never
wholly escape, that blacks and whites must be carefully kept separate.
Emancipation of the blacks, he said in his *Notes,* should be accompanied by colonization, whether in Africa, in the West Indies, or in a
separate state in the West.

At age seventy-one he wrote privately, and with some bitterness,
that "amalgamation" of blacks and whites "produces a degradation to
which no lover of his country, no lover of excellence in the human
character can innocently consent." And at seventy-seven, in his un-
finished *Autobiography,* he wrote, "Nothing is more certainly written
in the book of fate, than that these people are to be free; nor is it
less certain that the two races, equally free, cannot live in the same
government."

Yet, ironically, one of the stories that clings tenaciously to Jefferson
is that he actually had a family by a slave woman. The so-called Sally
Hemings story broke into the press in great detail in 1802; public
scoldings and bawdy ballads humiliated President Jefferson well into
1805. Throughout the 1830's and 1840's abolitionists elaborated the
story to suggest that Jefferson had had a whole seraglio of black women
and that one of his black mistresses and two of his daughters had been
sold at a slave auction in New Orleans. Jefferson biographers, on the
other hand, have almost unanimously denounced the stories as libellous.

On March 13, 1873, there appeared in an obscure Ohio newspaper,
the *Pike County Republican,* a memoir by one of Sally Hemings' sons,

Madison. The account was lucidly written, suggesting considerable education; when checked with Jefferson's *Farm Book*, the details were remarkably but not totally accurate. Madison Hemings wrote simply, even drily, that his mother had indeed borne Jefferson several children of whom he was one and that she was his only "concubine." This revelation caused a shudder among Jefferson scholars. Since its publication the memoir has been cited often for various details of life at Monticello, but its basic claim of paternity has been totally rejected almost without exception. Curiously, the piece itself has never been reprinted.

Although today's biographers still repudiate the Sally Hemings story, comment on the great Jefferson taboo does not disappear. Instead, we have the spectacle of ever-increasing numbers of pages devoted to its refutation. Merrill Peterson, in *The Jefferson Image in the American Mind*, looked at the documentation with some care, and in his recent biography, *Thomas Jefferson and the New Nation*, he writes:

> The evidence, highly circumstantial, is far from conclusive, however, and unless Jefferson was capable of slipping badly out of character in hidden moments at Monticello, it is difficult to imagine him caught up in a miscegenous relationship. Such a mixture of the races, such as ruthless exploitation of the master-slave relationship, revolted his whole being.

Dumas Malone devotes a whole appendix in his recent volume, *Jefferson the President, First Term 1801–1805*, to a refutation of the charge. He writes:

> It is virtually inconceivable that this fastidious gentleman whose devotion to his dead wife's memory and to the happiness of his daughters and grandchildren bordered on the excessive could have carried on through a period of years a vulgar liaison which his own family could not have failed to detect.

And Professor Malone suggests that Sally Hemings may have told her children that Jefferson was their father out of "vanity."

Certain black historians, on the other hand, including Lerone Bennett, believe that the miscegenation was real and that Jefferson's descendants dot the country from Cambridge, Massachusetts, to San Francisco. Any defense of this thesis causes anguish and outrage among

Jefferson admirers. Why does this story nevertheless persist? Does it touch some chord in fantasy life? Or do people feel that the scholars protest too much? Jefferson, after all, was a widower at thirty-nine. Defenders of Jefferson assure us again and again that miscegenation was out of character for him. But the first duty of a historian is to ask not "Is it out of character?" but "Is it true?"

What one might call "the family's official denial," begun by Jefferson's grandson, Thomas Jefferson Randolph, holds, first, that Jefferson was not at Monticello when Sally Hemings' children were conceived and, second, that they were fathered by Jefferson's nephews, Peter and Samuel Carr. This denial has been gratefully accepted by Jefferson biographers, his admirers, and his heirs. Still, one must note the fact, as Winthrop Jordan has done in his *White Over Black, American Attitudes Toward the Negro,* 1550–1812—and he was the first to say it in print—that Jefferson actually was at Monticello nine months before the births of each of Sally Hemings' children that are recorded in the *Farm Book.* And there is no evidence that she ever conceived a child when he was not there. Moreover, it takes very little research in the enormous file of family letters at the University of Virginia to demonstrate that Peter and Samuel Carr were elsewhere, managing plantations with slaves of their own, during most of the years that Sally Hemings was bearing children at Monticello.

Professor Jordan is the first white historian in our own time to describe dispassionately evidence for the Sally Hemings liaison, as well as the case against it, writing on the one hand that it was unlikely, a "lapse from character unique in his mature life," but noting on the other that it could have been evidence of deep ambivalence and that Jefferson's "repulsion" toward blacks may have hidden a powerful attraction. Jordan finds the story distasteful, however, and regrets that the charge is "dragged after Jefferson like a dead cat through the pages of formal and informal history." Still, he calls for an "unexcited" discussion of the facts.

It is possible to keep such a discussion "unexcited," though the material is dramatic and, at times, tragic. There are many facts that Jefferson scholars have overlooked, and some that have been ignored, apparently because they were too painful to consider. This is not uncommon with biographers, especially those whose sense of identification with their subject is almost total. In all fairness to Sally Hemings, as well as to Jefferson, whether one believes the story or not, phrases like "vulgar liaison," "ruthless exploitation of the master-slave relationship," and even "dragged after Jefferson like a dead cat" simply do not apply.

As everyone knows, Jefferson was a man of very great gifts and special sensibility. Yet we know little about Sally Hemings except that she was a quadroon of considerable beauty and that she was the half sister of his wife. Several of her brothers could read and write, and one may assume that this was true also of Sally. But no letter from her has been preserved, nor any by Jefferson to her.

Still, if it is true that Sally's seven children were also his children, this already illuminates the length and steadiness of their affection for each other and suggests that there may have been much suffering because it could not publicly be honored. A careful marshalling of the facts surely helps to throw light on Jefferson's life and character, and discovering a liaison does not degrade him or her. It may help explain some mysteries, such as why he never married again, and why he lapsed in his later years into ever-increasing apathy toward emancipation of slaves. For it may well be that this special involvement peculiarly incapacitated him for action in helping to change the national pattern of white over black. In any case, the facts may serve to illuminate his general ambivalence—his mixture of love and hate—concerning race.

Jefferson knew and revered two men who had children by slave women. One was his law teacher, George Wythe, whom he called his second father. Wythe, having no children of his own by two white wives, took a black mistress, Lydia Broadnax, whom he had freed. She bore a son, whom he raised with affection, teaching him Greek and Latin and promising him an inheritance in his will. Wythe even named Jefferson in his will as trustee in charge of the boy's education. But this provision was never to be fulfilled. An envious grandnephew of Wythe's named Sweney forged Wythe's name on several checks; seeking to avoid prosecution and also to win the total inheritance, Sweney put arsenic in the coffee and on some strawberries at Wythe's house. The mulatto child died quickly; Wythe lived long enough to disinherit Sweney. Lydia Broadnax, though very ill, survived. But because the only people who could testify against the murderer were blacks, he was acquitted.

Almost as close to Jefferson as George Wythe, at least for a time, was Jefferson's father-in-law, John Wayles. Wayles had had three white wives, who bore him four daughters. When his third wife died, he turned to Elizabeth Hemings, a slave on his plantation and the daughter of an English sea captain and an African slave woman. "Betty" Hemings bore Wayles six children, the youngest a girl named Sally, all of whom came to Monticello with their mother in the inheritance of Jefferson's wife, Martha Wayles. So it can be seen that although Jefferson may have been intellectually opposed to miscegenation, he grew up seeing it close at hand, and in his adult life he had two important models. He could hardly have believed it to be a grave sin.

Jefferson was greatly blessed in his marriage. He loved his wife passionately, and described their union in his *Autobiography* as "ten years of unchecquered happiness." Still, it was full of tragedy. Three of their six children died in infancy. After the birth of their sixth child, on May 8, 1782, Martha Jefferson hovered between life and death for months. When she finally died, on September 6, 1782, Jefferson fainted and, according to his oldest daughter, who was then ten, "remained so long insensible that they feared he never would revive."

> He kept his room for three weeks and I was never a moment from his side. He walked almost incessantly night and day only lying down occasionally when nature was completely exhausted on a pallet that had been brought in during his long fainting fit. My Aunts remained constantly with him for some weeks, I do not remember how many. When at last he left his room he rode out and from that time he was incessantly on horseback rambling about the mountain in the least frequented roads and just as often through the woods; in those melancholy rambles I was his constant companion, a solitary witness to many a violent burst of grief.

Most Jefferson biographers believe that he never again felt any deep or lasting affection for any woman. Gilbert Chinard wrote in 1928 that "there is no indication that he ever fell in love again," and in one fashion or another Jefferson scholars have adhered to the tradition that he became essentially passionless, monastic, and ascetic. Yet this view has had to be reconciled with the fact that Jefferson had a romance in

Paris in the 1780's with an Englishwoman, Maria Cosway. One solution has been to describe it as "superficially frantic," temporary, and playful rather than passionate. But the episode resulted in what are certainly the greatest love letters in the history of the American Presidency—letters whose copies were carefully preserved by Jefferson (and mostly kept hidden by his heirs until 1945), despite the fact that he is thought to have destroyed all his correspondence with both his wife and his mother. Moreover, passion does not usually disappear in a man's life unless his capacity for passion is constricted and warped from the beginning. When at forty-three, four years after his wife's death, he met the enchanting artist-musician and sensed at once the unhappiness of her marriage to the decadent and foppish Richard Cosway, he fell in love in a single afternoon. They saw each other alone many times during five happy weeks in the autumn of 1786, and in August, 1787, she returned to Paris for a second visit, without her husband. She remained four months. The story of this romance, told in *American Heritage* in August, 1971, need not be repeated here, except as it relates in a subtle fashion to the Sally Hemings story.

Jefferson had taken his eldest daughter Martha (Patsy) with him to Paris, leaving Maria (Polly) and baby Lucy with his wife's sister. When Lucy died of whooping cough, Jefferson in a frenzy of anxiety insisted that Polly be sent to Paris. He ordered that a middle-aged slave woman accompany her, one who had had the smallpox. But when Abigail Adams met the ship in London, she saw with some consternation that the maid accompanying the eight-year-old Polly was a young slave girl of striking beauty. It was Sally Hemings. Though Sally was only fourteen, Abigail believed her to be "about 15 or 16" and described her unhappily in a letter to Jefferson as "quite a child . . . wanting even more care" than Polly, and "wholly incapable" of looking after her young charge properly by herself.

It had been a lively voyage, with no other females on the ship, and Captain John Ramsay had quite won Polly's affection. She had become, Abigail reported grimly, "rough as a little sailor." The captain readily agreed with Abigail that Sally Hemings would be of "little Service" to Jefferson and suggested that "he had better carry her back with him." It takes no special imagination to see why, for quite different reasons, Abigail Adams and Captain Ramsay agreed that it would be better if Sally Hemings did not go on to Paris. But Jefferson sent his trusted French servant Petit to fetch them, and they arrived in July, 1787.

Sally Hemings was later described by a Monticello slave as "very handsome" and "mighty near white" with "long straight hair down her back." Jefferson's grandson, Thomas Jefferson Randolph, said she was "light colored and decidedly good looking," and at Monticello she was described as "Dashing Sally." If she resembled her half sister Martha Wayles Jefferson in any fashion, there is no record of it. But certainly she brought to Paris the fresh, untainted aura of Jefferson's past, the whole untrammeled childhood with the quantities of slave children, the memory of the easy, apparently guiltless miscegenation of his father-in-law, the many-faceted reality of black and white in Virginia.

Sally Hemings arrived in Paris shortly before Maria Cosway returned for her second visit, without her husband. There are some indications that Maria was troubled and guilt-ridden, and there were many reasons why such an affair could not continue. She was a devout Catholic, and besides, divorce was virtually impossible for an Englishwoman, even a Protestant. Her husband, increasingly restive in London, became nastier in his letters. She went back to England in December, 1787, and Jefferson was again left lonely and bereft. Earlier he had written to her, "I am born to lose everything I love."

Sally Hemings was now fifteen. She was learning French, as was her older brother James, who was in Paris as Jefferson's personal servant. We know from Jefferson's account books that he paid 240 francs to a Dr. Sutton on November 6, 1787, for Sally's smallpox inoculation, and that by January, 1788, he had begun for the first time to pay wages to both James and Sally Hemings, thirty-six francs a month to James and twenty-four to his sister. The French servants received fifty and sixty francs. By French law both were free if they chose to make an issue of it, and they knew it.

The circumstances were propitious for an attachment. Sally Hemings must certainly have been lonely in Paris, as well as supremely ready for the first great love of her life. She was thrown daily into the presence of a man who was by nature tender and gallant with women. He was, moreover, the man whom all the children at Monticello, whether white or black, had looked upon as a kind of deity. What is more, if Jefferson had a model in the person of his father-in-law, who

had turned to a slave woman after the death of his third wife, Sally
Hemings, too, had a model in her mother, that Betty Hemings who
had apparently dominated the private life and passions of John Wayles
until his death.

In his *Notes on the State of Virginia* Jefferson had described blacks
as more "ardent" than whites, a preconception that could have served
only to heighten an interest in Sally at this moment, whatever dilemma it might produce. Moreover, he liked warmly domestic women.
Though he took pleasure in intellectual female companions, enjoying
the sharp, witty, and inquiring minds of Abigail Adams and several
talented Frenchwomen, he did not fall in love with them. In this respect he resembled Goethe and Rousseau, both of whom loved and
lived with unlettered women for many years before marrying them.
Furthermore, during this Paris sojourn, Jefferson wrote to an American friend, the beautiful Anne Bingham, deploring the new preoccupation of Frenchwomen with politics:

> Society is spoilt by it. . . . You too, have had your political
> fever. But our good ladies, I trust have been too wise to wrinkle
> their foreheads with politics. They are contented to soothe and
> calm the minds of their husbands returning ruffled from politi-
> cal debate. . . . Recollect the women of this capital, some on
> foot, some on horses, and some in carriages hunting pleasure in
> the streets, in routs and assemblies, and forgetting that they have
> left it behind them in their nurseries; compare them with our
> own countrywomen occupied in the tender and tranquil amuse-
> ments of domestic life, and confess that it is a comparison of
> Amazons and Angels.

Maria Cosway was no Amazon. Nor, it can be assumed, was Sally
Hemings. Her son Madison tells us nothing of his mother's education
or temperament. But he does write of what happened to her in Paris:

> Their stay (my mother and Maria's) was about eighteen months.
> But during that time my mother became Mr. Jefferson's concu-
> bine, and when he was called home she was *enceinte* by him. He
> desired to bring my mother back to Virginia with him but she
> demurred. In France she was free, while if she returned to Vir-
> ginia she would be re-enslaved. So she refused to return with
> him. To induce her to do so he promised her extraordinary privi-
> leges, and made a solemn pledge that her children should be

freed at the age of twenty-one years. In consequence of his promises, on which she implicitly relied, she returned with him to Virginia. Soon after their arrival, she gave birth to a child, of whom Thomas Jefferson was the father.

Is there any evidence other than Madison Hemings' memoir that a liaison between Jefferson and Sally Hemings began in Paris? If a man is in love, in however clandestine an affair, he must tell someone, if only unconsciously and with inadvertence. This is what happened to Jefferson. In March, 1788, he went to Holland on a diplomatic mission and then continued as a tourist into Germany. Not usually a diary keeper, he did write an almost daily journal of this seven-week trip. It is a matter of great curiosity that in this twenty-five-page document he uses the word *mulatto* eight times:

> The road goes thro' the plains of the Maine, which are mulatto and very fine. . . .
> It has a good Southern aspect, the soil a barren mulatto clay. . . .
> It is of South Western aspect, very poor, sometimes grey, sometimes mulatto. . . .
> These plains are sometimes black, sometimes mulatto, always rich. . . .
> . . . the plains are generally mulatto. . . .
> . . . the valley of the Rhine . . . varies in quality, sometimes a rich mulatto loam, sometimes a poor sand. . . .
> . . . the hills are mulatto but also whitish. . . .
> Meagre mulatto clay mixt with small broken stones. . . .

This appears to be evidence of both a preoccupation and a problem. If, moreover, one contrasts this journal with another he kept when touring southern France in the spring of 1787, before Sally Hemings' disturbing mulatto presence had come to trouble him, one will see that in that account, numbering forty-eight pages, he uses the word *mulatto* only once. The rest of the time he describes the hills, plains, and earth as dark, reddish-brown, gray, dark-brown, and black.

There is another quotation, too, in Jefferson's Holland journal that bears repeating:

> The women here [in Holland], as in Germany, do all sorts of work. While one considers them as useful and rational com-

panions, one cannot forget that they are also objects of our pleasures. Nor can they ever forget it. While employed in dirt and drudgery some tag of ribbon, some ring or bit of bracelet, earbob or necklace, or something of that kind will shew that the desire of pleasing is never suspended in them. . . . They are formed by nature for attentions and not for hard labour.

This is all very tender, and suggests that he was thinking not at all of the splendidly dressed Maria Cosway when he wrote it.

Upon his return to Paris, Jefferson found a letter from Maria Cosway reproaching him for not writing, which he had not done for three months. His reply was affectionate; he described his trip to Germany, and in mentioning the art gallery at Düsseldorf, he made what would seem to be a wholly unconscious confession of his new love:

> At Dusseldorpf I wished for you much. I surely never saw so precious a collection of paintings. Above all things those of Van der Werff affected me the most. His picture of Sarah delivering Agar to Abraham is delicious. I would have agreed to have been Abraham though the consequence would have been that I should have been dead five or six thousand years.

Hagar the Egyptian, it will be remembered, was Abraham's concubine, given to him by his wife Sarah when she could not bear a child. Known through legend as mother of the Ishmaelites, she was depicted by artists as having a dark skin.

Jefferson continued in this letter to Maria Cosway: "I am but a son of nature, loving what I see & feel, without being able to give a reason, nor caring much whether there be one." Shortly afterward he formulated what became the most provocative of all his moral directives to society: "The earth belongs to the living and not to the dead." He wrote this in a famous letter to James Madison on September 6, 1789, repeating it in slightly different fashion: "The earth belongs always to the living generation. . . . They are masters too of their own persons, and consequently may govern them as they please."

In another fascinating letter, written to Maria Cosway on January 14, 1789, he described himself as "an animal of a warm climate, a mere Oran-ootan." In 1789 the word *orang-utan* meant for most people not one of the great apes but "wild man of the woods," the literal translation of the Malay words from which it is derived. There was much confusion about the relation of the great apes to man; even the gorilla was as yet unknown in Europe and America. In his *Notes on the State of Virginia*, published only a few months before Sally Hemings' arrival, Jefferson had indiscreetly written that blacks preferred white women, just as "the Oran-ootan" preferred "the black woman over those of his own species." We do not know exactly what Jefferson conceived an "Oran-ootan" to be in 1787, but we do know that in Paris on October 2, 1788, he sent away to his London bookseller for a list of books which included E. Tyson's *Oran-outang, or an anatomy of a pigmy* (1699), a work that tried to clarify the problem of whether an orang-utan was an ape or a man. All of this would indicate that Jefferson was suddenly uncomfortable about what he had written in his book. And well he might be. For when the Federalist press in America later heard rumors about his slave paramour, it needled Jefferson mercilessly on this very passage. For example, on September 29, 1802, the editor of the Frederick-Town, Virginia, *Herald* quoted from Jefferson's *Notes*, adding that "by the same criterion he might be making himself out to be an 'Oranootan.' . . . there is merriment on the subject."

There is also what one might call "hard," as well as psychological, evidence that Jefferson was treating Sally Hemings with special consideration. A curious item for April 29, 1789, in Jefferson's Paris account book reads as follows:

> pd Dupré 5 weeks board of Sally 105"
> washing &c 41–9
> 146–9

This suggests the possibility that when Jefferson went to Holland and Germany he saw to it that Sally was properly chaperoned in a French home and not left as prey to the French servants in his ministry on the Champs Elysées. Jefferson's account book shows, too, that in April, 1789, he spent a surprising amount of money on Sally Hemings' clothes. His figures for that month include ninety-six francs for "clothes for Sally on April 6," seventy-two more on the sixteenth, and an additional twenty-three francs on the twenty-sixth for "making clothes for servts," which might also apply to her wardrobe. The total, including the last, was 191 francs, almost as much as the 215 francs he had spent on his daughter Martha the previous June.

The basic "proof" of the liaison, of course, would be Sally Hemings' pregnancy in Paris at age sixteen. To support this, we have the statement of her son Madison, who could have learned it only from his mother and who, perhaps, learned from her at the same time the French word for pregnant, *enceinte*. But there is additional evidence, for which one must jump ahead almost thirteen years to 1802, when Jefferson was President. Madison Hemings tells us that the child was born "soon after" their arrival back in America, which was in late October, 1789. On September 2, 1802, James T. Callender, co-editor of the Richmond *Recorder*, published the following:

> It is well known that the man, *whom it delighteth the people to honor*, keeps and for many years has kept, as his concubine, one of his slaves. Her name is SALLY. The name of her oldest is Tom. His features are said to bear a striking though sable resemblance to the president himself. The boy is ten or twelve years of age.

Most Jefferson biographers give the impression that Callender was a lying renegade who was determined to destroy Jefferson politically. It is true that he was obsessively a defamer of the great, and that after calling Jefferson a hero for some years he had turned against him venomously. But while Callender repeated and exaggerated scandal, he did not invent it. He had been the first to publish the story of Alexander Hamilton's affair with Mrs. Reynolds, which Hamilton later admitted. He was also the first to publish the ancient rumor that Jefferson before his own marriage had tried to seduce Betsey Walker, the wife of one of his best friends. Poor Jefferson, terribly besieged, and even threatened by Walker with a challenge to a duel in 1803, finally in 1805 admitted privately in a now-famous letter, "When young and single I offered love to a handsome lady; I acknolege its incorrectness."

Callender in 1802 was told by Jefferson's neighbors that Sally Hemings by then had borne Jefferson five children, and he reported this additional scandal in the *Recorder* on September 15. Though Jefferson's *Farm Book* records are scanty up to 1794, we know from scattered entries after that date that Sally Hemings bore four children from 1795 to 1802, and that two of them, both daughters, died in infancy. Once Callender broke the story, other newspapermen felt free to join the attack, and it soon became evident that some of them had been quietly circulating among themselves since 1800 the rumors that Jefferson had a slave mistress. Now those who had not heard of it began checking on their own.

The editor of the Lynchburg, Virginia, *Gazette*, who scolded Jefferson like an indignant parish vicar for not marrying a nice white girl, said that he had waited two months for a Presidential denial of Callender's charges, and then made inquiries and found "nothing but proofs of their authenticity." The Frederick-Town *Herald* editor wrote that he had waited three months before personally checking, and then concluded:

> Other information assures us that Mr. Jefferson's Sally and their children are real persons, and that the woman herself has a room to herself at Monticello in the character of semstress to the family, if not as house-keeper, that she is an industrious and orderly creature in her behaviour, but that her intimacy with her master is well known, and that on this account she is treated by the rest of his house as one much above the level of his other servants. Her son, whom Callender calls president Tom, we are assured, bears a strong likeness to Mr. Jefferson.

This description of Sally's position is very like that given by Madison Hemings:

> We were always permitted to be with our mother, who was well used. It was her duty all her life which I can remember, up to the time of father's death, to take care of his chamber and wardrobe, and look after us children and do such light work as sewing &c.

Jefferson's staunch editor friend, Meriwether Jones, in defending the President in the Richmond *Examiner* on September 25, 1802, made a rare and astonishing public admission that mulatto children were born by the thousands on southern plantations. He admitted also that there was a "mulatto child" at Monticello but denied that Jefferson was the father:

> That this servant woman has a child is very true. But that it is M. Jefferson's, or that the connection exists, which Callender mentions, *is false*—I call upon him for his evidence. . . .

In gentlemen's houses everywhere, we know that the virtue of the unfortunate slaves is assailed with impunity. . . . Is it strange therefore, that a servant of Mr. Jefferson's at a house where so many strangers resort, who is daily engaged in the ordinary vocations of the family, like thousands of others, should have a mulatto child? Certainly not.

John Adams, one of the few statesmen of the time who could testify firsthand about Sally Hemings' beauty, fully believed the Callender story. He said, privately, that it was "a natural and almost unavoidable consequence of that foul contagion in the human character—Negro slavery." But he found circulation of the story saddening. It is said that young John Quincy Adams wrote a ballad about the President and Sally, as did a great many other bad poets at the time.

Jefferson, despite enormous public and private pressure, made no public denial of either the Sally Hemings or the Mrs. Walker story. He insisted that he would not dignify calumny by answering it in the press, though actually he did delegate friends, to whom he supplied material, quietly, to write defenses on his behalf. We know he wrote at least one article during the crisis of these scandals and published it under the pseudonym Timoleon, but curiously it answered only one charge, both obscure and false, namely, that he had paid one Gabriel Jones a debt of £50 in depreciated currency.

There were other defenses made, however, that touched on Sally Hemings. William Burwell, Jefferson's private secretary in 1805, in an unpublished memoir now in the Library of Congress, tells us that at Jefferson's request he wrote a series of articles for the Richmond *Enquirer* in 1805 in reply to accusations of a Virginia plantation owner, Tom Turner, in the Boston *Repertory*. Turner had accused Jefferson of a whole list of misdemeanors, including the favorite Federalist canard that he had acted as a coward when, during the Revolution, the British invaded Virginia while he was governor of the state. Turner had also insisted that the Sally Hemings story was "unquestionably true." The Burwell articles, called "Vindication to Mr. Jefferson," appeared serially in the Richmond *Enquirer* in August and September of 1805. They consisted chiefly of a vigorous defense of Jefferson's wartime governorship. But of the slave-paramour charge Burwell, on September 27, 1805, said only that it was "below the dignity of a man of understanding."

Finally, in 1805, apparently under great pressure, Jefferson wrote a private letter, now missing, to his Attorney General, Levi Lincoln. In it, presumably, he answered more, possibly all, of the many charges being heaped upon him in the venomous Federalist press. He sent a copy to Robert Smith, Secretary of the Navy, on July 1, 1805, with a covering letter, part of which we have already quoted, in which he acknowledged offering love to Betsey Walker. But he then added that this story was "the only one founded in truth among all their allegations against me." Because of that statement, some Jefferson scholars believe that this covering letter is "a categorical denial" by Jefferson of the Sally Hemings story.

And yet the original letter to Levi Lincoln, the copy to Robert Smith, and presumably the letterpress copy Jefferson almost always made of his letters have all inexplicably disappeared. One wonders why. If this letter contained the denial Jefferson's friends had been hoping to see for almost three years, what became of it and the copies? The covering letter to Robert Smith is very ambiguous. Who knows exactly which "allegations against me" Jefferson had chosen to list in the missing letter? It is conceivable that this letter and its copies disappeared because there was something essentially and inadvertently damaging to Jefferson in them.

The story of the abuse heaped upon Jefferson during his Presidency in regard to his intimate life has never been told in full detail. Nor have the evidences of his anguished reaction to this abuse ever been pieced together in such a fashion that one can see the extent of his humiliation and his suffering. Nevertheless, despite the savagery of the attacks, despite the dozen or so published pornographic ballads, Jefferson kept Sally Hemings and her children at Monticello. In 1805 and 1808 she bore two more sons.

Years later Thomas Jefferson Randolph, Jefferson's favorite grandson, who was born in 1792 and spent many summers at Monticello, in effect growing up with Sally Hemings' children, talked to biographer Henry Randall confidentially about the controversy. Randall reported privately that Randolph described one of the children as looking so much like Jefferson that "at some distance or in the dusk the slave, dressed in the same way, might have been mistaken for Mr. Jefferson." Since he was a house servant, Randall noted, "the likeness between master and slave was blazoned to all the multitudes who visited this political mecca." When Randall asked Randolph why Jefferson did not send this family away from Monticello to another of his plantations, the grandson replied that though "he had no doubt his mother would have been very glad to have them thus removed," still "all venerated Mr. Jefferson too deeply to broach such a topic to him," and "he never betrayed the least consciousness of the resemblance."

One is reminded here of Tolstoi, also a great egalitarian, who had an illegitimate son by a serf on his estate before marrying the Countess Sophia. This son became Tolstoi's coachman—similarly visible for everyone to see. But he was never educated like Tolstoi's numerous legitimate children nor made part of the inner family.

Both Thomas Jefferson Randolph and his sister, Ellen Randolph Coolidge, blamed their uncles, Peter and Samuel Carr, instead of their grandfather, for the paternity of Sally Hemings' children. Randolph told Randall in all seriousness that he himself had "slept within sound of his [Jefferson's] breathing at night," and "had never seen a motion, or a look, or a circumstance" that was suspicious. Still, in an article about his grandfather, he wrote that Jefferson's bedroom-study was his sanctum sanctorum, and that even his own daughters never sat in it.

In the end, much evidence is contained in the history of Sally Hemings' seven children. Despite the strenuous "family denial" and the secrecy Jefferson himself, not surprisingly, seems to have encouraged, a considerable amount of information is available about them. Ellen Randolph Coolidge, in discussing the "yellow children" at Monticello in an unpublished letter, wrote that she knew of her "own knowledge" that Jefferson permitted "each of his slaves as were sufficiently white to pass for white to withdraw quietly from the plantation; it was called running away, but they were never reclaimed." "I remember," she wrote, "four instances of this, three young men and a girl, who walked away and staid away—their whereabouts was perfectly known but they were left to themselves—for they were white enough to pass for white."

TOM

There are three runaways listed in Jefferson's *Farm Book*. Jamy, son of Critta Hemings, born in 1787 when Jefferson was still in Paris, ran away in April, 1804. Beverly and Harriet, two children of Sally Hemings, ran away in 1822. It is possible that the fourth runaway referred to by Ellen Coolidge was the oldest son of Sally Hemings, the one Callender derisively called "president Tom." Though he is described in the newspapers of 1802 as resembling Jefferson, in one respect he remains the most mysterious of all Sally Hemings' children because he is not listed in the *Farm Book* under the name of his mother, as are the others. Since there are at least six different slaves named Tom recorded at various times in the *Farm Book*, only one listed with a birth year, absolute identification of "Tom Hemings" in this old record is not possible.

Jefferson listed his slaves first in 1774, again in 1783, but not again till 1794. During his Presidency, 1801 through March, 1809, he neglected his *Farm Book* altogether. Almost all his slaves are listed by first name only except Betty, Peter, and John Hemings and two or three others, including an old slave, Tom Shackleford. Sally Hemings is easily identified, both by her birth year, 1773, and by the names of her children, listed and indented under her own, at least when they were small. Of the several slaves in the *Farm Book* named Tom, one appears frequently among the Hemings family slaves, which are usually listed together. He does not appear on the official inventories of 1794, 1798, and 1810, but shows up consistently on the food and clothing distribution lists from 1794 to 1801. It can be argued that this "Tom" represents Tom Shackleford without his last name. If true, then it would seem that Jefferson did not choose to list Sally Hemings' oldest son regularly among his slaves and may have considered him free from birth.

Martha Jefferson Randolph mentions a "Tom" in a letter to her father on January 22, 1798, describing an epidemic of sickness in the neighborhood:

> Our intercourse with Monticello has been almost *daily*. They have generally been well there except Tom and Goliah who are both *about* again and poor little Harriot who died a few days after you left us.

This "Harriot," we know from *Farm Book* entries, was Sally Hemings' daughter, and the "Tom" may have been her son. There were two slaves named Goliah at Monticello, one an old man and the other a child of seven.

There are no listings in the *Farm Book* between 1801 and 1810. By this time Tom Shackleford had died, but there are several listings of a "hired" Tom in 1810 and 1811. One can speculate that this was "Tom Hemings," and that he was by then old enough for regular wages. Since no slave named Tom appears after 1811 in the *Farm Book*, it is possible that Sally Hemings' son left Monticello in that year, when he was twenty-one. This would have been a fulfillment of Jefferson's promise to Sally, as described by her son Madison.

Madison Hemings, who was born in 1805, makes no mention of an older brother Tom. It is possible that the "president Tom" who was the subject of all the ribald publicity from 1802 through 1805 was persuaded to leave the shelter of Monticello after he became old enough to make the transition into white society on his own. Even in 1805 he would have been fifteen, old enough to leave. He could have returned for the summers of 1810 and 1811, long enough to appear in various distribution lists. Madison Hemings wrote that the child his mother conceived in France "lived but a short time." Here he is obviously confusing him with the two small daughters who died in 1796 and 1797. It is conceivable that Sally Hemings, burned by the scandal-mongering publicity of 1802–1805, chose not to discuss this son with anyone after his departure and made every effort to protect his identity in the white society by a mantle of silence. Such behavior is common even today among relatives of a black who "passes."

HARRIET AND EDY

Jefferson was in political semiretirement at Monticello from January 16, 1794, to February 20, 1797. He wrote to Edward Rutledge on November 30, 1795, "Your son . . . found me in a retirement I doat on, living like an Antediluvian patriarch among my children & grandchildren, and tilling my soil." The celebrated French rationalist, Comte de Volney, a fugitive from the French Revolution, visited Jefferson in Monticello in 1796. He noted in his journal some astonishment at seeing slave children as white as himself: "Mais je fus étonné de voir appeler noirs et traiter comme tels des enfants aussi blancs que moi." They resulted, he said, from miscegenation between mulatto slave women and the white workmen Jefferson hired. But were some of these children in fact Jefferson's?

Two daughters were born to Sally Hemings during this temporary retirement: Harriet, on October 5, 1795, and Edy, whose name is listed twice in 1796 in the *Farm Book* under Sally's name and then disappears. Edy, it can be assumed, died in 1796, since she appears in no slave listings under her mother's name thereafter. We know that Harriet died in 1797, not only because she disappears from *Farm Book* listings after that year, but also by Martha Jefferson's report in January, 1798, already quoted. If Jefferson wrote a letter of sympathy to Sally Hemings, there is no record of it. What has been preserved is his reply to Martha, a letter of such melancholy that it suggests something more than peripheral involvement. He said in part:

> Indeed I feel myself detaching very fast, perhaps too fast, from every thing but yourself, your sister, and those who are identified with you. These form the last hold the world will have on me, the cords which will be cut only when I am loosened from this state of being. I am looking forward to the spring with all the fondness of desire to meet you all once more.

BEVERLY

Beverly, a son, was born to Sally Hemings on April 1, 1798, eight months and twenty days after Jefferson's arrival in Monticello from Philadelphia on July 11, 1797. We know nothing of Beverly's youth except a tantalizing reference in the reminiscences of the Monticello slave named Isaac, who referred to "the balloon that Beverley sent off," and the fact that he is listed as a runaway at age twenty-four. Madison Hemings wrote that "Beverly left Monticello and went to Washington as a white man. He married a white woman in Maryland, and their only child, a daughter, was not known by the white folks to have any colored blood coursing in her veins. Beverly's wife's family were people in good circumstances." All of this suggests that Beverly had some schooling at Monticello and could have had some financial assistance from Jefferson, as did his sister Harriet.

HARRIET (No. 2)

A second Harriet, named after the child that died in 1797, was born in May, 1801, and it must be noted that Jefferson was in Monticello from May 29 to November 24, 1800. Harriet was listed as a runaway in the *Farm Book* in 1822. Edmund Bacon, an overseer at Monticello, said later of this slave girl:

> He [Jefferson] freed one girl some years before he died, and there was a great deal of talk about it. She was nearly as white as anybody and very beautiful. People said he freed her because she was his own daughter. She was not his daughter: she was _____'s daughter. I know that. I have seen him come out of her mother's room many a morning when I went up to Monticello very early. When she was nearly grown, by Mr. Jefferson's direction I paid her stage fare to Philadelphia and gave her fifty dollars. I have never seen her since and don't know what became of her. From the time she was large enough, she always worked in the cotton factory. She never did any hard work.

Bacon, however, did not come to Monticello as overseer till 1806, after six of Sally's seven children were born, and he never lived in the big house.

Madison Hemings wrote of his sister Harriet with a touch of irony:

> Harriet married a white man in good standing in Washington City, whose name I could give, but will not, for prudential reasons. She raised a family of children, and so far as I know they were never suspected of being tainted with African blood in the community where she lived or lives. I have not heard from her for ten years, and do not know whether she is dead or alive.

MADISON

Madison Hemings, named after James Madison, was born January 19, 1805. Jefferson was not in Monticello at his birth, but had been there from April 4 to May 11, 1804. Madison's reminiscences, on the whole remarkable for their accuracy of detail concerning Monticello, show evidence of considerable education, though he insists he learned to read "by inducing the white children to teach me." Of his relations with Jefferson he writes in his memoir:

> He was uniformly kind to all about him. He was not in the habit of showing partiality or fatherly affection to us children. We were the only children of his by a slave woman. He was affec-

tionate toward his white grandchildren, of whom he had fourteen, twelve of whom lived to manhood and womanhood.

The slave Isaac in his reminiscences reported that "Sally had a son named Madison, who learned to be a great fiddler," but we do not know whether it was Jefferson, himself an able violinist, who taught the young slave who claimed to be his son. Freed by Jefferson in his will, Madison lived for a time with his mother (by then also free) in Albermarle County, Virginia, married a free black woman in 1834, and after his mother's death in 1835 went west to Ohio, where he made his living as a carpenter.

ESTON

Jefferson was in Monticello from August 4 to October 1, 1807. Eston Hemings was born May 21, 1808. As with Beverly, Harriet, and Madison, his name appears many times in the *Farm Book* under the name of Sally Hemings. He was one of the five slaves freed in Jefferson's will, all of whom were members of the Hemings family. Madison Hemings wrote that Eston married a free black woman, immigrated to Ohio, and then went on to Wisconsin.

Jefferson's will contained the request that the Virginia legislature be petitioned to permit Madison and Eston Hemings to stay in the state if they so chose. Otherwise, by Virginia law, which barred free Negroes, they would automatically have been banished. Still, it must be noted, by Jefferson's own reckoning, based on Virginia's legal definitions of the time, these youths were white. When a friend wrote to him in 1815 asking at what point a black man officially changes into a white man, Jefferson replied explicitly, "Our canon considers two crosses with the pure white, and a third with any degree of mixture, however small, as clearing the issue of negro blood."

And what, in the end, was "the condition" of Sally Hemings? Jefferson did not free her in his will, but left this service for his daughter Martha to perform, which she did two years after Jefferson's death in 1826. Had Jefferson freed her during his lifetime and made the necessary request from the Virginia legislature that she be allowed to remain in the state, the news would have been trumpeted over the nation. This publicity he was probably unwilling to subject himself to, and it is conceivable that Sally Hemings never requested it. Still, it is a melancholy discovery to find her listed on the official inventory of Jefferson's estate, made after his death, as an "old woman" worth thirty dollars. She was then fifty-three.

Madison Hemings wrote that his mother lived with him and Eston Hemings in a rented house until her death in 1835. The U.S. Census of Albermarle County in 1830 listed Eston Hemings as head of a family, and as a white man. The other members of this family are listed under his name by age and sex only, as was traditional at the time. There is a listing of a woman—fifty to sixty years of age—described as white. This is Sally Hemings. So the census taker, in making this small descriptive decision, underlined the irony and tragedy of her life.

As for Jefferson, he had watched with increasing despair over the years as Virginia permitted slavery to expand and as the laws controlling slaves became ever more repressive. He had seen the social degradation imposed upon Sally Hemings' five living children by the taboos and rituals of the slave society in which he was inextricably enmeshed. So rigid were these taboos that he could not admit these children to be his own, even when they passed into white society, without social ostracism and political annihilation. Whether one believes they were his children or not, one cannot deny that he paid dearly for their presence on that enchanted hill. He could not abandon the slave society in Virginia if he would, and he would not if he could. Overwhelmed at the end with a crushing burden of debt—$107,000—he could not find his way to free in his will more than five of his hundred-odd slaves. He had lived almost half of his life, in the phrase he used to describe himself to Maria Cosway at age seventy-seven, "like a patriarch of old." And so his ambivalence—which may well have served to lessen for him the sense of the tragedy of it all—was continually compounded.

II THE YOUNG REPUBLIC

9

The Old Northwest

JAMES E. DAVIS

• An ongoing theme in American history has revolved around what is believed to have been the real participatory democracy that existed on the frontier. It was a democracy, so it is said, that eroded with the industrialization and urbanization of the landscape. From the romantic French settler J. Hector St. Jean de Crèvecoeur to Thomas Jefferson to Alexis de Toqueville this idea of an idyllic rural ideal was handed down. No one, however, elaborated it more fully than Frederick Jackson Turner, who gave the Presidential address at the 1893 convention of the American Historical Association in Chicago. It was the West, he said, which focused American energies; and it was the West—wild, isolated, and infinitely challenging—which formed that peculiarly adventurous democrat, the American. "Stand at the Cumberland Gap," Turner asserted, "and watch the procession of civilization marching single file." A century later one could have watched the same parade at the South Pass in the Rockies.

Much of the rhetoric and style of political life in the United States can be traced to the persistent appeal of the frontier concept. President Jimmy Carter's visits to Midwestern farms and to town meetings in New England were clearly attempts to appeal to the sentiment and/or the belief that the heart of American democracy is and always has been in the hamlets and rural areas.

This idealized portrait of early American life has been challenged by many historians since the end of World War II. Richard C. Wade has argued that it was the cities, not the farms, that were the spearheads of the frontier; others have questioned whether the entire vision of Jeffersonian democracy was a myth from the start. But the view that the frontier

From James E. Davis, "New Aspects of Men and New Forms of Society: The Old Northwest, 1790–1820," *Journal of the Illinois State Historical Society* 69 (August 1976): 164–72.

fostered a special kind of egalitarianism and democratic spirit
is one that will not die. In the essay which follows, Professor
James E. Davis brings out evidence that grass-roots democracy was more than just a dream for early settlers. Whether
Davis's view of Old Northwest society as being characterized
by "creativity and egalitarianism" is accurate or just Jeffersonian mythology in a new form is up to the reader to decide.

They came to the lands north of the Ohio River from many places:
the valleys and highlands of the Upper South, the coastal plains and
inland regions of the Middle Atlantic states, and the boulder-strewn
hills of New England. Between the end of the American Revolution
and the admission of Illinois to the Union in 1818, settlers hacked
their way through dense forests, established farms and communities
along waterways, and pushed on to the broad expanses of prairie
country. Their reasons for migrating were as numerous as their origins. Perhaps the majority were enticed westward by hopes of economic gain. Some were motivated by curiosity and a sense of adventure; others by misfortune—economic disaster, death in the family, a
brush with the law, or persecutions accompanying the French Revolution and Napoleonic upheavals.

The lands were not empty when the newcomers arrived. The Indian population, although decreasing, was still powerful enough in the
1790s to inflict stinging defeats on federal forces in Ohio, and as late
as the War of 1812 the Indians and their British sponsors lashed into
the region with surprising strength. After the war the influence of
Great Britain diminished, and the Indians—their offensive power cur-
tailed—grudgingly yielded vast tracts of land to the Americans. The
newcomers also encountered French and French-Indian residents,
whose way of life was in eclipse. In short, those whose livelihood was
dependent upon furs, Indians, and isolated outposts yielded to those
who cleared the land, broke the prairie, and sank the taproot of rural
family life.

Usually disdainful of the French and the Indians, the American settlers sought to subdue the wilderness and re-create the best aspects of
their own cultures. In that attempt they were only partially successful.

The society that did evolve was a curious hybrid of outside ideas, aspirations, customs, and institutions, altered somewhat by elements of the French and Indian cultures and tempered by the sometimes harsh realities of the wilderness.

Two traits of the new settlers seem to have predominated: creativity and egalitarianism or republicanism. The purpose of this paper is to examine those traits and their likely causes, and to suggest, in turn, how life in the Old Northwest was influenced by them.

Republicanism in the late 1700s and early 1800s assumed several forms. One was a high, perhaps inflated, self-confidence that was reflected everywhere, particularly in the independent, even haughty and surly, attitudes of hired workers. Elias Pym Fordham, who came to the region in 1817, observed: "No white man or woman will bear being called a servant. . . . Hirelings must be spoken to with Civility and cheerfulness." Observing the republican West shortly after the War of 1812, Isaac Holmes warned, "Male and female servants, or, as they are there called 'helps,' must eat and drink with the family." From early Princeton, Indiana, it was reported that even servants brought from England to America were soon "on a happy equality, rising up last and lying down first, and eating freely at the same time and table. None here permit themselves to have a master, but negroes." A friend of Henry Bradshaw Fearon's, having the temerity to ask a pioneer woman for her master, received this bristling republican response, "In this country there is no mistresses nor masters; I guess I am a woman citizen." If it is true that republican spirit and democratic institutions have as their basis a self-confident population, then the opening years of the nineteenth century in the lands north of the Ohio augured well for an egalitarian society.

The accessibility of public officials further illustrates the prevalence of republicanism. Unlike the East, where magistrates, military officers, and politicians were held in awe, the Old Northwest was characterized by an easy familiarity between the public and authorities. One observer, perhaps somewhat carried away, wrote: "I wish I could give you a correct idea of the perfect equality that exists among these republicans. A Judge leaves the Court house, shakes hands with his fellow citizens and retires to his loghouse. The next day you will find him holding his own plough. The Lawyer has the title of Captain, and serves in his Military capacity under his neighbour, who is a farmer and a Colonel." Richard Flower wrote from his farm near Albion, Illinois: "I went into my field the other day, and began a conversation with my ploughman: his address and manner of speech, as well as his conversation surprised me. I found he was a colonel of militia, and a member of the legislature." The unpretentiousness of public officials was also observed by John Palmer, traveling near Cincinnati in 1817. After meeting a certain Judge Lowe, who was also a tavern-keeper, Palmer commented, "It no doubt seems singular to the English reader, to hear of judges and captains keeping taverns . . . but it is very common in this republican country." The accessibility of public officials and the familiarity with which they were treated appears to have bred, among their constituents, a healthy suspicion of government and politicians.

Yet the spirit of republicanism was liveliest when ordinary citizens plunged headlong into politics. It was widely believed that eligible voters should participate, or be willing to participate, in public affairs. In the early settlements, according to one historian: "Candidates were perpetually scouring the country . . . defending and accusing, defaming and clearing up, making licentious speeches, treating to corn whiskey, violating the Sabbath, and cursing the existing administration. . . . And every body expected at some time to be a candidate for something." Newcomers to the Old Northwest cast off habits of social deference, and for the first time in their lives scrambled after the numerous public positions that had to be filled if society was to function. In every village and courthouse, inexperienced people were thrust into roles of leadership. More important, the problems with which those political novices grappled were fundamental, dealing as they did with transportation, education, defense, and administration. Furthermore, the solutions arrived at in the early days of settlement established the tone of the community for decades to come.

The resolution of problems of frontier life illustrates the creativity of the pioneers in the Old Northwest. The Western waterways, filled with snags and subject to seasonal fluctuations, called for particularly creative solutions. By the 1820s, strange-looking, shallow-draft boats, powered by high-pressure, lightweight engines, were successfully navigating the Western waters.

Other problems generated equally creative, if not always completely effective, solutions. The difficulties encountered in breaking the unyielding prairie grass and constructing adequate fencing elicited from nimble minds a host of solutions. When settlement outstripped the effective reach of territorial or state government, popular *ad hoc* committees sprang into existence. New sicknesses, as well as old ones, prompted strange cures from quack and doctor alike. Richard Lee Mason, traveling through Indiana in 1819, commented on the strange food substitutions: "Yolk of egg, flour and water mixed is a good substitute for milk and is often used in coffee in this country. Rye is frequently substituted for coffee and sage tea in place of the Imperial." Such commonplace solutions to daily problems were only part of the unending experimentation that occurred at all levels of society and in all aspects of life. The numerous difficulties accompanying settlement produced an impressive amount of inventiveness and adaptability.

The economy of the Old Northwest, unlike that of the East, was not specialized. Few settlers were *full-time* judges, teachers, clergymen, legislators, or even farmers. Professional men performed manual tasks and suffered no loss of esteem as a result. One traveler in early Ohio noted: "The doctor returns from his rounds . . . feeds his pigs; and yet his skill as a physician is not doubted on that account. Nor is the sentence of the magistrate . . . esteemed less wise or impartial, even by the losing party of his wrangling disputants, because Cincinnatus-like, he is called from the plough tail to the bench of justice." Other settlers turned from one job to another and still another; such jacks-of-all-trades could be found in the Northwest long after Illinois achieved statehood. A Swedish traveler, Gustaf Unonious, wrote of that kind of mobility: "The speed with which people here change their life calling and the slight preparation generally needed to leave one calling for another are really surprising, especially to one that has been accustomed to our Swedish guild-ordinances. . . . A man who today is a mason may tomorrow be a doctor, the next day a cobbler, and still another day a sailor, druggist, waiter, or school master." Unonious may have exaggerated somewhat, but it is undeniably true that many early Illinoisans sampled a dozen occupations over the course of a lifetime—learning from each and transferring knowledge and skills from one activity to the next.

There are several reasons for the growth of republicanism and creativity in the Old Northwest. One was the diverse nature of those who settled the land. Each migratory group and each household arrived with its own ideas concerning the future of the new society. The resulting suspicions and disputes between Protestant and Catholic, Southerner and Northerner, and native and immigrant insured that there would be no deferential society in the Old Northwest. Family name, religious affiliation, and political influence probably counted for less in the unfolding society of the Old Northwest than in the more highly ordered and structured society of the East. The pluralism of the new society guaranteed that common problems would be attacked from a number of directions. And solutions were probably found more quickly than would have been the case if only one cultural group had settled the region.

The very act of migration also fostered republicanism and creativity. Migration was selective, beckoning to the fresh lands a disproportionately large number of young adult males and generally discouraging the old and females. Selective migration, it appears, also discouraged the very wealthy, the very poor, and the timid and trouble-laden. It is clear that society in the Old Northwest from 1790 to 1820 was no mere reproduction of Eastern society, efforts to the contrary notwithstanding. Rather, the selective nature of migration created vacuums, and those vacuums generated a republican rush for the political and social positions formerly held by those who stayed behind.

Those who even considered migrating were precisely those who were able, and perhaps eager, to see new possibilities and new ways of doing things. Timothy Flint, for example, asked, "What mind ever contemplated the project of moving from the old settlements over the Alleghany mountains . . . without forming pictures of new woods and streams, new animals and vegetables, new configurations of scenery, *new aspects of men and new forms of society?*" For many, the promise of the Old Northwest began not with actual arrival in the region but with creative and liberating dreams of "new aspects of men and new forms of society."

The trek westward removed the immigrants from scenes of defeat and frustration and gave them an exhilarating and immediate success, which encouraged them to seize further opportunities for advancement. A variety of people were thrown together and enriched each other by swapping bits of news, methods of travel, and farming techniques.

In short, the act of migration performed several functions: it selectively eliminated certain kinds of settlers, raised expectations, heightened confidence, and generated a creative mix of diverse people. As we have seen, settlers in the new lands scrambled for new positions, moved from occupation to occupation, and refused to have masters. Habitual deference collapsed, at least temporarily, and a number of years passed—perhaps a decade or two—before the fabric of society was tightly drawn. In the early days, it was virtually impossible for a settler to awe his fellows with his name, past social standing, or connections. Rather, people exerted themselves—they *willed* themselves—into new roles and thereby transformed themselves and their society.

The abundance and availability of good land were crucial to that transformation. That fact was not lost on Francis Hall, who traveled in the Old Northwest shortly after the War of 1812. Of the pioneer, he wrote, "With his axe on his shoulder, his family and stock in a light waggon, he plunges into forests, which have never heard the woodman's stroke, clears a space sufficient for his dwelling, and first year's consumption, and gradually converts the lonely wilderness into a flourishing farm." Farmers were relatively self-sufficient—making much of what they needed from materials at hand, and selling only

Physicians' advertisements from a Kaskaskia (Illinois) newspaper

DR. W. L. REYNOLDS,

Has removed to his new shop, on Charter street, where he can always be found. He has fresh and genuine *Cow Pock Matter,* and those who wish to avail themselves of its salutary effects, had better make early application. He continues to practice *Physic, Surgery and Midwifery* with the most unremitted attention. Those who have accounts of more than six months standing with him will please to call and settle, as his shop cannot be supplied without money.   Aug. 22

DOCTOR JOEL C. FRASER

Determining on a permanent residence at St. Charles, solicits the patronage of a general and liberal public as a practitioner of *Medicine* and *Surgery*—All calls in the line of his profession will be attended to with cheerfulness, and promptitude.

He has on hand some genuine *Vaccine or Cow-Pock Matter,* a safe and effectual preventive of the Small Pox. Those who wish to enjoy the advantage of the vaccine discovery, will please to call immediately. The poor will be inoculated GRATIS.   Sept. 17, 1817.

rarely to distant markets. (It appears that almost every farmer supplemented his income by providing overnight shelter for travelers.) That many settlers were self-sufficient farmers was regarded with favor by such agrarian critics as Johann David Schoepf: "These incessant emigrations, of which there will be no end so long as land is to be had for little or nothing, hinder the taking up of manufactures. . . . It is more befitting the *spirit* of this population, and that of all America, to support themselves on their own land . . . than to live better continually employed for wages."

Writing of immigrants from England who settled near Olive-green Creek in Ohio, William Tell Harris noted, "Though they have not been here more than fourteen months, they have grown corn, potatoes, pumpkins, cucumbers, greens, melons, and tobacco, sufficient to render them *independent* of their neighbours for support." Traveling in Ohio in 1819, Richard Lee Mason wrote of "*Independent* people in log cabins. They make their own clothes, sugar and salt, and paint their own signs." Land was within the reach of the average citizen in the Old Northwest and even the average alien. To a considerable degree the availability of land created, however briefly, something approaching an *economic* democracy in the Old Northwest; and that condition in turn provided the security necessary for people to express their republican tendencies and engage enthusiastically in political democracy.

Although land was plentiful and cheap, labor was not. According to William Faux, "Nothing is reckoned for land; land is nothing; labour every thing. In England it was almost vice versa." Artisans, craftsmen, and ordinary laborers were at a premium in the Old Northwest, and they knew it. Their economic independence was greater than it had been elsewhere and so, too, was their self-confidence. Until there were large pools of surplus farm labor—which were not available before perhaps the late 1830s—laborers strutted about in good republican style, confident in the knowledge that their services commanded premium wages.

Business and professional success in the Old Northwest required fewer skills, less capital, and less experience than were needed in the East or the Sweden of Gustaf Unonius. The cobbler who grew weary of mending boots and shoes could associate with a man practicing medicine, observe him as he concocted and dispensed cures, pay him a fee for a kit of pills and instruments, and then himself begin to practice medicine. Ease of changing jobs undoubtedly promoted republicanism and, according to Unonious, creativity as well. After noting, "A man who today is a mason may tomorrow be a doctor, the next day a cobbler," Unonious admitted that "distinct inconveniences arise from this situation; yet undeniably this unlimited freedom is exactly one of the important reasons why America has advanced with such tremendous speed. It has indeed given opportunity for many humbugs to flourish, but at the same time it has called forth many able men and has spurred them on to greater efforts." The virtual absence of restraining professional societies encouraged people to go from occupation to occupation, learning from each and transferring knowledge to each.

Republicanism and creativity were also fostered by generally inactive or ineffective state and federal governments. Government, it is true, did help to pave the way for settlement through diplomacy, warfare, purchase, and survey. But even with the consolidation of national power during the 1790s, the federal government was unable to enforce treaty provisions, subdue Indians north of the Ohio, or remove illegal squatters on public lands. More important, what we now consider the basic responsibilities of government—local defense, transportation, education, and protection from criminals—often rested primarily with *ad hoc* committees of local settlers. Just as diversity prevented one strain of culture from dominating all of the other strains, the absence of a strong and pervasive government insured that republican assertiveness and creativity would not be crushed or inhibited by exclusionary tests of religion, political correctness, or ideological purity. Francis Hall was well aware of that fact. Of the nation's expansion, he said, "Such is the growth, and such the projects of this transatlantic republic, great in extent of territory, in an active and well-informed population; but above all, in a *free government*, which not only leaves individual talent unfettered, but calls it into life by all the incitements of ambition most grateful to the human mind."

One observer, witnessing the influx of settlers into the region, was moved to write: "A sense of relative consequence is fostered by their growing possessions, and by perceiving towns, counties, offices and candidates springing up around them. One becomes a justice of the peace, another a county judge and another a member of the legislative assembly. Each one assumes some municipal function, pertaining to schools, the settlement of a minister, the making of roads, bridges, and public works. A sense of responsibility to public opinion, self respect, and a due estimation of character and correct deportment are the consequence."

Those arriving late in the settlement process often found that the best land—the town sites, bridge sites, mill sites, and simply the best soil—was either occupied or prohibitively expensive. They also found that entrenched interests controlled county and state political offices and social positions. Some of the late arrivals stayed on as hired help or tenant farmers; others, realizing that opportunity lay farther to the west, pushed on. In short, whether or not a settler in the Old Northwest became a creative republican depended, at least in part, upon the date of his arrival.

It is impossible to make a characterization that would apply to all the settlers who came to the Old Northwest. Yet today's historian would almost certainly agree with an 1818 visitor to the Old Northwest, who wrote, "The thinking man who wants to witness the expansion and development of a new people in a new land will here find a sweeping and an interesting field for his studies."

IO

Indian Policy in the Jacksonian Era

RONALD N. SATZ

• As Frederick Jackson Turner, Bernard De Voto, Richard A. Bartlett, William H. Goetzmann, and dozens of other historians have noted, the expansion of the United States from its narrow base along the Eastern Seaboard to almost continental size has been a central fact of American development. The story of the confrontation and eventual domination of the vast and empty spaces by successive waves of pioneer Americans has become our national epic.

Much less attention has been focused on the fact that the settlement of the West ranks among the many examples of naked aggression offered by history. In simple terms, an entire people was removed, a people whose claims to the land often dated back hundreds of years before it was even seen by the first white man. Those Indians that did not die in battle, or from hunger, or from diseases introduced by the new "Americans" were pressed onto reservations that kept getting smaller and smaller, despite treaties and guarantees from the federal government.

That this history was largely ignored for a century and more is hardly surprising given the treachery and the shameful methods used to separate the Indians from what was once theirs. Scholars who did write on the subject were usually so convinced of their own racial and cultural superiority over the native people that their accounts are properly suspect.

The essay by Ronald N. Satz is part of a reappraisal by younger historians of the assumptions held by nineteenth-century policymakers concerning the removal of Indian tribes. Were the claims of these relatively nomadic Indians greater than those of the pioneers who wanted to cultivate the land

From *Michigan History* 60 (Spring, 1976): 71–93. Reprinted by permission of the Michigan History Division, Lansing, Michigan.

and create a cornucopia of plenty in the midst of a wilderness?
Or would you agree with twentieth-century historian Satz
(and nineteenth-century English traveler Frances Trollope)
that, as Satz puts it, "Indian removal epitomized everything
despicable in American character"?

There has long been a tendency among scholars to view the Indian removal policy of the Jacksonian era in dualistic terms—the forces of evil supported removal while the forces of humanity opposed it. Recently, Francis Paul Prucha, George A. Schultz, and Herman J. Viola have attempted to show that enlightened thought supported Indian removal as a means of rescuing the eastern Indians from the evil effects of close contact with the advancing white frontier. Yet even these historians admit that the actual removal process entailed numerous hardships for the Indians.

This paper is an attempt to assess the goals, execution, and results of the Indian removal policy in the 1830s and 1840s by focusing on the application of that policy in the Old Northwest. The events surrounding the removal of the Five Civilized Tribes from the South have long been, to use the words of Grant Foreman, "a chapter unsurpassed in pathos and absorbing interest in American history." This dramatic episode has, to some extent, obscured similar events taking place farther north during the same period of time. The Old Northwest provides an interesting test case for an examination of the differences between the rhetoric and the reality of the removal policy. The Indians in this region were not the beneficiaries of anything approaching the tremendous outpouring of public sympathy for the Cherokees and their neighbors in the Southeast. If the Cherokees faced a "Trail of Tears" in spite of the great volume of petitions, letters, and resolutions presented to Congress in their behalf, what happened to the Indians in the Old Northwest who lacked such enthusiastic public support?

An essential ingredient to an understanding of the Indian policy in this period is the recognition that President Jackson and his successors in the White House, the War Department, the Office of Indian Affairs, and Indian agents maintained that the removal policy would bring at least four major benefits to the Indians. These included:

1. fixed and permanent boundaries outside of the jurisdiction of American states or territories;
2. isolation from corrupt white elements such as gamblers, prostitutes, whiskey vendors, and the like;
3. self-government unfettered by state or territorial laws; and
4. opportunities for acquiring the essentials of "civilized" society—Christianity, private property, and knowledge of agriculture and the mechanical arts.

Such were the benefits that government officials claimed the removal policy would bring the Indians. As a test case of the application of this policy, let us focus our attention on events in the Old Northwest.

President Jackson asked Congress on December 8, 1829, to provide him with authority to negotiate treaties to transfer Indians living east of the Mississippi River to a western location. Jackson and his congressional supporters, in their great rush to push through such legislation, seemed unconcerned about the technical aspects of any great migration of eastern Indians to the trans-Mississippi West. Opponents of the scheme, however, raised several important questions: Would emigration be purely voluntary? Would treaty commissioners negotiate only with acknowledged tribal leaders or would land be purchased from individuals? How many Indians would go? What kind of preparations and resources would be necessary for them? What would be the specific boundaries between emigrant tribes? How would the indigenous tribes in the West react to the intrusion of new people? During the debates on the Removal Bill, Tennessean David Crockett warned that it was a dangerous precedent to appropriate money for the executive branch without specifically knowing how the president intended to use it. Crockett warned that if Congress turned a deaf ear to the rights of the Indians then "misery must be their fate."

Unfortunately for the Indians, Congress passed the Removal Act in May 1830, and, despite the opposition of the nascent Whig party, Indian removal became a generally accepted policy in the ensuing decades. Throughout this period, congressional interest focused on patronage, partisan politics, and retrenchment to the detriment of the administration of Indian affairs. While the Whigs found it expedient to condemn aspects of the removal policy when they were struggling to capture the White House, they found it desirable to continue the policy once in office. Henry R. Schoolcraft, an Indian agent in Michigan Territory, poignantly described a serious defect of American Indian policy when he noted that "the whole Indian race is not, in the political scales, worth one white man's vote." The result of this situation, as David Crockett had warned, was misery for the Indians.

Among those who witnessed the actual dispossession of the eastern tribes in the Jacksonian era were two foreign travelers who, while not being authorities on the American Indians, nevertheless clearly recognized the deceptions involved in the treaty-making process. French traveler Alexis de Tocqueville poignantly observed that American officials, "inspired by the most chaste affection for legal formalities," obtained Indian title "in a regular and, so to say, quite legal manner." Although bribery and threats often accompanied treaty making and the formal purchases of Indian land, the United States had legal confirmation of its acquisitions. Indeed treaty negotiators were able to "cheaply acquire whole provinces which the richest sovereigns in Europe could not afford to buy" by employing such tactics as bribery or intimidation. Another European visitor, English Captain Frederick Marryat, accurately reported that "the Indians . . . are *compelled* to sell—the purchase money being a mere subterfuge, by which it may *appear* as if the lands were not being wrested from them, although, in fact, it [*sic*] is."

President Jackson had early indicated that his primary interest was the removal of the southeastern tribes. Although congressmen from the Old Northwest advised him following the passage of the Removal Act that the time for securing removal treaties in their region was "auspicious," Old Hickory informed them that his immediate concern was to set into motion a great tide of southern Indian emigration. Events in Illinois in the spring of 1832, however, played into the hands of the supporters of Indian removal in the Old Northwest.

In the spring of 1832, a hungry band of a thousand Sac and Fox Indians and their allies left their new home in Iowa Territory and crossed the Mississippi River en route to their old capital on the Rock River. Under the leadership of the proud warrior Black Hawk, this band, which included women and children, entered Illinois in search of food and as a means of protesting against their treatment by white frontiersmen. Mass hysteria swept the Illinois frontier with the news that the Indians had crossed the river. Governor John Reynolds called up the state militia to repel the "invasion" despite the fact that Black

Hawk's band was clearly not a war party. The result was a short, bloody conflict brought on largely as a consequence of the actions of drunken state militia. The ruthless suppression of the so-called "Indian hostilities" in Illinois and neighboring Wisconsin in 1832, and the seizure of a large part of the trans-Mississippi domain of the Sac and Fox Indians as "indemnity" for the war, broke the spirit of other tribes in the Old Northwest. Under pressure from the War Department, the Winnebagos in Wisconsin soon signed a removal treaty ceding their land south of the Wisconsin River. One by one, other tribes succumbed to similar pressure.

As critics of the Removal Act of 1830 had feared, the War Department obtained many of these land cessions by bribery. Agents courted influential tribal leaders by offering them special rewards including money, merchandise, land reserves, and medals, among other things. Sometimes treaty commissioners selected chiefs to represent an entire tribe or group of bands. The Jackson administration, for example, secured the title to the land of the United Nation of Chippewa, Ottawa, and Potawatomi Indians in northeastern Illinois, southeastern Wisconsin, and southern Michigan by "playing Indian politics." Indeed, the very existence of the United Nation was the result of the government's insistence on dealing with these Indians as if they were a single unit. Yet neither the great majority of the Chippewas and Ottawas nor all of the Potawatomi bands recognized the authority of the so-called United Nation. The government's policy of dealing with the entity as the representative of all Chippewas, Ottawas and Potawatomis was a clever maneuver to oust these Indians from their lands. By working closely with mixed-blood leaders and by withholding Indian annuities, the War Department secured the desired land cessions from the United Nation in the early 1830s.

During the Jacksonian era, the War Department frequently used economic coercion as a means of securing Indian title in the Old Northwest. Since the 1790s, the department had invested funds appropriated by Congress for purchasing Indian land in state banks or stocks and had paid the Indians only the annual interest on the amount owed them under treaty stipulations. This annuity or trust fund system gave government bureaucrats virtual control over funds legally belonging to the Indians. Although Thomas Jefferson played an important role in establishing the precedent of withholding Indian annuities as a means of social control, this procedure became a standard policy after 1829.

Treaty commissioners, Indian agents, and other field officers of the War Department found that withholding annuities was a convenient means of inducing recalcitrant Indians to sign treaties and to emigrate. Commissary General of Subsistence George Gibson advised the Jackson administration, "Let the annuities be paid west of the Mississippi [River], and there is no reason to doubt that the scheme of emigration would meet with little future opposition." American officials maintained considerable influence over tribal politics by determining who would receive the annuities.

Another measure used to encourage Indians to make land cessions was the inclusion of provisions in removal treaties for the granting of land reserves to chiefs, mixed-bloods, or other influential members of the tribes. The motivation behind this practice was twofold. First, it allowed government officials to combat Indian and American opposition to the removal policy based on the fact that some Indians had demonstrated a willingness and capability of accepting the white man's "civilization." When Andrew Jackson encountered strong opposition to his efforts to remove the Cherokees and the other so-called Civilized Tribes from their Southern domain, he conceded that Indians willing to accept the concept of private property should be allowed to remain in the East on individual reserves and become citizens of the states in which they resided. Secondly and more importantly for the Old Northwest, the practice of providing reserves of land to certain Indians was an ingenious device for bribing chiefs or influential tribesmen into accepting land cession treaties and for appeasing white traders into whose hands their reserves were certain to fall.

Treaty commissioners in Indiana found it impossible to secure land cessions from the Miami and Potawatomi Indians without the approval of the Wabash Valley traders to whom they were heavily in debt. Land speculators and settlers regarded the Miami and Potawatomi reserved sections adjacent to the Wabash River and the route of the Wabash and Erie Canal as choice lands. Wabash Valley traders, Indian agents, and even United States Senator John Tipton ultimately secured most of these lands from the Indians and rented them to white settlers for high profits after the Panic of 1837. By 1840 treaties with the Miamis and Potawatomis of Indiana had provided for nearly two hundred thousand acres of individual reserves. The largest holders of these reserves were not Indians but Wabash Valley traders W. G. and G. W. Ewing and Senator Tipton. Thousands of acres of Indian land elsewhere in the Old Northwest also fell into the hands of speculators.

In spite of the fact that speculators and traders often pressured the Indians into relinquishing their reserves before the government even surveyed the ceded tribal land, little was done to protect the Indians from such swindlers. Indiana Whig Jonathan McCarty, a bitter political adversary of Senator Tipton, introduced a resolution in Congress in 1835 calling for an investigation of the handling of Indian reserves, but no action resulted. Jackson, and his successors in the White House, were anxious to tone down investigations of alleged frauds in Indian affairs in order to avoid possible political embarrassments. Even some of the staunchest opponents of the removal policy benefited directly from the sale of Indian lands. Daniel Webster, Edward Everett, Caleb Cushing and Ralph Waldo Emerson were among those who speculated in Indian lands in the Old Northwest.

In addition to granting land reserves to Indians, the War Department followed the practice of including provisions in removal treaties for the payment of Indian debts to traders as a means of promoting removal. Since the Indians relied heavily on traders for subsistence and advice in the Old Northwest, the inclusion of traders' debts was often crucial to successful treaty negotiations. Although the recognition of these debts helped to promote the signing of land cession treaties, the practice also meant that the Indians lost huge sums of money to men who frequently inflated the prices of the goods they sold or falsified their ledgers. Transactions at treaty negotiations relative to the sale of Indian land, the adjustment of traders' claims, and the like were a complex business, yet many Indians, especially the full bloods, did not know the difference between one numerical figure and another.

The administration of Indian affairs in the mid-1830s was particularly vulnerable to criticism. The Panic of 1837 led many traders to exert political influence on treaty commissioners to have phoney Indian debts included in removal treaties. Commissioners Simon Cameron and James Murray awarded the politically influential American Fur Company over one hundred thousand dollars in alleged debt claims against the Winnebagos in Wisconsin in 1838 in return, according to rumor, for a large kickback. Only the military disbursing agent's refusal to pay the traders ultimately led to the exposure of the fraud. One eyewitness to this episode subsequently claimed that it was worse than the Crédit Mobilier scandal. An English visitor to Wisconsin several years after the incident reported that the acknowledgment of traders' claims during annuity payments was still a "potwallopping affair" in which the Indians left as empty-handed as when they had arrived. Both the Tyler and Polk administrations, in response to complaints from some congressmen, honest Indian agents, and concerned frontier residents, denounced the practice of acknowledging traders' debts in treaties. But the tremendous political influence of the traders, together with the War Department's emphasis on the speedy removal of Indians from areas desired by whites, led the government to follow the path of expediency. Traders continued to receive payments for their claims throughout the Jacksonian era.

If the techniques already mentioned failed to entice the Indians to emigrate, there was always brute force. The state of Indiana probably had one of the worst records in this respect. The Potawatomis ceded their last holdings in Indiana in 1836, but the treaty provisions allowed them two years to emigrate. Whites quickly began moving onto their land in order to establish preemption rights. As tension between the Indians and the whites grew, the Indiana militia rounded up the Potawatomis in 1838. When Chief Menominee, who had refused to sign the removal treaty, objected to the proceedings, the soldiers lassoed him, bound him hand and foot, and threw him into a wagon. The militia then hastily set into motion the Potawatomi exodus to the West—the "Trail of Death" along which about one hundred and fifty men, women, and children died as a result of exposure and the physical hardships of the journey. Several years later the Indiana militia also rounded up the Miami Indians in similar fashion to expedite their removal to the West.

By the end of Jackson's second term, the United States had ratified nearly seventy treaties under the provisions of the Removal Act and had acquired about one hundred million acres of Indian land for approximately sixty-eight million dollars and thirty-two million acres of land in the trans-Mississippi West. While the government had relocated forty-six thousand Indians by 1837, a little more than that number were still in the East under obligation to remove. According to the Office of Indian Affairs, only about nine thousand Indians, mostly in the Old Northwest and New York, were without treaty stipulations requiring their relocation, but there is evidence to indicate that the number of such Indians east of the Mississippi River at this time was much larger than the Indian Office reported. Indeed, there were probably more than nine thousand in Wisconsin Territory alone! The dearth of reliable population statistics for Indians during the Jacksonian era is a perplexing problem. By 1842, however, the United States had acquired the last area of any significant size still owned by the Indians in the Old Northwest. Only scattered remnants of the great tribes that had once controlled the region remained behind on reservations or individual holdings, chiefly in Michigan and Wisconsin.

The removal treaties of the Jacksonian era contained liberal provisions for emigrants and those remaining behind on reserves. They offered emigrants rations and transportation, protection en route to their new homes, medicine and physicians, reimbursement for abandoned property, funds for the erection of new buildings, mills, schools, teachers, farmers and mechanics, and maintenance for poor and orphaned children. The treaties read as if they were enlightened agreements. Yet there were several inherent defects in the treaty-making process. One of these was the assumption that the Indian leaders dealing with the government commissioners represented the entire tribe. Another was the assumption that the Indians clearly understood the provisions of the agreements. Still another was the fact that the Senate often amended or deleted treaty provisions without prior consultation with tribal leaders. Although treaty stipulations were provisional until ratified by the Senate, settlers rarely waited for formal action before they inundated Indian land. While Alexis de Tocqueville noted that "the most chaste affection for legal formalities" characterized American treaty making with the Indians, he also argued that "it is impossible to destroy men with more respect to the laws of humanity."

In spite of the favorable terms promised in removal treaties, most emigrants faced numerous hardships on their journeys to their new homes. A major reason for their misery was the system of providing them food and transportation by accepting the lowest bid from contractors. Many unscrupulous expectant capitalists furnished the Indians with scanty or cheap rations in order to make a sizeable profit from their contracts. The contractors were businessmen out to make money, and they were quite successful. Thomas Dowling, who received a contract in 1844 to remove six hundred Miami Indians from Indiana for nearly sixty thousand dollars, boasted to his brother that he would make enough profit to "rear the superstructure of an independence for myself, family, and relations."

In addition to the evils of the contract system, Indian emigrants also suffered from the government's perpetual concern for retrenchment. Although removal treaties provided for the medical care of emigrants, the War Department prohibited agents from purchasing medicine or surgical instruments until "actually required" during the economic hard times after 1837. Such instructions greatly hampered the effectiveness of the physicians accompanying migrating parties. To make matters worse, emigrants from the Old Northwest, many of them weakened by their constant battle with the elements of nature en route to the trans-Mississippi West, found themselves plagued with serious afflictions. Efforts to economize in removal expenditures by speeding up the movement of emigrants also led to much suffering. The War Department ordered in 1837 that only the sick or very young could travel west on horseback or by wagon at government expense. Even before this ruling, efforts to speed up the movement of migrating parties under orders from Washington officials proved detrimental to the Indians. An agent in charge of the removal of the Senecas from Ohio earlier in the 1830s, for example, wrote his superior that "I charge myself with cruelty in forcing these unfortunate people on at a time when a few days' delay might have prevented some deaths, and rendered the sickness of others more light, and have to regret this part of my duty."

Now let us examine the success of the removal policy in terms of the so-called benefits that government officials had argued it would bring to the Indians after their relocation. The first benefit was fixed and permanent boundaries outside the jurisdiction of American states and territories. Even before the Black Hawk War, the French travelers Alexis de Tocqueville and Gustave de Beaumont had voiced concern over the government's failure to establish a permanent Indian country for the northern Indians comparable to the one it was setting off west of Arkansas for the southern tribes. Sam Houston, a good Jacksonian Democrat, assured the travelers that Indian-white relations in the Old

Northwest were not as critical as in the South. He pointed out that permanent boundaries were unnecessary for the northern tribes since they would eventually be "pushed back" by the tide of white settlement. Following the Black Hawk War, Houston's contention proved correct.

The history of the relocation of the Winnebago Indians from Wisconsin illustrates the government's failure to systematically plan fixed boundaries for emigrants from the Old Northwest. When the War Department pressured the Winnebagos into signing a removal treaty at the cessation of the Black Hawk War, it left them with two alternative locations. One was the so-called "neutral ground" in Iowa between the Sac and Fox Indians and their Sioux enemies to the north. This location proved too precarious for the Winnebagos, who quickly made their way back to the second designated area that was within the territorial limits of Wisconsin, north of the Wisconsin River. When the Winnebagos moved into this area, they found themselves too tightly crowded together to live according to their old life styles. As a result, they frequently returned to the sites of their old villages south of the Wisconsin River.

In returning to their old homesites, the Winnebagos encountered other Indians as well as white settlers. While the War Department had induced the Winnebagos to leave southern Wisconsin in order to free them from white contact in that area, it had relocated tribes from New York there in order to free them from white contact in New York. Both the Winnebagos and the New York Indians relocated in Wisconsin soon became the victims of the great land boom that swept the territory in the 1830s as whites eagerly sought Indian land for settlement and timber.

By 1838 the Winnebagos had ceded all of their land in Wisconsin and had promised to move to the neutral ground in Iowa, but the "final" removal of the last band of these Indians in 1840 required the use of troops. For several years after their relocation, the Indian Office attempted to transfer them from Iowa to the Indian country west of Missouri. In 1841 the Tyler administration planned to have them join other northern tribes in a new Indian territory north of the present Iowa-Minnesota border and south of, roughly, the 46th parallel. This new location would appease residents of Iowa who were clamoring for the removal of the Winnebagos and settlers in Wisconsin who were anxious to expel the Winnebago stragglers and the New York Indians who had settled there. Such a northern location would also placate the citizens of Arkansas and Missouri who opposed any additional influx of Indians on their western borders. The War Department favored this plan because it would provide a safe corridor for white expansion to the Pacific through Iowa and would place the Indians of the Old Northwest far south of the Canadian border thus luring them away from British-Canadian influence.

In spite of the War Department's plans, large numbers of Winnebagos drifted back to Wisconsin during the 1840s. Efforts to relocate them in present-day Minnesota between the Sioux and their Chippewa enemies led again to Winnebago defiance. Despite the use of military force to compel them to go to their "proper homes," the Winnebagos were greatly dispersed in Wisconsin, Iowa, and Minnesota at the end of the decade, to the annoyance of white settlers in those areas. The condition of these Indians clearly indicates that the War Department was lax in undertaking long-range planning for a permanent home for the tribes of the Old Northwest. The government continually reshuffled these Indians in order to make room for northeastern tribes and the growing pressures of white settlement. Whenever the white population pattern warranted it, the War Department merely redesignated new locations for the Indians. Nor did the government pay much attention to the needs of emigrants. Menominee Chief Oshkosh, in complaining about Winnebago intrusions on Menominee land in Wisconsin in 1850, cited several reasons why the Winnebagos continually left their new locations and returned to Wisconsin; these included the poor soil in their new country, the scarcity of game there, and, most importantly, their dread of their fierce Sioux neighbors.

The agony of the Winnebagos was not unique. Many other tribes faced the prospect of removing to an allegedly permanent location more than once. Continued white hostility following the Black Hawk War led the United Nation of Chippewas, Ottawas, and Potawatomis, for example, to give up their claims to northern Illinois, southeastern Wisconsin and several scattered reserves in southern Michigan in 1833 for a tract of land bordering the Missouri River in southwestern Iowa and northwestern Missouri. The new Potawatomi lands included the Platte Country, the region in present-day northwest Missouri watered by the Little Platte and Nodaway rivers. This area was not included in the original boundaries of Missouri in 1820. The inclusion of the Platte Country in the land designated for the Potawatomis demonstrates once again the poor planning of the War Department. In 1832 Missouri Governor John Miller had called for the annexation of this region and Missouri Senators Lewis F. Linn and Thomas Hart Benton joined him in arguing that the area was necessary for the political and economic growth of their state. Although over one hundred Potawatomis had signed the original treaty, the War Department, in its effort to appease Missourians, secured an amended treaty, signed by only seven Indians, that substituted a similar amount of land in Iowa for the Platte Country.

While the government was seeking to modify the original treaty to placate Missouri, Potawatomis who had signed that document moved to the Platte Country. The number of tribesmen there grew as small bands from Indiana continued to travel West in accordance with the provisions of the original treaty. Many Potawatomis came to view the government's new proposed location for them in Iowa as being too close to the Sioux. The Jackson administration reluctantly permitted them to settle temporarily in the Platte Country until they could find suitable sites for new villages in southeastern Iowa. There were still approximately sixteen hundred Potawatomis in the Platte Country in March 1837 when President Martin Van Buren proclaimed the area part of the state of Missouri. The War Department soon ejected them from there and resettled them in southwestern Iowa and Kansas. Government officials consolidated the Potawatomis into one reservation in northcentral Kansas in 1846 and subsequently relocated them in Oklahoma during the 1860s.

The experiences of the Winnebago and Potawatomi Indians clearly indicate that the new boundaries for emigrants from the Old Northwest were far from permanent. Treaty commissioners merely reshuffled the tribes around as frontiersmen, speculators, and state officials pressured the War Department to open more Indian land to white settlement. Federal officials failed to undertake long-range planning for the establishment of permanent boundaries for the emigrant tribes from this region. The sole effort in this direction before 1848, the Tyler administration's attempt to create a northern Indian territory, failed because the War Department had neglected the needs and the desires of the Indians.

At the end of the Jacksonian era, Indian Commissioner William Medill reported that the Polk administration had begun to mark off a northern Indian "colony" on the headwaters of the Mississippi River for "the Chippewas of Lake Superior and the upper Mississippi, the Winnebagoes, the Menomonies, such of the Sioux, if any, as may choose to remain in that region, and all other northern Indians east of the Mississippi (except those in the State of New York), who have yet to be removed west of that river." Together with the removal of Indians from the "very desirable" land north of the Kansas River to a southern "colony" west of Arkansas and Missouri, Medill hoped that the concentration of the northern Indians on the headwaters of the Mississippi River would provide "a wide and safe passage" for American emigrants to the Far West. Medill's report of November 30, 1848, was a tacit admission of the government's failure to provide Indian emigrants from the Old Northwest with fixed and permanent boundaries as guaranteed by the Removal Act of 1830. Throughout this period, the exigencies of the moment determined the boundaries that American officials provided for the Indians.

The second alleged benefit of removal was isolation from corrupt white elements such as gamblers, prostitutes, whiskey peddlers, and the like. The government's lack of planning for the permanent relocation of the tribes of the Old Northwest meant that these Indians were continually in the path of the westward tide of white settlement. Although Congress passed a Trade and Intercourse Act in 1834 to protect the Indians from land hungry whites, as well as whiskey peddlers and similar groups, nothing, including Indian treaty rights, stopped the advance of white settlement. Liquor was readily available to most tribes. In 1844 Thomas McKenney, an expert on Indian affairs, reported that the Menominees in Wisconsin, who had undergone several relocations, were "utterly abandoned to the vice of intoxication." Efforts to strengthen the Trade and Intercourse Laws in 1847 failed once again to halt the liquor traffic. Frontier citizens, especially the traders and their powerful political allies, blatantly refused to cooperate in enforcing the laws.

Tribal self-government unfettered by state or territorial laws was the third benefit that removal was supposed to bring the Indians. Yet the Trade and Intercourse Acts of 1834 and 1847 placed the Indians at the mercy of the white man's conception of justice. The legislation clearly provided that American laws would take precedence over Indian laws and customs in all cases involving both groups. Since the local judicial officers in the white communities adjoining Indian settlements reflected the dominant attitudes of their respective communities and often had ties with local businessmen and traders, they were not always effective administrators of the federal laws designed to protect the Indians from whiskey peddlers or other avaricious whites. The presence of federal Indian agents and military detachments near Indian settlements, moreover, meant that the Indians were not completely sovereign. Indian agents and the commanding officers of frontier posts often played "Indian politics." They found it much easier to deal with a central tribal authority rather than a series of chiefs or headmen and encouraged the recognition of one individual as the principal tribal leader. One vehicle used to accomplish this purpose was the allocation of Indian annuities. By determining who would receive the annuities, the War Department manipulated tribal politics. The result of such efforts was the emasculation of tribal self-government.

The fourth alleged benefit of removal was "civilization." American officials involved in the formulation and execution of Indian policy argued that the Indians lacked the essentials of civilized society—Christianity, private property, and knowledge of agriculture and the mechanical arts. Indian removal, they maintained, would provide ample opportunities for the uplifting of the Indians. Yet the removal policy did not bring great benefits, in terms of the white man's "civilization," to a significant number of Indians.

The constant reshuffling of tribes to new "permanent" locations failed to promote Indian interest in the white man's "civilization." How could the Winnebagos who had suffered tremendous social and psychological strains as a result of their continuous uprooting and relocation be expected to have interest in, or make significant advances in, the adoption of Christianity or any of the other so-called prerequisites of "civilized" society? Other Indians had similar reactions.

The events surrounding the acquisition of Chippewa and Ottawa lands in Michigan demonstrate some of the reasons for the failure of government efforts to promote its "civilization" program among the Indians of the Old Northwest. In 1836 the Chippewas and Ottawas had ceded their lands with the understanding that the government would allot them permanent reservations in northern Michigan and

provide blacksmiths, farmers, and teachers to help them learn white
trades and farming techniques. The land cession treaty provided federal funds to accomplish the "civilization" of these Indians, but the
entire project was doomed before it began.

When the Senate considered the ratification of the treaty, it
amended the document so that the reserves in northern Michigan
would only be temporary residences. The Indians were understandably
disturbed by this unilateral alteration of the treaty, and they were reluctant to move to temporary reserves in order to clear the land and to
take up farming. Commissioner of Indian Affairs Carey Allen Harris,
moreover, urged that government funds for these Indians be kept to a
minimum until they settled at a permanent location.

Because their "permanent" boundaries always seemed to be temporary ones, the Indians of the Old Northwest found it more convenient
to live off their annuities than to labor in their fields. As Chippewa Indian George Copway lamented, "no sooner have the Indians gone on
and made improvements, and our children began to like to go to the
school houses which have been erected, than we hear the cry of the
United States government, 'We want your lands'; and, in going from
one place to another, the Indian looses [sic] all that he had previously
learned." As a result of this situation, the Indians paid more attention
to the fur traders than to the school teachers. The tribes in this region
relied heavily on the traders for food and goods. Government officials
tended to see this dependence on the traders as a sign of idleness or
weakness of character. Their ethnocentricism blinded them to the fact
that farming had long been women's work among these tribes. The fur
trade, wild grain, and fish were traditionally much more important to
the livelihood of these Indians than American agricultural products.

Other problems inherent in the "civilization program" included the
personnel employed to "civilize" the Indians. Such appointments offered patronage-hungry politicians a means of rewarding their supporters. Consequently, the teachers hired to work with the Indians did
not always bring altruistic motives to their jobs. Some of them were
even "indolent and shif[t]less." The employment of missionaries as
civilizing agents caused special problems. Interdenominational rivalries
greatly impeded their work. Some Indians demonstrated open hostility
to missionaries because they associated them with efforts to remove
their people from their ancient homes. Presbyterian minister Peter

Dougherty found that his preaching of the Gospel to the Chippewa Indians in Michigan was greatly impeded by the belief of "heathen" Chippewas that the acceptance of Christianity would lead to their removal. For several reasons, therefore, the "civilization" program actually suffered because of the removal policy.

Regardless of the intentions of federal officials, the Indian removal policy in the Jacksonian era did not bring the tribesmen the benefits that they had predicted. Scholars such as Prucha, Schultz, and Viola have argued that the architects of the removal policy had thought that it was in the best interests of the Indians. If the formulators and executors of the policy actually believed this, their assumption proved erroneous for the Indians of the Old Northwest. While there was no policy of racial extermination or genocide perpetrated against the Indians of this region, there can be no doubt that the removal policy led to tribal demoralization. Whether noble intentions or nefarious ones lay behind the removal policy, the results were disastrous for the Indians. As one scholar recently asserted, "it is sometimes difficult to tell whether the Indian has suffered more at the hands of his 'friends' or at the hands of his 'enemies.' "

Frances Trollope, an English visitor to the United States, wrote in 1832 that Indian removal epitomized everything despicable in American character, especially the "contradictions in their principles and practice." "You will see them one hour lecturing their mob on the indefeasible rights of man," she wrote, "and the next driving from their homes the children of the soil, whom they have bound themselves to protect by the most solemn treaties." American Indian policy in the Old Northwest during the Jacksonian era serves as a grim reminder of what can happen to a politically powerless minority in a democratic society. It also demonstrates that scholars must be careful not to confuse the rhetoric of government policies with the realities involved in executing these policies.

II

The Founding of Mount Holyoke College

KATHRYN KISH SKLAR

• During the colonial period, women were not often required to be ladies. There was little opportunity for such frivolous roles; all hands were needed for simple survival. Women were valued for their much-needed economic contributions to their families and were engaged in providing such necessities of daily life as food and clothing through the backbreaking labor that was the norm. Even the Southern lady, usually described as a carefree belle forever waltzing among magnolia blossoms, was engaged in the continual and arduous task of planning and managing plantation life.

Between 1820 and 1860, however, a new "cult of true womanhood" insisted that every female—meaning, of course, only white, middle-class ones—was a lady and should follow a prescribed code of behavior. In these years, when men were busily expanding geographic and economic frontiers, intent on materialistic concerns, it gave them a sense of security to believe that the spiritual and moral side of life was being taken care of by their women, safe at home. Thus, the cult of the lady had a very important function to society at large; it provided assurance that at home and with the women were peace and stability, two qualities so lacking in the outside world of a nation on the move.

In such an environment, the education of the second sex for anything more than domestic duties was not accorded a high national priority, and it was not until the last third of the nineteenth century that such elite women's colleges as Vassar, Barnard, Smith, and Wellesley were founded. Long before these, however, in 1837, Mount Holyoke opened its

K. K. Sklar, "The Founding of Mount Holyoke College," in Carol Berkin and Mary Beth Norton (eds.): *Women in America*. Copyright © 1979 by Houghton Mifflin Company. Used by permission.

doors. *Never the largest, richest, or most famous of women's institutions, it nevertheless initiated, as Professor Kathryn Kish Sklar of the University of California at Los Angeles demonstrates in the following essay, "a new era in female education."*

The 1830s marked a turning point in many dimensions of American female experience. Especially important were the changes the decade witnessed in women's education, epitomized by the founding of Mount Holyoke Female Seminary in South Hadley, Massachusetts, in 1837. Even before the seminary opened its doors, its founder, Mary Lyon, predicted that it would inaugurate "an era in female education." "The work will not stop with this institution," she told a friend shortly after the ceremonial placement of the building's cornerstone, and subsequent years proved the accuracy of her statement. Mount Holyoke, innovative among female educational institutions because of its solid financial base, its commitment to instructing girls drawn from all economic levels, and its advanced curriculum, served as a model for many women's colleges founded later in the century. Accordingly, an examination of the circumstances surrounding its inception can reveal the impulses behind the significant advances made in female education during the antebellum period.

To some degree Mary Lyon's successful attempt to establish an institution of higher learning for women in 1837 was unique in the annals of female education in the nineteenth century. Her institution was designed for and funded by families of average wealth, unlike the seminaries that preceded it in the 1820s—such as Emma Willard's in Troy, New York, or Catharine Beecher's in Hartford, Connecticut—and unlike the colleges such as Vassar, Smith, and Wellesley, that followed it in the last third of the nineteenth century, which were designed for and funded by a wealthier constituency. Mount Holyoke was nevertheless a logical product of its time and place and of a founder whose own personal experience was replicated to some extent in the lives of many of her less-distinguished female contemporaries.

MARY LYON: THE EARLY YEARS

Born in 1797 in Buckland, Massachusetts, Mary Lyon was raised by her mother after her father died when she was only 5. Jemima Shepherd Lyon provided her daughter with a model of a woman who was a "presiding angel of good works" for the neighborhood, and in later years Mary called her "that dearest friend of my young heart." Certainly her father's death drew the girl closer to her mother, and her relationship with this "dearest friend" could well have been the source of her lifelong respect for and loyalty to her sex.

But the death of her father had another important effect on the shape of Mary Lyon's life: As a widow, Jemima Lyon had few financial resources, so her daughter was forced to contribute to her own support at an early age. In 1814, when she was 17 years old, Mary Lyon started her career as an educator by contracting to teach in a town school in nearby Shelburne during the summer months. Her pay was 75 cents a week, plus the board and room she received by "boarding round" with Shelburne families, who were in turn reimbursed for their expenses by the town selectmen.

FEMALE EDUCATION IN NEW ENGLAND, 1760–1840

In choosing to make her living by teaching, Mary Lyon was following in the footsteps of many other young New England women of her generation. But employment in the town schools had only recently become an occupation open to females. Before 1780 most publicly supported schools in Massachusetts towns had been attended exclusively by boys and were taught solely by men. Even though state education laws required all towns to maintain district schools to teach "children" reading, writing, and arithmetic, girls were usually denied access to these institutions, just as they were automatically excluded from the grammar schools (also town supported), which trained college-bound boys in Latin and Greek.

Thus, colonial parents who wanted their daughters to learn to read, write, and cipher had to pay for that privilege, sending them first to the dame schools that were also attended by younger boys, and then perhaps to a local female academy that offered instruction in music, fancy needlework, and dancing. The women who ran these schools, generally in their own homes, lacked any sort of special training for the task; they combined occasional instruction with other domestic duties in order to support themselves and their families.

Given the erratic nature of this education, it is not surprising that Kenneth Lockridge, who has investigated literacy patterns in prerevolutionary New England, has estimated the literacy rate of women there to be only half that of men (about 45 percent of women as opposed to 90 percent of men). But by the time Mary Lyon began to teach, this discriminatory pattern had been seriously eroded, if not completely eliminated. The federal census of 1850, which first measured literacy by sex, registered equal and universal literacy skills among white native-born New England men and women. Because such skills were acquired early in life, and because the population of 1850 included a sizable number of women who grew up between 1780 and 1820, it is obvious that a substantial improvement in female education occurred during those decades.

Although by approximately 1810 girls were accepted in town schools throughout Massachusetts (Mary Lyon attended a Buckland school in 1803), the process by which they were included varied considerably. One of the leaders in opening district schools to girls was Sutton, a relatively poor agricultural community in Worcester County, which as early as 1767 paid women teachers to run summer sessions for local girls.

Interestingly, Sutton violated state law by not supporting a grammar school until the 1790s, even though it had established a system of 14 district schools by the 1770s. This suggests that one factor in Sutton's commitment to the basic education of its daughters was its concomitant lack of interest in producing a well-educated male elite. By 1773 the selectmen of Sutton were already devoting half of their education appropriations to the instruction of girls—a proportion that continued throughout the rest of the century—and it is clear that the town fathers preferred to have all their children learn the rudiments rather than to concentrate their resources on the training of a few boys in Latin and Greek.

This trade-off between the basic instruction of all children and the advanced education of a small number of male youths is apparent when Sutton's actions are contrasted to those of Northampton, a commercial town in the Connecticut Valley located near South Hadley and the eventual site of Mount Holyoke Seminary. In 1800 the selectmen of Northampton spent as much to support one grammar schoolmaster as the leaders of Sutton spent year round on seven district schools, and as late as 1788 these selectmen voted explicitly "not to be at any expense for schooling girls."

In 1792 an outlying district of Northampton finally obtained the selectmen's permission to include girls in a coeducational summer session taught by a man, but not until several of the town's citizens won a ruling from the Massachusetts attorney general that "girls had rights and could not be excluded from school" did the selectmen begin to consider altering their policy. They implemented the change slowly and reluctantly, being prodded by a town committee's recommendation in 1801 that women be employed to teach girls. Only in 1810, however, were the committee's suggestions for the systematic employment of female teachers fully effectuated.

Mary Lyon and other women hired by town selectmen to teach in public schools between 1780 and 1820 differed markedly from their predecessors, the proprietors of dame schools, in two important ways. Whereas teaching in dame schools was a female occupation governed by custom, teaching in town schoolhouses meant entering a male occupation governed by state regulations that applied equally to both sexes. The first systematic revision of state school laws after the Revolution, in 1789, was also the first to mention schoolmistresses along with schoolmasters. That law required that teachers of either sex be certified as competent before being employed, and specified the ways public funds were to be raised for their salaries. Their positions of public authority gave young schoolmistresses a new kind of prestige in their communities. As one woman who taught in a district school in this period put it, "she who could preside with dignity in the school room commanded respect elsewhere."

Also, whereas women of all ages taught in home dame schools, the vast majority of those who taught in town schoolhouses were young and unmarried. Most were between the ages of 16 and 23, the average age at marriage, and turnover was high among them. Because women could be paid significantly less than men—perhaps one-half or even one-third the salary of a male schoolmaster—town selectmen increasingly hired females. By 1837 Massachusetts district schools employed three women for every two men, and by 1850 there were two women for every man employed. As a result of high turnover rates and the widespread employment of women, it has recently been estimated that by 1837 one of every five native-born white Massachusetts women had taught school at some point during her life, whereas the equivalent male proportion was one in seven.

Most of Mary Lyon's female contemporaries went no further than sporadic district school teaching. But in 1817, after three summers of teaching at that level and as many winters of instructing children in private families, she entered the coeducational Sanderson Academy in Ashfield "resolved," according to her biographer Edward Hitchcock, "to prepare herself particularly for teaching." She paid the tuition of two shillings a week with savings from her previous jobs and by doing spinning and weaving for local families.

The academy, located less than five miles from Mary Lyon's birthplace, had been founded in 1816 by Alvan Sanderson, the town's Congregational minister. It was one of a number of private academies that offered an equal education to men and women, emphasizing a practical curriculum and the study of natural philosophy (physics). Sanderson, like others of its type, neither provided training in such traditional female skills as sewing or music nor developed a specific vocational rationale for the education of women. Mary Lyon later described Sanderson as "the school where I was principally educated, and to which I feel in no small degree indebted." Certainly her later stress on an academic curriculum for women and her emphasis on the spiritual training of her charges can be traced in part to her experience at the academy.

Alvan Sanderson exemplified the vital links forged between church and school in this rocky and hilly hinterland west of the Connecticut River. Ashfield contained one of the largest Baptist communities in New England, and "awakened" or evangelical religion was especially strong there, imbuing all aspects of life with spiritual urgency. Mary Lyon's great-grandfather, Chileab Smith, had been a lay patriarch among Ashfield Baptists, "whose right to worship without taxation he had won in 1773 after a long struggle culminating in an appeal to London." Jemima Lyon had raised her children in the Baptist faith, which meant that they were not baptized until after they had experienced personal religious conviction, or "conversion from their sins."

The spiritual state of young children was therefore more than a nominal concern around Ashfield, and this concern prompted closer ties than usual between church and school.

These ties contained an unexploited potential for the advancement of female education. Ministers encouraged female teachers like Mary Lyon to exercise spiritual authority and leadership in their schools, transforming their task of instilling "virtue" in their pupils from a nominal to a vital responsibility, and viewing the training of female teachers as a sacred as well as a secular undertaking. When Mary Lyon was herself teaching at Sanderson a few years later, visiting ministers emphasized her spiritual responsibilities to the teachers she was training. As she described one visit:

> After expressing a great interest in the school on account of its influence on society, and on account of its containing so many teachers for district schools the ensuing summer, he said that he had been anxious for its *spiritual* prosperity. *He only said it*, but it found a resting place in my heart, and there it has rested.

This religious aspect of teacher training accounted for the uniqueness in Mary Lyon's later fund raising, which succeeded in raising a new scale of funding for female higher education for a new middle-class constituency.

MARY LYON'S FUND-RAISING TECHNIQUES

We can see this uniqueness in fund-raising circulars Mary Lyon wrote between 1834 and 1836 for Mount Holyoke. These circulars made four basic points: like male colleges, the seminary was to be permanently endowed by the whole Christian community; like male colleges, it was designed to cultivate Christian activism in its students; like male colleges, it was designed to draw students from moderate circumstances as well as from wealthy families; and unlike male colleges, but parallel to their chief goal of training ministers, Mount Holyoke's primary function was to train female teachers.

Thus, Mary Lyon imitated the funding principles on which new male colleges, especially Amherst, were founded—widespread support "from liberal Christians in common life" who contributed because "the prospect was held out that it would be a college of high standing where the expenses would be low, and that it would be accessible to all." When "the Christian public" responded with 15,000 dollars in two years' time, Mary Lyon concluded: "I doubt whether any benevolent object, not excepting even the missionary cause has ever, within two years from its commencement, made as great advance in gaining access to the understanding and hearts of the people."

This initial endowment was nearly four times greater than the financial resources with which Willard and Beecher began their seminaries in the 1820s. They were responsible to stockholders who expected a profitable return on their investment, and this profit was reflected in high tuition fees. As Reverend Mark Hopkins, President of Williams College, said in 1840: "In some cases the expense of sustaining a young lady in school for a year was more than double what was required to give a young man the advantages of a college course."

Mary Lyon succeeded in obtaining a new scale of funding, which freed her from placing the burden of profit or of institutional development on tuition fees. Costs at Mount Holyoke were one-third those paid by students at Willard's Troy Female Seminary. Lyon's new scale of funding therefore significantly benefited "the adult female youth in the common walks of life."

How did she do it? In this essay we view three factors that contributed to her success: the ideological and religious example of Reverend Joseph Emerson; the partnership she formed with Emerson's assistant, Zilpah Grant; and the loyalty she retained to her social and economic origins. Emerson's example provided her with theoretical and behavioral connections between evangelical religion and female teachers; Grant's assistance provided her with fund-raising experience; and her adherence to her origins made it possible for her to exploit an untapped source of support for higher female education—the same popular roots that had nourished change in female primary education before 1820.

Before enrolling at Emerson's Ladies Seminary in 1821 Lyon contributed to her support by "weaving heavy blue and white coverlets, a kind of work requiring strength equal to that of a man and therefore commanding more pay than common labor." After a harrowing three-day journey with a close friend from Ashfield and her father in their family carriage, the two young women joined others from nearby Boston and from towns throughout New England.

THE INFLUENCE OF AWAKENED RELIGION

Reverend Joseph Emerson had been dismissed from his pastoral labors by his Beverly congregation in 1816 due to ill health, but his insistence on religious conversion as a criterion for church membership, which was opposed by his more decorous parish, probably also contributed to his dismissal. The seminary he established in nearby Byfield infused vocational training for female teachers with the experiential and ideological power of awakened religion. His efforts were reinforced by the able assistance of his wife, Rebecca Hasseltine, sister of New England's first missionary heroine and martyr, Nancy Hasseltine Judson, and with the help of Abigail Hasseltine, "preceptress" for many years at Bradford Academy.

In the 1820s Joseph Emerson was one of the strongest supporters of and advocates for female teachers. As his biographer and brother, Ralph Emerson, wrote:

> He was born for the very work of teaching and especially of teaching females. His specific object now was, to render their education more solid and much more extensive. . . . His object was not merely to have a good seminary of his own, but also to benefit other teachers, and to raise up a multitude more, of the right stamp, and ultimately to fill the land with such seminaries and schools.

At Emerson's school all learned "an increased sense of the responsibility of the maternal relation," and in keeping with this emphasis, turned their attention "from the fancy work of the fingers to the great subjects of thought in science and religion." But the seminary's main purpose was to benefit female teachers.

Like Willard and Beecher, Emerson advocated a reorientation of female higher education away from the development of leisured skills (such as instrumental music or fancy sewing) designed to polish the rudiments of home learning. These skills, in Willard's words, merely fit women "for displaying to advantage the charms of youth and beauty," and prepared "them to please the other [sex]." Whereas higher education had formerly prepared young women for the marriage market and had focused on skills useful in establishing a husband-wife relationship, these innovators in the 1820s found a new rationale for female education in the mother-child relationship and its vocational equivalent—the female schoolteacher.

In her *Plan for Improving Female Education*, presented to the New York legislature in 1819, Emma Willard argued that female seminaries deserved the support of public funds because:

> properly fitted by instruction, women would be likely to teach children better than the other sex; they could afford to do it cheaper; and those men who would otherwise be engaged in this employment, might be at liberty to add to the wealth of the nation, by any of those thousand occupations, from which women are necessarily debarred.

Willard's argument did not succeed in gaining the financial support of the New York State Legislature for female seminaries, but it did represent the strongest grounds on which to base such an appeal.

In his 1822 *Discourse on Female Education* Joseph Emerson echoed Willard's view that more women should join men in "the business of teaching," because "their instructions are at once more excellent and less expensive." To this economic argument, however, Emerson added the buttresses of evangelical religion. Endowing the vocation of teaching with sacred agency, he said that teachers could "do more to enlighten and reform the world and introduce the millennium than persons of any other profession except the ministers of Christ," and he believed that females were as good as if not better than males in this redemptive work. Calling for improvements in female education commensurate with female responsibilities, Emerson urged that "something must be *done* in order that females may attain that dignified and elevated rank in society for which the God of nature, as well as the Bible, has manifestly designed them." In conclusion Emerson pointed to two hopeful portents of positive change in the immediate future: benevolent activism among mature women, and the desire among average women for improved education.

Emerson praised female benevolent activity in general and declared:

> As woman was the first in the transgression, so she appears to have been most active to deliver the world from the dreadful effects of her horrid apostasy. . . . The numerous and noble institutions that so distinguish and bless the present day have

been greatly promoted by female exertions. They have been urged forward by female hands, by female tongues, by female prayers.

Praising female support of education and the American Education Society in particular, he quoted from a recent report of that society, which was founded in 1815 to meet the rising demand for charitable support among the growing numbers of indigent young men preparing for the ministry at college.

> The Female Auxiliary Education Society of Salem and Vicinity, has been perseveringly engaged five years, and has contributed $695.03. The Contributions of the last year exceed those of any preceding year. The Female Auxiliary Society of Boston and Vicinity has in three years contributed to the funds $1,119.32. The Graham Society of Boston from Jan. 1817 to Jan. 1821, have aided 42 beneficiaries of the American Education Society, in articles of clothing to the amount of $626.27. . . . *Of fifty-eight societies which are auxiliary to this, thirty-one are composed of females.*

Educational auxiliaries, one of the most common forms of female benevolent activity, were described by Lucy Stone, later an important abolitionist and suffragist, and a member of such an auxiliary in West Brookfield when Mary Lyon spoke to it in 1837:

> Little sewing circles were formed where rich and poor women met to sew, either for a fair to raise money or for garments to be given directly to the young men whom the education societies aided. "Help educate young men! Help educate young men for ministers and for missionaries!" was the constant appeal made to women. Was it a wonder that as young women drew the needle they also drew the conclusion that if education was so necessary for men it must be valuable for women who were to stay at home?

In 1822 Joseph Emerson did not call on women to channel their fund raising into the support of female education. During the next 15 years, however, female benevolent associations grew in numbers and in experience, making them ripe for Mary Lyon's appeal.

Between 1776 and 1811, religious institutions ceased to be supported by taxes levied on all households regardless of their church attendance, and came instead to rely on voluntary contributions. Partly in response to this "disestablishment," an increasing number of churches and ministers revived the seventeenth-century emphasis on the church as a voluntary community whose membership was defined not only on the basis of geography, but also on the ability of each prospective communicant to experience a spiritual rebirth, the authenticity of which might be examined by the minister, deacons, or entire congregation. During the "Great Revival" of 1800 to 1840, the social and economic power of an awakened laity compensated for the withdrawal of state support and transformed female church members, who had since 1660 constituted a numerical majority within most churches, into an active agency for the redemption of the world.

Between 1810 and 1840 the numbers and size of New England female religious, charitable, or reform associations grew dramatically. At the peak of the Great Revival in the 1830s a significant proportion —at least one-third and probably a majority—of adult women were members of one or more such associations. The records of the Grafton Female Moral Reform Society, near Sutton, listed approximately one-third of the town's adult women as members between 1838 and 1840. This coalescing of the female religious laity into a variety of voluntary associations usually began under the nominal leadership of the minister, but frequently (as in the case of Female Moral Reform Societies) they developed into legally autonomous female corporations.

In such organizations single women often acted as treasurers, because married women could not hold and transfer money or engage in legal contracts. Although legally disabled upon marriage, around 1810 mature women, in combination with a few single or widowed women and in alliance with the church, began to exercise a new kind of collective power within their communities. During this period the American Education Society and its female auxiliaries also grew at a rapid pace. In a recent study David F. Allmendinger has estimated that by 1838 the society supported one out of seven young men enrolled in New England colleges.

As Nancy F. Cott recently pointed out in *The Bonds of Womanhood: Woman's Sphere in New England, 1780–1835*, male associations formed during this period for a variety of political, civic, and professional goals as well as for religious or charitable purposes, but female associations were almost exclusively religious or charitable.

One obvious reason for this distinction was the general exclusion of women from public life. Another reason can be found in the benefits women derived from such associations. Cott concluded that women supported religion faithfully because, "No other avenue of self-expression besides religion at once offered women social approbation, the encouragement of male leaders (ministers), and, most important, the community of their peers." At Emerson's Seminary Mary Lyon learned how this approbation, encouragement, and community could sustain the lives of young female teachers. She may also have realized that a connection could be made between the collective strength of organized female benevolence and the advancement of female education.

In addition to their "more excellent and less expensive" teaching as young women and their active enlistment in the cause of redemption as mature women, Emerson pointed to another hopeful sign for change in female education—the eagerness with which older women of average economic circumstances promoted their daughters' as well as their own schooling:

> So many thousands of American mothers, impressed with the importance of knowledge which they do not possess, are willing to rise up early, to sit up late, to eat the bread of the most rigid economy, to exert themselves to the utmost, that their daughters may be favored with the means of improvement, very greatly superior to what they themselves had possessed; and that so many females are making such vigorous efforts, to enjoy and improve the means of their education, and are not ashamed to become fellow pupils with those who have not seen half so many summers themselves.

ENCOURAGEMENT OF FEMALE EDUCATION

Emerson put his prescriptions into practice by raising funds for students who received little or no economic support from their families. His public announcement for a "Course of Lectures on Astronomy" in Boston in 1819 stated that the proceeds:

> are to be appropriated to the charitable purpose of aiding pious and indigent young ladies in obtaining an education, with a view to qualify themselves for the important business of teaching.

There are few objects for which charity is solicited, which, in proportion to the expense, promises greater benefit to society.

His announcement noted that class inequities in education affected females in ways they did not affect males:

> It is the happiness of the present age, that female education is much more attended to than it was in ages past. Indigent females, however, many of whom with the advantages of education, might embellish and improve society, are left without resource. They are destitute of various means of acquiring an education, which are possessed by the other sex; and the Education Society, it may be remarked, do nothing for females. This benevolent object, therefore . . . must commend itself, with peculiar claims to every friend to female improvement as well as to literature and religion.

At the end of his lecture series Emerson had "at least $350 to carry home to my poor scholars."

As well as generating economic support for less wealthy students, Emerson promoted what might be called ego strength or psychological autonomy in his students through the conversion processes of evangelical religion. At the beginning of each term he invited those who "were professors of religion, or hoped they had been renewed by divine grace," to remain in the seminary hall during a recess period. Then he urged them to use their influence on their fellow pupils and announced a weekly prayer meeting to which the whole school was invited.

Mary Lyon described the results of Emerson's policy in a letter to her mother, saying, "an increasing anxiety for a revival in the seminary began to prevail," with those who already considered themselves saved laboring for the conversion of the others. This conversion process had two stages: a recognition of the obstacles within one's own heart to the Savior's "special presence and works," and the transcendence of those obstacles through complete "trust in God." Students learned to monitor their own spiritual progress and to receive assistance from their peers while they were "passing this critical period, this all important moment of their lives." Lyon and others were especially grateful for "the solemnity, affection, and tender solicitude" of Zilpah Grant, Emerson's assistant, who spoke at religious meetings "in the most interesting and affecting manner."

Peer solidarity developed in a context removed from normal family influences. "Imagine to yourself," Lyon wrote her mother, " a little circle of about forty females, almost excluded from the rest of the human family, all appearing as solemn as eternity." This solidarity was reinforced the night before their departure for home at the end of the school term, when, Lyon wrote, several "met at our chamber after school for prayer. We had an impressive season." Religion was the basis of a "community of feeling" among Emerson's students in which, one observer noted:

> They were all led to drink into one and the same spirit; and to feel that they had a great work before them in life, and that they were to aid each other in this work. . . . This laid the foundation for a new and kindred feeling of an exalted and permanent character.

"We learned to consider each other as sisters," Zilpah Grant said, "and this feeling did not cease with our connection with the school." The benefits of awakened religion were therefore threefold. Conversion, or spiritual rebirth, promoted self-esteem in young women by giving them the feeling "that they had a great work before them in life." It promoted psychological autonomy by emphasizing God rather than family as the organizing principle of personal identity. It promoted solidarity among young women by encouraging them to express their "affection and tender solicitude" for one another.

THE CREATION OF A NEW INSTITUTION

In his address on *Female Education* Emerson concluded "that the period is not remote, when female institutions very greatly superior to the present, will not only exist, but be considered as important as are now our colleges for the education of our sons." But, he added, "Where such an institution shall be erected, by whom it shall be founded, and by whom instructed, is yet for the hands of Providence to develop."

In a manner that combined "the hands of Providence" with changing social and economic circumstances, Mary Lyon established during the winters between 1824 and 1831 the prototype of an institution "as important as" male colleges. At Buckland, near Ashfield, this school combined evangelical religion, prospective female teachers, and class consciousness in ways that earned extensive popular support and established the basis for her funding appeals of 1835 to 1837.

It was there Lyon first conceived of "a seminary which should be so moderate in its expenses as to be open to the daughters of farmers and artisans, and to teachers who might be mainly dependent for their support on their own exertions." Between 1824 and her decision in 1834 to devote herself to full-time fund raising for an endowed institution of her own design, however, Lyon's loyalties and energies were divided between her work at Buckland and the professional alliance she formed at Byfield with Zilpah ("Polly") Grant.

Polly Grant grew up in northwestern Connecticut in circumstances very similar to those Mary Lyon had known around Ashfield. Grant's father died in 1796 when she was 2 years old, and her widowed mother (also named Zilpah) raised five children on their small and isolated farm. But there was one salient difference between Lyon and Grant; Grant's mother committed suicide soon after her remarriage in 1820. From 1821 until her retirement and subsequent marriage around 1840, Zilpah Grant suffered long periods of emotional and physical collapse. Her partnership with Lyon dissolved in 1833, after they tried and failed to secure financial support from wealthy benefactors for an "Emersonian" approach to female education.

Their first joint venture between 1824 and 1827 at Adams Academy in Londonderry, New Hampshire, was a telling prediction for the future. Adams began as a coeducational academy with an endowment from a wealthy benefactor of 5,000 dollars. But after a bequest of 4,000 dollars by a "single gentleman" for the female department only, it reincorporated on a new basis in 1823 and became one of the first institutions endowed exclusively for girls. Grant agreed to manage the school on the condition that "one seventh of the study time should be devoted to the Bible," and "there was to be special instruction for those who wished to become teachers." She and Lyon eliminated "ornamental branches" of study, emphasized "solid training," and promoted "guidance and control of the heart" through religious awakening and commitment. "The plan may be called *Emersonian*, though considerably altered to meet our particular purpose," Lyon wrote.

In 1824 theirs was the first female academy to issue diplomas or a

"testimonial of approbation" to those who had completed a full course
of study. Their spiritual leadership was much in evidence. Lyon, who
had recently joined the Congregational church, wrote her sister, Free-
love: "We believe the Holy Spirit is now with us by his special operations. It is now a very critical period." They also recruited the older
generation in this effort, asking "several mothers who have daughters
here to supplicate the influence of the Spirit on this institution every
Wednesday morning between eight and nine oclock."

Using religion to gain the loyalty and support of mothers as well
as daughters, Adams Academy might have marked "an era in female
education" if its (male) trustees had not put a stop to these Emersonian methods by unilaterally announcing that "music and dancing"
would be offered at the school in the future, and teachers would be
selected "who will not attempt to instill into the minds of their pupils
the peculiar tenets of any denomination of Christians, but will give
that general instruction wherein all Christians agree."

The evangelical movement was growing rapidly in New England
churches in the 1820s, but all Christians did not agree that spiritual
rebirth was a necessary part of a godly or moral life. Unitarians were
first among these, and most of Adams's trustees were adherents of this
theologically "liberal" and nonevangelical outgrowth of Congregation-
alism. By reinstating music and dancing, the trustess endorsed genteel
female skills appropriate to the parlor or the sitting room. By substituting more general ethical training for the psychological processes
of conversion, they lessened the degree to which pupils could "drink
into one and the same spirit; and feel that they had a great work
before them in life." Refusing to teach dancing on grounds that it
would disrupt their schedule, Grant left for the newly incorporated
Ipswich Female Seminary near Boston, and Lyon returned to Buckland, where she cultivated more intensely the winter school she had
been developing since 1824.

THE BUCKLAND AND IPSWICH SCHOOLS

Buckland school began with 25 female pupils, doubled its size the next
year, grew to 74 when Lyon returned to it in 1828, and had an en-
rollment of 99 the next year. Its low tuition of 3 dollars a term was less
than half that charged at Ipswich Female Seminary, making it accessi-

ble to "the daughters of farmers and artisans" and self-supporting teachers. Her Buckland school

> became the resort of many who had been or expected to be teachers. The celebrity of the school in that region was such, that to have attended it one or more terms became a letter of recommendation to a candidate for teaching. . . . Though the word had not yet found its way thither, it was, to all interests and purposes, a *normal* school.

Neighboring towns began to appoint school committeemen in the fall instead of the spring in order to make their selections from pupils in Mary Lyon's school. Local religious leaders were equally strong in their endorsement, since "ministers in the sanctuary, when they prayed for colleges, did not forget the school at Buckland." To the churches in the vicinity the school became a "consecrated spot," and "in many a working man's house, at many a family altar, that school was remembered with earnest prayer and with pious gratitude," because "daughters who went thither thoughtless and bent on pleasure, returned home serious, and bent on doing good."

Some of them, however, would not return home. By 1820 parents in this declining farming region were experiencing a massive loss of their young, especially of their sons, through migration west. But unmarried daughters were less free to seek their fortunes elsewhere. As Hitchcock dramatized the conflict such departures entailed:

> Fathers, with trembling lips, would ask, "Why do you want to go away? Is not your father's house a pleasant home to you? Is there anything you do not have? Why do you wish to leave us?" The daughter pleaded that a younger sister would be company, eyes and feet for her parents; that *she* could be spared, and not much missed; that, in some other spot, she might minister to the wants of young minds; and by such considerations would win the father's consent to her departure.

Thus, religious commitment allowed young women to resist the "family claim" on their services and greatly facilitated their entrance into the larger world of social service.

Mary Lyon's advice to students in 1832 showed how religious commitment also provided psychological assistance in such moments of risk-taking and personal choice, allowing a young woman to take a first step, even though she might not know where it would lead her.

> Take all the circumstances, and weight them candidly, taking the Bible for your guide, and asking God to enlighten your mind. . . . You may see but one step where you can place your foot; but take that, and another will then be discovered, and if you can see one step at a time, it is all you ought to ask.

This was good advice for a generation that faced new occupational options. Religion supplied the means for young women to develop autonomous personal goals commensurate with their new economic ability to support themselves away from home. "I would have all contented, wherever Providence may place them," Mary Lyon said in 1829, "whether or not they may be favored with the society of father or mother, brother or sister."

Such migration-assisting religious advice became even more important in Mary Lyon's teaching after 1830, when she left Buckland to work with Zilpah Grant at Ipswich Female Seminary. About 20 of her Buckland students went with her. Ipswich attracted students from greater distances and propelled them further, as missionaries and teachers. There she and Grant engaged in extensive fund raising, building Ipswich into one of the leading female seminaries in the country. They employed Emersonian principles, concentrating on training female teachers and supplying them with religious commitment.

Like Emerson's school, theirs lacked a rent-free structure, and students were scattered in neighboring homes rather than boarding together as a collective unit. But Grant and Lyon saw collective living as essential to their character-building and academic goals. In the words of their first fund-raising circular: "The whole should resemble a well-regulated voluntary association." They first sought funds for "a seminary building" and "a boardinghouse . . . for one-hundred and fifty boarders," but due partly to apathy among the prospective trustees and partly to illness affecting Grant, this effort collapsed in 1831. Subsequently they designed an ambitious new institution, the New England Female Seminary for Teachers, which closely resembled Willard's proposal of 1818 except that it appealed to private sources of funding among "friends of education and of evangelical religion" rather than the state legislature.

When this proposal also failed, one prospective trustee concluded: "I must confess that the best men in the community do not favor our plan of a female seminary as much as I anticipated." Mary Lyon's analysis of their failure was perceptive. She concluded that "the attention of the community" could not be gained on the purely educational grounds they had used to argue for "the superior literary and scientific advantages of a permanent school." Rather, "some peculiar and tangible feature, addressing itself to the feelings and perceptions of the middling classes of society, must be used as a lever for moving public opinion and obtaining the needed funds."

Realizing that her own creative energy was best expressed in class as well as religious terms, Mary Lyon wrote to Hannah White, her assistant at Buckland:

> During the past year, my heart has so yearned over the adult female youth in the common walks of life, that it has sometimes seemed as though a fire were shut up in my bones. I should esteem it a greater favor to labor in this field than in any other on which I have ever fastened my attention.

Recognizing that Zilpah Grant's preference for a life-style that transcended her own social origins prevented her from joining Lyon in such a field, Lyon wrote Grant in 1833: "If I should separate from you, I have no definite plan. But my thoughts, feelings, and judgment are turned toward the middle classes of society. For this class I want to labor, and for this class I consider myself rather peculiarly fitted to labor."

Believing that the cultural institutions of religion were the best means of reaching this class, she wrote Grant: "If the institution is ever founded, it will be safe only in the hand of God, and under God, in the arms of the whole benevolent community, including not only the rich, but the poor." Lyon adopted the "peculiar and tangible feature" of religious sponsorship in her independent fund raising after 1833. This allowed her to combine two powerful support systems reaching deep into the "middling classes" of New England life—the ministry and the female evangelical associations. Although the former provided her with endorsements and protection, she relied on women to generate most of her funds.

FUND RAISING FOR MOUNT HOLYOKE

"Skilled in the art of dealing with the 'gentlemen,'" in September 1834 Lyon selected trustees who endorsed the religious and class principles of her fund-raising efforts, and protected her from "fear of the effect on society of so much female influence, and what some will call female greatness." One trustee, Reverend Theophilus Packard of Shelburne, had four months earlier gained the official endorsement of the Association of Ministers in both Franklin and Hampshire counties for the establishment of an endowed female seminary under Mary Lyon's direction. Packard's daughter, Louisa, had been a student and assistant teacher at Lyon's Buckland school.

Powerful male supporters like Amherst's Edward Hitchcock defended her fund-raising efforts against religious conservatives, who attacked her educational qualifications, her right to identify her cause with the church, and her masculine style. In her defense Hitchcock spoke for the religious constituency to which Mary Lyon appealed, saying:

> Let the Ipswich and Mount Holyoke Seminaries be blest, as Amherst has been, with revivals of religion every year, nay almost every term, and they may be sure, however they may be sneered at and ridiculed by [some] individuals, that they stand fast in the affections and may rely upon the pecuniary support, of the greater part of the religious community.

And he spoke for the economic constituency for which she labored, asking:

> Is it no honor for females to make efforts and sacrifices of a masculine character, that they may elevate the literary and religious condition of their sex, especially of those who for want of pecuniary means have been unable to enjoy the best opportunities?

Half of Lyon's trustees were enthusiastic supporters from her home region, and half were prestigious and nominal eastern supporters who had been associated with fund raising for Ipswich. Therefore, Lyon could recruit funds from both regions. She began, however, not with wealthier or influential gentlemen, but with "the ladies of Ipswich."

Because students at Ipswich Female Seminary "had been accustomed, once or twice a year," to contribute to local benevolent societies, Lyon's appeal "exclusively to ladies" for 1,000 dollars in seed money fell on fertile ground. Calling for "a separate and independent institution, similar in character to the Ipswich Seminary," but "founded and sustained by the Christian public" and expenses "reduced one third or one half," she "held before them the object dear to her heart—the bringing of a liberal education within the means of the daughters of the common people, till it loomed up to them, for the time, as it did before her eyes."

Walking from door to door in Ipswich, Lyon "told the husbands, in a very good-natured but earnest way, that she had come to get them to cut off one little corner of their estates, and give it to their wives to invest in the form of a seminary for the daughters of the common people." The result was that "Ladies who in ordinary subscriptions to benevolent objects, did well to put down their fifty-cents, gave her five or ten dollars of hard-earned money, collected by the slow gains of patient industry." Lyon subsequently distributed a large number of circulars through her male support system, such as the packet she sent Thomas White Ashfield saying, "I do wish our farmers would look at this and see what can be done." But women remained the central focus of her fund-raising campaign of 1835–1837.

Finding her bodily presence more powerful than her letters, "she went to many towns and met the ladies, to inspire them with zeal for the work," and "with her impassioned eloquence, she stirred up the spirit of emulation by holding up the example of the Ipswich ladies."

As Lucy Stone described the effect of Lyon's appeal on her sewing circle:

> Those who had sewed and spent time, strength and money to help educate young men, dropped the needle and toil and said "Let these men with broader shoulders and stronger arms earn their own education, while we use our scantier opportunities to educate ourselves."

Relying on organizations like sewing circles or on individual local women, such as Mrs. Abby Allen in South Hadley, a former teacher and "the acknowledged leader in all benevolent enterprises," to organize local donations, Lyon described her seminary as "another stone in the foundation of our great system of benevolent operations." By transcending local boundaries, this system made possible a new scale of funding for female education. As Lyon declared in a printed letter addressed to "Dear Madame" soon after the cornerstone was dedicated, "hundreds of individuals in more than sixty different towns" had proved untrue "the principle so long acted upon that Christians are not required to contribute for the building up of any female seminary, unless it be established in their own town!"

Grass-roots financial support within the "Christian community" meant, she said, that "it will no longer be doubted whether the work of supplying our country with well qualified female teachers shall be allowed a standing among the benevolent operations of the day." Less than three months later, in January 1837, her contributors had increased to more than 1,800 individuals in 90 towns, who pledged 27,000 dollars in addition to South Hadley's 8,000 dollars and Ipswich's 1,000 dollars.

To critics who thought her aggressive fund raising was unseemly in a woman, Lyon said:

> What do I do that is wrong? . . . I ride in the stage coach or cars without an escort. Other ladies do the same. I visit a family where I have been previously invited, and the minister's wife, or some leading woman, calls the ladies together to see me, and I lay our object before them. Is that wrong? . . . If there is no harm in doing these things once, what harm is there in doing them twice, thrice, or a dozen times? My heart is sick, my soul is pained with this empty gentility, this genteel nothingness. I am doing a great work. I cannot come down.

When questioned as to the motives of women who donated "under her persevering eloquence and prolonged urgency," she would reply: " 'Get the money,' closing her hand to suit the action to the word, 'Get the money; the money will do good.' "

By December 1841, a new wing had been added to the original building and more than 50,000 dollars had been raised and expended for the seminary. By the time Lyon died in 1849, Mount Holyoke annually trained more female teachers than any other institution, including the three state normal schools established by the Massachusetts Board of Education in 1839 to 1840 through an allocation of 20,000 dollars, half of which came from a private donor. As of 1851 the seminary had received donations worth 70,300 dollars. Until 1853 tuition and boarding fees at Mount Holyoke were 60 dollars a year.

The significant change and innovation that Mount Holyoke promised at its founding seems to have been amply fulfilled in practice after 1837. At least three-quarters of its students during the seminary's first 50 years became teachers. By the 1840s the missionary movement was as strong there as it was among their brothers at Amherst or Yale. Because they were systematically recruited for such partnerships by spiritually ambitious young men in about a dozen New England colleges, and because missionary organizations denied sponsorship to single women, many found higher callings in foreign fields as wives of missionaries.

Mount Holyoke's curriculum matched this seriousness of purpose. Latin, the language of the church, was ambitiously emphasized in the curriculum and was required for admission by 1847. Science classes were frequently taught by Professor Hitchcock, who gave lectures on human anatomy in the 1840s illustrated by the most advanced equipment, including a manikin with detachable organs. David F. Allmendinger is currently studying the social origins of early Mount Holyoke students and has estimated that they closely resembled the class composition of contemporary male colleges, in which approximately one-third were to some degree self-supporting, or came from families who could not afford to pay all or part of their expenses.

Historians have generally assumed that the ideological context in which female institutions first achieved collegiate parity with male colleges was the secular or scientific milieu of the last third of the nineteenth century, when Vassar, Smith, and Wellesley were founded. By the time these institutions were founded college students of both sexes, probably including those at Mount Holyoke, were drawn almost exclusively from wealthy or professional families, and historians have generally assumed that funding for the first significant advance in female education came primarily from wealthy sources. But Mount Holyoke's early history requires us to re-examine these assumptions, since it was established at the height of the greatest religious revival in American history, and initiated a "new era in female education" for "the adult female youth in the common walks of life."

12

Women, Work, and Protest in the Early Lowell Mills

THOMAS DUBLIN

• The United States underwent a profound industrial transformation in the years between 1820 and 1860. At the earlier
date, agriculture and foreign trade dominated the economy,
and more than three-fourths of the labor force worked on
farms. Such manufacturing as there was typically took place
in houses or in very small establishments serving a local market. By the outbreak of the Civil War, the proportion of the
work force employed outside agriculture had jumped to 41
percent, and the cotton textile and boot and shoe industries
were well developed.

No section of the nation was more affected by the impact
of early industrialization than the Northeast. In 1790, Samuel
Slater set up the first permanent spinning mill in Pawtucket,
Rhode Island; in 1793, Alexander Hamilton established the
Society for Useful Manufacturers in Paterson, New Jersey;
and in 1813, the first fully integrated textile factory began op-
erating in Waltham, Massachusetts. Soon thereafter, the factory system began to dominate the economies of the growing
urban centers throughout the region.

As Thomas Dublin indicates in the following essay, women
had an important place in this emerging industrial economy.
The new mills tempted farmers' daughters to leave their rural
homes—at least temporarily—to accumulate savings for marriage. By 1860, more than 60,000 women were employed in
the cotton textile industry in New England alone. The pattern for such work was set in Massachusetts at the junction of
the Merrimack and Concord rivers just below the Pawtucket
Falls. In 1821, a group of Boston businessmen began to buy
land secretly in the area, and the following year they began to

From *Labor History* 16 (Winter 1975), 99-116. Reprinted by permission.

build the Merrimack Manufacturing Company. The town which grew up there was incorporated as Lowell in 1826, and by 1850 it was the leading textile center in the United States. More importantly, it was seen as an experiment, as a vindication of American methods that would prove superior to those of the Old World. As Dublin indicates, however, the experiment was not as idyllic as its proponents wanted to believe, and the dream of a new United States industrial order soon gave way to the grim realities of debilitating factory work and labor strife.

In the years before 1850 the textile mills of Lowell, Massachusetts, were a celebrated economic and cultural attraction. Foreign visitors invariably included them on their American tours. Interest was prompted by the massive scale of these mills, the astonishing productivity of the power-driven machinery, and the fact that women comprised most of the workforce. Visitors were struck by the newness of both mills and city as well as by the culture of the female operatives. The scene stood in sharp contrast to the gloomy mill towns of the English industrial revolution.

Lowell was, in fact, an impressive accomplishment. In 1820, there had been no city at all—only a dozen family farms along the Merrimack River in East Chelmsford. In 1821, however, a group of Boston capitalists purchased land and water rights along the river and a nearby canal, and began to build a major textile manufacturing center. Opening two years later, the first factory employed Yankee women recruited from the nearby countryside. Additional mills were constructed until, by 1840, ten textile corporations with thirty-two mills valued at more than ten million dollars lined the banks of the river and nearby canals. Adjacent to the mills were rows of company boarding houses and tenements which accommodated most of the eight thousand factory operatives.

As Lowell expanded, and became the nation's largest textile manufacturing center, the experiences of women operatives changed as well. The increasing number of firms in Lowell and in the other mill towns brought the pressure of competition. Overproduction became a problem and the prices of finished cloth decreased. The high profits of the early years declined and so, too, did conditions for the mill operatives. Wages were reduced and the pace of work within the mills was stepped up. Women operatives did not accept these changes without protest. In 1834 and 1836 they went on strike to protest wage cuts, and between 1843 and 1848 they mounted petition campaigns aimed at reducing the hours of labor in the mills.

These labor protests in early Lowell contribute to our understanding of the response of workers to the growth of industrial capitalism in the first half of the nineteenth century. They indicate the importance of values and attitudes dating back to an earlier period and also the transformation of these values in a new setting.

The major factor in the rise of a new consciousness among operatives in Lowell was the development of a close-knit community among women working in the mills. The structure of work and the nature of housing contributed to the growth of this community. The existence of community among women, in turn, was an important element in the repeated labor protests of the period.

The organization of this paper derives from the logic of the above argument. It will examine the basis of community in the experiences of women operatives and then the contribution that the community of women made to the labor protests in these years as well as the nature of the new consciousness expressed by these protests.

The pre-conditions for the labor unrest in Lowell before 1850 may be found in the study of the daily worklife of its operatives. In their everyday, relatively conflict-free lives, mill women created the mutual bonds which made possible united action in times of crisis. The existence of a tight-knit community among them was the most important element in determining the collective, as opposed to individual, nature of this response.

Before examining the basis of community among women operatives in early Lowell, it may be helpful to indicate in what sense "community" is being used. The women are considered a "community" because of the development of bonds of mutual dependence among them. In this period they came to depend upon one another and upon the larger group of operatives in very important ways. Their experiences were not simply similar or parallel to one another, but were inextricably intertwined. Furthermore, they were conscious of the existence of community, expressing it very clearly in their writings and in labor protests. "Community" for them had objective and subjective dimensions and both were important in their experience of women in the mills.

The mutual dependence among women in early Lowell was rooted in the structure of mill work itself. Newcomers to the mills were particularly dependent on their fellow operatives, but even experienced hands relied on one another for considerable support.

New operatives generally found their first experiences difficult, even harrowing, though they may have already done considerable hand-spinning and weaving in their own homes. The initiation of one of them is described in fiction in the *Lowell Offering*:

> The next morning she went into the Mill; and at first the sight of so many bands, and wheels, and springs in constant motion, was very frightful. She felt afraid to touch the loom, and she was almost sure she could never learn to weave . . . the shuttle flew out, and made a new bump on her head; and the first time she tried to spring the lathe, she broke out a quarter of the treads.

While other accounts present a somewhat less difficult picture, most indicate that women only became proficient and felt satisfaction in their work after several months in the mills.

The textile corporations made provisions to ease the adjustment of new operatives. Newcomers were not immediately expected to fit into the mill's regular work routine. They were at first assigned work as sparehands and were paid a daily wage independent of the quantity of work they turned out. As a sparehand, the newcomer worked with an experienced hand who instructed her in the intricacies of the job. The sparehand spelled her partner for short stretches of time, and occasionally took the place of an absentee. One woman described the learning process in a letter reprinted in the *Offering*:

> Well, I went into the mill, and was put to learn with a very patient girl. . . . You cannot think how odd everything seems. . . . They set me to threading shuttles, and tying weaver's knots, and such things, and now I have improved so that I can take care of one loom. I could take care of two if only I had eyes in the back part of my head.

After the passage of some weeks or months, when she could handle the normal complement of machinery—two looms for weavers during the 1830s—and when a regular operative departed, leaving an opening, the sparehand moved into a regular job.

Through this system of job training, the textile corporations contributed to the development of community among female operatives. During the most difficult period in an operative's career, the first months in the mill, she relied upon other women workers for training and support. And for every sparehand whose adjustment to mill work was aided in this process, there was an experienced operative whose work was also affected. Women were relating to one another during the work process and not simply tending their machinery. Given the high rate of turnover in the mill workforce, a large proportion of women operatives worked in pairs. At the Hamilton Company in July 1836, for example, more than a fifth of all females on the Company payroll were sparehands. Consequently, over forty percent of the females employed there in this month worked with one another. Nor was this interaction surreptitious, carried out only when the overseer looked elsewhere; rather it was formally organized and sanctioned by the textile corporations themselves.

In addition to the integration of sparehands, informal sharing of work often went on among regular operatives. A woman would occasionally take off a half or full day from work either to enjoy a brief vacation or to recover from illness, and fellow operatives would each take an extra loom or side of spindles so that she might continue to earn wages during her absence. Women were generally paid on a piece rate basis, their wages being determined by the total output of the machinery they tended during the payroll period. With friends helping out during her absence, making sure that her looms kept running, an operative could earn almost a full wage even though she was not physically present. Such informal work-sharing was another way in which mutual dependence developed among women operatives during their working hours.

Living conditions also contributed to the development of community among female operatives. Most women working in the Lowell mills of these years were housed in company boarding houses. In July 1836, for example, more than 73 percent of females employed by the Hamilton Company resided in company housing adjacent to the mills. Almost three-fourths of them, therefore, lived and worked with each other. Furthermore, the work schedule was such that women

had little opportunity to interact with those not living in company
dwellings. They worked, in these years, an average of 73 hours a week.
Their work day ended at 7:00 or 7:30 P.M., and in the hours between
supper and the 10:00 curfew imposed by management on residents
of company boarding houses there was little time to spend with friends
living "off the corporation."

Women in the boarding houses lived in close quarters, a factor that
also played a role in the growth of community. A typical boarding
house accommodated twenty-five young women, generally crowded
four to eight in a bedroom. There was little possibility of privacy
within the dwelling, and pressure to conform to group standards was
very strong (as will be discussed below). The community of operatives
which developed in the mills it follows, carried over into life at home
as well.

The boarding house became a central institution in the lives of
Lowell's female operatives in these years, but it was particularly important in the initial integration of newcomers into urban industrial
life. Upon first leaving her rural home for work in Lowell, a woman
entered a setting very different from anything she had previously
known. One operative, writing in the *Offering*, described the feelings
of a fictional character: "The first entrance into a factory boarding
house seemed something dreadful. The room looked strange and
comfortless, and the women cold and heartless; and when she sat
down to the supper table, where among more than twenty girls, all
but one were strangers, she could not eat a mouthful."

In the boarding house, the newcomer took the first steps in the
process which transformed her from an "outsider" into an accepted
member of the community of women operatives.

Recruitment of newcomers into the mills and their initial hiring
was mediated through the boarding house system. Women generally
did not travel to Lowell for the first time entirely on their own. They
usually came because they knew someone—an older sister, cousin, or
friend—who had already worked in Lowell. The scene described
above was a lonely one—but the newcomer did know at least one
boarder among the twenty seated around the supper table. The
Hamilton Company Register Books indicate that numerous pairs of
operatives, having the same surname and coming from the same
town in northern New England, lived in the same boarding houses.

If the newcomer was not accompanied by a friend or relative, she was usually directed to "Number 20, Hamilton Company," or to a similar address of one of the other corporations where her acquaintance lived. Her first contact with fellow operatives generally came in the boarding houses and not in the mills. Given the personal nature of recruitment in this period, therefore, newcomers usually had the company and support of a friend or relative in their first adjustment to Lowell.

Like recruitment, the initial hiring was a personal process. Once settled in the boarding house a newcomer had to find a job. She would generally go to the mills with her friend or with the boarding house keeper who would introduce her to an overseer in one of the rooms. If he had an opening, she might start work immediately. More likely, the overseer would know of an opening elsewhere in the mill, or would suggest that something would probably develop within a few days. In one story in the *Offering*, a newcomer worked on some quilts for her house keeper, thereby earning her board while she waited for a job opening.

Upon entering the boarding house, the newcomer came under pressure to conform with the standards of the community of operatives. Stories in the *Offering* indicate that newcomers at first stood out from the group in terms of their speech and dress. Over time, they dropped the peculiar "twang" in their speech which so amused experienced hands. Similarly, they purchased clothing more in keeping with urban than rural styles. It was an unusual and strongwilled individual who could work and live among her fellow operatives and not conform, at least outwardly, to the customs and values of this larger community.

The boarding houses were the centers of social life for women operatives after their long days in the mills. There they ate their meals, rested, talked, sewed, wrote letters, read books and magazines. From among fellow workers and boarders they found friends who accompanied them to shops, to Lyceum lectures, to church and church-sponsored events. On Sundays or holidays, they often took walks along the canals or out into the nearby countryside. The community of women operatives, in sum, developed in a setting where women worked and lived together, twenty-four hours a day.

Given the all-pervasiveness of this community, one would expect it to exert strong pressures on those who did not conform to group standards. Such appears to have been the case. The community influenced newcomers to adopt its patterns of speech and dress as described above. In addition, it enforced an unwritten code of moral conduct. Henry Miles, a minister in Lowell, described the way in which the community pressured those who deviated from accepted moral conduct:

> A girl, suspected of immoralities, or serious improprieties, at once loses caste. Her fellow boarders will at once leave the house, if the keeper does not dismiss the offender. In self-protection, therefore, the patron is obliged to put the offender away. Nor will her former companions walk with her, or work with her; till at length, finding herself everywhere talked about, and pointed at, and shunned, she is obliged to relieve her fellow-operatives of a presence which they feel brings disgrace.

The power of the peer group described by Miles may seem extreme, but there is evidence in the writing of women operatives to corroborate his account. Such group pressure is illustrated by a story (in the *Offering*)—in which operatives in a company boarding house begin to harbor suspicions about a fellow boarder, Hannah, who received repeated evening visits from a man whom she does not introduce to the other residents. Two boarders declare that they will leave if she is allowed to remain in the household. The house keeper finally informed Hannah that she must either depart or not see the man again. She does not accept the ultimatum, but is promptly discharged after the overseer is informed, by one of the boarders, about her conduct. And, only one of Hannah's former friends continues to remain on cordial terms.

One should not conclude, however, that women always enforced a moral code agreeable to Lowell's clergy, or to the mill agents and overseers for that matter. After all, the kind of peer pressure imposed on Hannah could be brought to bear on women in 1834 and 1836 who on their own would not have protested wage cuts. It was much harder to go to work when one's roommates were marching about town, attending rallies, circulating strike petitions. Similarly, the ten-hour petitions of the 1840s were certainly aided by the fact of a tight-knit community of operatives living in a dense neighborhood of boarding houses. To the extent that women could not have completely private lives in the boarding houses, they probably had to conform to group norms, whether these involved speech, clothing, relations with men, or attitudes toward the ten-hour day. Group pressure to conform, so important to the community of women in early Lowell, played a significant role in the collective response of women to changing conditions in the mills.

In addition to the structure of work and housing in Lowell, a third factor, the homogeneity of the mill workforce, contributed to the development of community among female operatives. In this period the mill workforce was homogeneous in terms of sex, nativity, and age. Payroll and other records of the Hamilton Company reveal that more than 85 percent of those employed in July 1836 were women and that over 96 percent were native-born. Furthermore, over 80 percent of the female workforce was between the ages of 15 and 30 years old; and only ten percent was under 15 or over 40.

Workforce homogeneity takes on particular significance in the context of work structure and the nature of worker housing. These three factors combined meant that women operatives had little interaction with men during their daily lives. Men and women did not perform the same work in the mills, and generally did not even labor in the same rooms. Men worked in the picking and initial carding processes, in the repair shop and on the watchforce, and filled all supervisory positions in the mills. Women held all sparehand and regular operative jobs in drawing, speeding, spinning, weaving and dressing. A typical room in the mill employed eighty women tending machinery, with two men overseeing the work and two boys assisting them. Women had little contact with men other than their supervisors in the course of the working day. After work, women returned to their boarding houses, where once again there were few men. Women, then, worked and lived in a predominantly female setting.

Ethnically the workforce was also homogeneous. Immigrants formed only 3.4 percent of those employed at Hamilton in July 1836. In addition, they comprised only 3 percent of residents in Hamilton company housing. The community of women operatives was composed of women of New England stock drawn from the hill-country farms surrounding Lowell. Consequently, when experienced hands made fun of the speech and dress of newcomers, it was understood that they, too, had been "rusty" or "rustic" upon first coming to Lowell. This common background was another element shared by women workers in early Lowell.

The work structure, the workers' housing, and workforce homogeneity were the major elements which contributed to the growth of community among Lowell's women operatives. To best understand the larger implications of community it is necessary to examine the labor protests of this period. For in these struggles, the new values and attitudes which developed in the community of women operatives are most visible.

II

In February 1834, 800 of Lowell's women operatives "turned-out"—went on strike—to protest a proposed reduction in their wages. They marched to numerous mills in an effort to induce others to join them; and, at an outdoor rally, they petitioned others to "discontinue their labors until terms of reconciliation are made." Their petition concluded:

> Resolved, That we will not go back into the mills to work unless our wages are continued . . . as they have been.
> Resolved, That none of us will go back, unless they receive us all as one.
> Resolved, That if any have not money enough to carry them home, they shall be supplied.

The strike proved to be brief and failed to reverse the proposed wage reductions. Turning-out on a Friday, the striking women were paid their back wages on Saturday, and by the middle of the next week had returned to work or left town. Within a week of the turn-out, the mills were running near capacity.

This first strike in Lowell is important not because it failed or succeeded, but simply because it took place. In an era in which women had to overcome opposition simply to work in the mills, it is remarkable that they would further overstep the accepted middle-class bounds of female propriety by participating in a public protest. The agents of the textile mills certainly considered the turn-out unfeminine. William Austin, agent of the Lawrence Company, described the operatives' procession as an "amizonian [sic] display." He wrote further, in a letter to his company treasurer in Boston: "This afternoon we have paid off several of these Amazons & presume that they will leave town on Monday." The turn-out was particularly offensive to the agents because of the relationship they thought they had with their operatives. William Austin probably expressed the feelings of other agents when he wrote: "Notwithstanding the friendly and disinterested advice which has been on all proper occasions [sic] communicated to the girls of the Lawrence mills a spirit of evil omen . . . has prevailed, and overcome the judgment and discretion of too many, and this morning a general turn-out from most of the rooms has been the consequence."

Mill agents assumed an attitude of benevolent paternalism toward their female operatives, and found it particularly disturbing that the women paid such little heed to their advice. The strikers were not merely unfeminine, they were ungrateful as well.

Such attitudes notwithstanding, women chose to turn-out. They did so for two principal reasons. First, the wage cuts undermined the sense of dignity and social equality which was an important element in their Yankee heritage. Second, these wage cuts were seen as an attack on their economic independence.

Certainly a prime move for the strike was outrage at the social implications of the wage cuts. In a statement of principles accompanying the petition which was circulated among operatives, women expressed well the sense of themselves which prompted their protest of these wage cuts:

UNION IS POWER

Our present object is to have union and exertion, and we remain in possession of our unquestionable rights. We circulate this paper wishing to obtain the names of all who imbibe the spirit of our Patriotic Ancestors, who preferred privation to bondage, and parted with all that renders life desirable—and even life itself—to procure independence for their children. The oppressing hand of avarice would enslave us, and to gain their object, they gravely tell us of the pressure of the time, this we are already sensible of, and deplore it. If any are in want of assistance, the Ladies will be compassionate and assist them; but we prefer to have the disposing of our charities in our own hands; and as we are free, we would remain in possession of what kind Providence has bestowed upon us; and remain daughters of freemen still.

At several points in the proclamation the women drew on their Yankee heritage. Connecting their turn-out with the efforts of their "Patriotic Ancestors" to secure independence from England, they interpreted the wage cuts as an effort to "enslave" them—to deprive them of their independent status as "daughters of freemen."

Though very general and rhetorical, the statement of these women does suggest their sense of self, of their own worth and dignity. Elsewhere, they expressed the conviction that they were the social equals of the overseers, indeed of the mill owners themselves. The wage cuts, however, struck at this assertion of social equality. These reductions made it clear that the operatives were subordinate to their employers, rather than equal partners in a contract binding on both parties. By turning-out the women emphatically denied that they were subordinates; but by returning to work the next week, they demonstrated that in economic terms they were no match for their corporate superiors.

In point of fact, these Yankee operatives were subordinate in early Lowell's social and economic order, but they never consciously accepted this status. Their refusal to do so became evident whenever the mill owners attempted to exercise the power they possessed. This fundamental contradiction between the objective status of operatives and their consciousness of it was at the root of the 1834 turn-out and of subsequent labor protests in Lowell before 1850. The corporations could build mills, create thousands of jobs, and recruit women to fill them. Nevertheless, they bought only the workers' labor power, and then only for as long as these workers chose to stay. Women could always return to their rural homes, and they had a sense of their own worth and dignity, factors limiting the actions of management.

Women operatives viewed the wage cuts as a threat to their economic independence. This independence had two related dimensions. First, the women were self-supporting while they worked in the mills and, consequently, were independent of their families back home. Second, they were able to save out of their monthly earnings and could then leave the mills for the old homestead whenever they so desired. In effect, they were not totally dependent upon mill work. Their independence was based largely on the high level of wages in the mills. They could support themselves and still save enough to return home periodically. The wage cuts threatened to deny them this outlet, substituting instead the prospect of total dependence on mill work. Small wonder, then, there was alarm that "the oppressing hand of avarice would enslave us." To be forced, out of economic necessity, to lifelong labor in the mills would have indeed seemed like slavery. The Yankee operatives spoke directly to the fear of dependency based on impoverishment when offering to assist any women workers who "have not money enough to carry them home." Wage reductions, however, offered only the *prospect* of a future dependence on mill employment. By striking, the women asserted their actual economic independence of the mills and their determination to remain "daughters of freemen still."

While the women's traditional conception of themselves as independent daughters of freemen played a major role in the turn-out, this factor acting alone would not necessarily have triggered the 1834 strike. It would have led women as individuals to quit work and return to their rural homes. But the turn-out was a collective protest. When it was announced that wage reductions were being considered, women began to hold meetings in the mills during meal breaks in order to assess tactical possibilities. Their turn-out began at one mill when the agent discharged a woman who had presided at such a meeting. Their procession through the streets passed by other mills, expressing a conscious effort to enlist as much support as possible for their cause. At a mass meeting, the women drew up a resolution which insisted that none be discharged for their participation in the turn-out. This strike, then, was a collective response to the proposed wage cuts— made possible because women had come to form a "community" of operatives in the mill, rather than simply a group of individual workers. The existence of such a tight-knit community turned individual opposition of the wage cuts into a collective protest.

In October 1836, women again went on strike. This second turn-out was similar to the first in several respects. Its immediate cause was also a wage reduction; marches and a large outdoor rally were organized; again, like the earlier protest, the basic goal was not achieved; the corporations refused to restore wages; and operatives either left Lowell or returned to work at the new rates.

Despite these surface similarities between the turn-outs, there were some real differences. One involved scale: over 1,500 operatives turned out in 1836, compared to only 800 earlier. Moreover, the second strike lasted much longer than the first. In 1834 operatives stayed out for only a few days; in 1836, the mills ran far below capacity for several months. Two weeks after the second turn-out began, a mill agent reported that only a fifth of the strikers had returned to work: "The rest manifest *good 'spunk'* as they call it." Several days later he described the impact of the continuing strike on operations in his mills: "We must be feeble for months to come as probably not less than 250 of our former scanty supply of help have left town." These lines read in sharp contrast to the optimistic reports of agents following the turn-out in February 1834.

Differences between the two turn-outs were not limited to the increased scale and duration of the later one. Women displayed a much higher degree of organization in 1836 than earlier. To co-ordinate strike activities, they formed a Factory Girls' Association. According to one historian, membership in the short-lived association reached 2,500 at its height. The larger organization among women was reflected in the tactics employed. Strikers, according to one mill agent, were able to halt production to a greater extent than numbers alone could explain; and, he complained, although some operatives were willing to work, "it has been impossible to give employment to many who remained." He attributed this difficulty to the strikers' tactics: "This was in many instances no doubt the result of calculation and contrivance. After the original turn-out they [the operatives] would assail a particular room—as for instance, all the warpers, or all the warp spinners, or all the speeder and stretcher girls, and this would close the mill as effectually as if all the girls in the mill had left."

Now giving more thought than they had in 1834 to the specific tactics of the turn-out, the women made a deliberate effort to shut down the mills in order to win their demands. They attempted to persuade less committed operatives, concentrating on those in crucial departments within the mill. Such tactics anticipated those of skilled mule-spinners and loomfixers who went out on strike in the 1880s and 1890s.

In their organization of a Factory Girls' Association and in their efforts to shut down the mills, the female operatives revealed that they had been changed by their industrial experience. Increasingly, they

acted not simply as "daughters of freemen" offended by the imposi-
tions of the textile corporations, but also as industrial workers intent
on improving their position within the mills.

There was a decline in protest among women in the Lowell mills
following these early strike defeats. During the 1837–1843 depression,
textile corporations twice reduced wages without evoking a collective
response from operatives. Because of the frequency of production
cutbacks and lay-offs in these years, workers probably accepted the mill
agents' contention that they had to reduce wages or close entirely. But
with the return of prosperity and the expansion of production in the
mid-1840s, there were renewal labor protests among women. Their
actions paralleled those of working men and reflected fluctuations in
the business cycle. Prosperity itself did not prompt turn-outs, but it
evidently facilitated collective actions by women operatives.

In contrast to the protests of the previous decade, the struggles
now were primarily political. Women did not turn-out in the 1840s;
rather, they mounted annual petition campaigns calling on the State
legislature to limit the hours of labor within the mills. These campaigns reached their height in 1845 and 1846, when 2,000 and 5,000
operatives respectively signed petitions. Unable to curb the wage cuts,
or the speed-up and stretch-out imposed by mill owners, operatives
sought to mitigate the consequences of these changes by reducing the
length of the working day. Having been defeated earlier in economic
struggles, they now sought to achieve their new goal through political
action. The Ten Hour Movement, seen in these terms, was a logical
outgrowth of the unsuccessful turn-outs of the previous decade. Like
the earlier struggles, the Ten Hour Movement was an assertion of the
dignity of operatives and an attempt to maintain that dignity under
the changing conditions of industrial capitalism.

The growth of relatively permanent labor organizations and institutions among women was a distinguishing feature of the Ten Hour
Movement of the 1840s. The Lowell Female Labor Reform Association was organized in 1845 by women operatives. It became Lowell's
leading organization over the next three years, organizing the city's
female operatives and helping to set up branches in other mill towns.
The Association was affiliated with the New England Workingmen's
Association and sent delegates to its meetings. It acted in concert with
similar male groups, and yet maintained its own autonomy. Women

elected their own officers, held their own meetings, testified before a State legislative committee, and published a series of "Factory Tracts" which exposed conditions within the mills and argued for the ten-hour day.

An important educational and organizing tool of the Lowell Female Labor Reform Association was the *Voice of Industry*, a labor weekly published in Lowell between 1845 and 1848 by the New England Workingmen's Association. Female operatives were involved in every aspect of its publication and used the *Voice* to further the Ten Hour Movement among women. Their Association owned the press on which the *Voice* was printed. Sarah Bagley, the Association president, was a member of the three-person publishing committee of the *Voice* and for a time served as editor. Other women were employed by the paper as travelling editors. They wrote articles about the Ten Hour Movement in other mill towns, in an effort to give ten-hour supporters a sense of the large cause of which they were a part. Furthermore, they raised money for the *Voice* and increased its circulation by selling subscriptions to the paper in their travels about New England. Finally, women used the *Voice* to appeal directly to their fellow operatives. They edited a separate "Female Department," which published letters and articles by and about women in the mills.

Another aspect of the Ten Hour Movement which distinguished it from the earlier labor struggles in Lowell was that it involved both men and women. At the same time that women in Lowell formed the Female Labor Reform Association, a male mechanics' and laborers' association was also organized. Both groups worked to secure the passage of legislation setting ten hours as the length of the working day. Both groups circulated petitions to this end and when the legislative committee came to Lowell to hear testimony, both men and women testified in favor of the ten-hour day.

The two groups, then, worked together, and each made an important contribution to the movement in Lowell. Women had the numbers, comprising as they did over eighty percent of the mill workforce. Men, on the other hand, had the votes, and since the Ten Hour Movement was a political struggle, they played a crucial part. After the State committee reported unfavorably on the ten-hour petitions, the Female Labor Reform Association denounced the committee chairman, a State representative from Lowell, as a corporation "tool." Working for his defeat at the polls, they did so successfully and then passed the following post-election resolution: *"Resolved, That the members of this Association tender their grateful acknowledgements to the voters of Lowell, for consigning William Schouler to the obscurity he so justly deserves."* Women took a more prominent part in the Ten Hour Movement in Lowell than did men, but they obviously remained dependent on male voters and legislators for the ultimate success of their movement.

Although co-ordinating their efforts with those of working men, women operatives organized independently within the Ten Hour Movement. For instance, in 1845 two important petitions were sent from Lowell to the State legislature. Almost ninety percent of the signers of one petition were females, and more than two-thirds of the signers of the second were males. Clearly the separation of men and women in their daily lives was reflected in the Ten Hour petitions of these years.

The way in which the Ten Hour Movement was carried from Lowell to other mill towns also illustrated the independent organizing of women within the larger movement. For example, at a spirited meeting in Manchester, New Hampshire, in December 1845—one presided over by Lowell operatives—more than a thousand workers, two-thirds of them women, passed resolutions calling for the ten-hour day. Later, those in attendance divided along male-female lines, each meeting separately to set up parallel organizations. Sixty women joined the Manchester Female Labor Reform Association that evening, and by the following summer it claimed over three hundred members. Female operatives met in company boarding houses to involve new women in the movement. In their first year of organizing, Manchester workers obtained more than 4,000 signatures on ten-hour petitions. While men and women were both active in the movement, they worked through separate institutional structures from the outset.

The division of men and women within the Ten Hour Movement also reflected their separate daily lives in Lowell and in other mill towns. To repeat, they held different jobs in the mills and had little contact apart from the formal, structured overseer-operative relation. Outside the mill, we have noted, women tended to live in female boarding houses provided by the corporations and were isolated from men. Consequently, the experiences of women in "these early" mill towns were different from those of men, and in the course of their daily lives they came to form a close-knit community. It was logical that women's participation in the Ten Hour Movement mirrored this basic fact.

The women's Ten Hour Movement, like the earlier turnouts, was based in part on the participants' sense of their own worth and dignity as daughters of freemen. At the same time, however, it also indicated the growth of a new consciousness. It reflected a mounting feeling of community among women operatives and a realization that their interests and those of their employers were not identical, that they had to rely on themselves and not on corporate benevolence to achieve a reduction in the hours of labor. One woman, in an open letter to a State legislator, expressed this rejection of middle-class paternalism: "Bad as is the condition of so many women, it would be much worse if they had nothing but your boasted protection to rely upon; but they have at last learnt the lesson which a bitter experience teaches, that not to those who style themselves their 'natural protectors' are they to look for the needful help, but to the strong and resolute of their own sex." Such an attitude, underlying the self-organizing of women in the ten-hour petition campaigns, was clearly the product of the industrial experience in Lowell.

Both the early turn-outs and the Ten Hour Movement were, as noted above, in large measure dependent upon the existence of a close-knit community of women operatives. Such a community was based on the work structure, the nature of worker housing, and workforce homogeneity. Women were drawn together by the initial job training of newcomers; by the informal work sharing among experienced hands; by living in company boarding houses; by sharing religious, educational, and social activities in their leisure hours. Working and living in a new and alien setting, they came to rely upon one another for friendship and support. Understandably, a community feeling developed among them.

This evolving community as well as the common cultural traditions which Yankee women carried into Lowell were major elements that governed their response to changing mill conditions. The pre-industrial tradition of independence and self-respect made them particularly sensitive to management labor policies. The sense of community enabled them to transform their individual opposition to wage cuts and to the increasing pace of work into public protest. In these labor struggles women operatives expressed a new consciousness of their rights both as workers and as women. Such a consciousness, like the community of women itself, was one product of Lowell's industrial revolution.

The experiences of Lowell women before 1850 present a fascinating picture of the contradictory impact of industrial capitalism. Repeated labor protests reveal that female operatives felt the demands of mill employment to be oppressive. At the same time, however, the mills provided women with work outside of the home and family, thereby offering them an unprecedented [opportunity]. That they came to challenge employer paternalism was a direct consequence of the increasing opportunities offered them in these years. The Lowell mills both exploited and liberated women in ways unknown to the pre-industrial political economy.

13

The Case of the *Creole* Slave Revolt

HOWARD JONES

• The institution of slavery started on the North American continent as an attempt to cope with severe labor shortages. The first boatload of Africans arrived in 1619, and for the next forty years blacks were sometimes treated as indentured servants—workers who toiled for a fixed period of time and were then free to pursue their own lives—and sometimes kept forever in bondage. Not until the 1660s did the custom develop to keep all Afro-Americans in permanent servitude. Thereafter the African slaves provided the bulk of the laboring force in the Southern colonies. Slavery existed in the North also during this period, but the institution was generally curbed, and the bondsmen released, before the Civil War. In the South, by contrast, the invention of the cotton gin in 1793 created an enormous need for slaves to support an essentially agricultural economy.

In recent years, historians have done valuable work on the nature of racist thought, on the conditions of plantation life, on the effect of bondage upon personality, and on the profitability of slavery. More recently, Alex Haley has pioneered in the effort to discover the ancestral roots of black Americans. Historical attention has also turned to the efforts at resistance by the oppressed; Nat Turner's famed uprising in Virginia in 1831 has been the subject of both scholarly and fictional treatments. Less well-known to the general public, though, is the slave mutiny which is the subject of the following essay.

From "The Peculiar Institution and National Honor: The Case of the *Creole* Slave Revolt," *Civil War History* 21 (March 1975): 28-50. Copyright Kent State University Press. Used by permission.

The slave mutiny on the brig *Creole* in 1841 has long been of interest to historians. Not only did it involve American domestic politics, it intimately concerned relations between the governments of the United States and Great Britain. Disposition of the case raised arguments and counterarguments similar to those which were to echo through American politics for two decades and result in the Civil War; it also indirectly affected the negotiation of the Webster-Ashburton Treaty in 1842. Because the *Creole* revolt occurred in 1841, not 1861, it eventually took its place as a minor incident in antebellum history; yet its potentially explosive nature justifies more attention than it has received. As far as this writer can tell, there has been no full, scholarly treatment of the *Creole* affair. Partially because of this, many accounts of the event have been either misleading or mistaken. The reader is left with the erroneous impression that the British government won a diplomatic victory over the United States, that the incident was indicative of the spontaneous, disorganized nature of slave revolts, and that it caused many Southerners to consider seriously the possibility of having to fight England again.

The purposes of this essay are to dispel some of the myths surrounding the *Creole* affair, to describe how such a seemingly unimportant event evoked serious questions of national honor, and to offer an explanation of the South's surprisingly subdued behavior in the latter stages of the controversy. By the 1830's that section of the United States, just embarking on the politics of slavery, was interested in almost any method to keep the peculiar institution intact. One of these was to prevent incendiary talk about the subject. Indeed, some Southern states passed laws against publications designed to encourage abolitionism, while freedom of the press on the slavery question did not exist in many Southern states after the 1830's. William W. Freehling has shown, in the South Carolina nullification controversy of 1832, that some Southerners sought to prevent widespread criticism of slavery by diverting attention from it to the tariff. In cases involving British interference with America's coastal trade in slaves, many in the South protested such actions as violations of the nation's honor. It is almost impossible to determine if they meant what they said, but it is a fact that some of the Southern press argued for maritime rights and national integrity when their real concern was the effect these British abuses could have on encouraging more slave rebellions.

In its details—the event itself, and its ramifications—the *Creole* case constituted a microcosm of the ideas and actions of later years. The vessel had sailed from Hampton Roads, Virginia, for New Orleans in October 1841 with eight crew members, five sailors, a cargo of tobacco, 135 slaves, and six white passengers (three men in charge of the slaves, together with the captain's wife, child, and niece). For nearly eleven days the brig made its way down the coast, and during the evening of November 7 prepared to enter harbor at Abaco Island in the Bahamas the following morning. About 9:30 that night the chief mate, Zephaniah Gifford, discovered a male slave in the main hold with the females. When he and William Merritt, the white man overseeing the slaves, entered the hold, they found Madison Washington, the slaves' head cook. Merritt tried to seize him, but was unable to hold on to Washington as the slave ran up the ladder. When Washington got on deck, he shoved Gifford and nearly knocked him back down into the hold. At the same time another slave fired a pistol, the ball of which grazed the back of the mate's head. With the firing of this shot Washington called for other blacks to join him.

Only nineteen slaves participated in the ensuing mutiny, but they easily took control of the brig, partly because the remainder of the crew and the white passengers had been asleep when the revolt began. The takeover had been well executed, even though no evidence has appeared to support the rumor that a plan had originated in Richmond. Since the crew had taken no precautions against an insurrection, the nineteen had little trouble arming themselves with pistols, bowie knives, and handspikes. Gifford ran below and warned others of the mutiny, and the captain, Robert Ensor, ordered everyone out of the cabin. By this time several blacks, armed with knives and clubs, were waiting at the cabin door.

Casualties were light on both sides because there was little resistance to the revolt and because Washington and another mutineer, Elijah Morris, restrained the others from killing the whites. There was indeed only a single death among the whites, John Hewell, owner of thirty-nine of the slaves, had frantically searched for a gun and found a musket in the stateroom. Breaking past the blacks at the door, he reached the deck. To his dismay the musket was not loaded. After he was knocked down and stabbed repeatedly, he staggered back into the cabin, fell into his berth, and died. Captain Ensor had fought with a bowie knife alongside Hewell, but soon realized the contest was hopeless. Wounded severely, he joined the mate, Gifford, in a race for the maintop. Two crew members meanwhile also climbed wildly up the rigging. The captain, reaching the top but bleeding profusely, soon fainted, but Gifford secured him to the rigging. With the *Creole* under control of the mutineers, Gifford was told to come down or be shot. He did so. Eight hours passed before a crew member brought Ensor down in a sling and placed him in the forecastle with the passengers. Two of the five sailors on board also were hurt, but their wounds were dressed by the mutineers. Two of the blacks in the revolt were seriously wounded, one of them later dying.

The mutineers then decided to steer for Nassau. Merritt, hiding under a mattress, was found, pulled out, and threatened with death unless he cooperated. Believing the captain and crew dead, he complied. After he convinced Washington that there were not enough provisions to go to Liberia, several blacks demanded that the ship be taken to the British islands. The mutineers had heard that an American schooner, the *Hermosa*, had shipwrecked the year before at Abaco, and that English wreckers had taken the slaves on the ship to Nassau where officials set them free. Around a table laden with brandy, whiskey, wine, applies, and bread, the leaders of the revolt watched Merritt plot the course to Nassau on the chart.

The *Creole* arrived at Nassau, New Providence, about eight o'clock on the morning of November 9. The mutineers, apparently deciding to place themselves at the mercy of British authorities, disposed of their weapons before entering the harbor, and allowed the mate to inform the American consul, John Bacon, of what had happened. Bacon arranged for the wounded to be taken ashore and asked the colonial governor, Francis Cockburn, to place a guard on board to prevent the blacks from escaping. Though expressing doubt about his authority to intervene, Cockburn did so. About noon, twenty-four black soldiers under command of a white officer boarded the *Creole*. Meanwhile the council of Nassau went into special session and after a hurried discussion declared that municipal courts had no jurisdiction over mutiny and murder at sea. It nonetheless announced that an investigation (to begin that day) would take place before the soldiers brought the accused ashore, and that after the inquiry all nonparticipants in the revolt would go free. A full account of the affair would be sent to the British minister in Washington.

Soon afterward, the blacks aboard the *Creole* were released by something approaching mob action. When the attorney general of Nassau, G. C. Anderson, boarded the *Creole* on the ninth, he noticed several boats nearby filled with black islanders. They had begun gathering ashore and in craft around the *Creole* around noon. By 1:30 the boats had increased to almost fifty. Someone warned the consul that when the troops withdrew from the ship there would be an attempt to free the blacks. When Bacon urged Cockburn to take preventive measures, the governor assured him that British subjects would not "act so improperly." Anderson then warned those in the boats not to interfere with the proceedings.

Bacon appealed for cooperation from Nassau at a second meeting of the governor and council. He first asked them to hold the blacks of the *Creole* in custody until an American ship of war could come from Indian Key in Florida, nearly 400 miles away. He also wanted permission for the American ships then at Nassau to conduct the *Creole* and its passengers and crew to New Orleans. Finally, he asked the governor to send the nineteen blacks to the United States to stand trial. The governor refused all his requests. Bacon then ordered the mate to return to the *Creole* and protest any attempts by Anderson's party to free the slaves. By now Anderson was describing the blacks of the *Creole* as "passengers," and black soldiers of the island were telling female slaves on the ship that they were free. The white commander of the company, according to Gifford, told the slaves that they should have killed all whites on board and run the ship ashore.

Early on the morning of November 12 there was an abortive attempt by a group of Americans to rescue the *Creole* from Nassau. Under Bacon's auspices the captain of an American sailing vessel then in port, the *Louisia*, along with four sailors of the American brig *Congress*, determined to take the *Creole* to Indian Key. Before dawn the men rowed to the *Creole*, their muskets and cutlasses wrapped in an American flag at the bottom of the boat. While on their way to the brig, however, a black islander who had been watching their activities from another boat nearby warned the British officer in command of the *Creole*. When the party approached the ship, it looked up to twenty-five British soldiers, armed with muskets and fixed bayonets. The Americans hastily withdrew.

Bacon claimed that later that same morning, the twelfth, British officials released the slaves before the soldiers left the ship. Two white clergymen from Nassau who had boarded the *Creole* seemed to be giving directions to the slaves, and telling them that they soon would be free. When the attorney general boarded the brig, he explained that all slaves had had to stay on the ship until witnesses identified those accused of the mutiny. But now the innocent were free. The mutineers were to be imprisoned until the governor received instruction from London about the place of the trial. Anderson privately warned the *Creole*'s mate and crew that resistance to the slaves' liberation could incite the islanders and cause bloodshed. After he left, British officials on the brig gave a signal, and with a shout the blacks eased their craft alongside. While the soldiers were on deck, the blacks of the *Creole* boarded the small boats. Cheers arose as they reached shore. Accompanied by hundreds of islanders the ex-slaves registered at the office of the superintendent of police, while Anderson arranged to have the nineteen prisoners taken ashore. The other blacks went free in the islands, though five who had hidden in the hold of the *Creole* would eventually return to the United States. According to several crew members of the *Creole*, many of the freed slaves had wanted to return to the United States, but were prevented from doing so by threats from the islanders.

Cockburn vehemently disagreed with Bacon's account. British officials, he argued, had had nothing to do with the slaves' leaving the *Creole*. Anderson claimed that after he informed the slaves not involved in the mutiny that he had no reason to hold them, Merritt, now virtually in command of the *Creole*, expressed no desire to detain any slave wanting to leave the ship. The attorney general did not say it, but Merritt undoubtedly feared that the blacks in the surrounding boats would board the *Creole* when the military left. Anderson said that before he had gone many yards he saw the slaves climb into the boats. Their departure, he asserted, was voluntary and met no protests from Merritt.

The fact is that neither Anderson nor Merritt could have stopped the slaves from going free. The attorney general might have resisted the black islanders, but they outnumbered the whites at Nassau about four to one. In addition, he did not act illegally by informing the blacks of the *Creole* that British officials had no right to hold them. The slaves should go free, he implied, for they belonged to the *Creole*, and it was the responsibility of the ship's officers to control them. Merritt's actions were likewise predictable. The ship's crew was disabled, the captain was helpless, and Merritt was surrounded by black islanders; he was in no position to dispute Anderson's announcement that all slaves innocent of the mutiny could go free. The situation at Nassau did not allow a choice.

When the *Creole* finally arrived at New Orleans on December 2, many people in the South, already sensitive about British interference with American maritime affairs, were demanding compensation for the slaves. The New Orleans *Commercial Bulletin* called for the United States government to rebuke Great Britain, while the city's *Advertiser* declared that England should make redress. The Washington *National Intelligencer*, the Charleston *Mercury*, the Mobile *Register & Journal*, the Nashville *Union*, and the *Southron* of Jackson, Mississippi, denounced British actions, while the legislatures of Louisiana, Mississippi, and Virginia passed resolutions demanding restitution for British violation of American rights. Throughout the South, according to the Baltimore *Sun* and the Charleston *Courier*, the *Creole* incident had caused condemnation of Great Britain. In the Senate, Thomas Hart Benton criticized England for encouraging mutiny and murder; Henry Clay warned of the danger to America's coasting trade; and John C. Calhoun appealed to national honor and property rights. If the United States could not sail its ships down the Atlantic coast with slaves on board, the South Carolinian warned, there would be no way to stop England from interfering with its coastal trade in cotton as well.

Some Southerners declared that earlier, in March 1841, the United States Supreme Court had handed down a decision in a remarkably similar case which now seemed to support the *Creole* protests. The *Amistad*, a Spanish slaver, had been carrying fifty-three blacks (secured in Africa) from Havana to another Cuban port in 1839 when they mutinied and killed the captain and crew. Federal authorities enventually imprisoned the blacks, and the Spanish minister in Washington appealed to the treaties between Spain and the United States in 1795 (Pinckney's Treaty), and 1821 (Adams-Onis Treaty), which called for each nation to restore ships and property rescued from pirates and robbers on the high seas. President Martin Van Buren, perhaps wanting to avoid a major issue on the eve of a presidential election, would have complied with Spain's demand, but the United States Supreme Court refused. The blacks' counsel, former President John Quincy Adams and now Representative from Massachusetts, argued for their freedom on the basis of humanity, but Justice Joseph Story ruled in favor of the blacks on other grounds: They were kidnapped Africans entitled to freedom because Spain had outlawed the African slave trade in 1820. In the *Creole* case, some Southerners argued that while there had been no reparation for the *Amistad* because its owners had been illegally engaged in the African slave trade, there *should* be redress for the *Creole*'s losses because the blacks had belonged to a nation which recognized slavery.

Other observers drew analogies between the *Creole* affair and earlier slave incidents involving the British Bahamas. Three American ships, the *Comet*, the *Encomium*, and the *Enterprise*, also had been driven into British islands by forces beyond their control (bad weather), and in all cases the slaves on board had been set free by the colonial governor. And less than a year before the *Creole* revolt, the *Formosa*, an American ship bound for Louisiana from Virginia with thirty-eight slaves on board, wrecked near Nassau, and British officials on the island again set them free. The Louisiana Insurance Company of New Orleans made payment for the loss of the slaves of the *Formosa* and then sent a memorial to the United States Congress, which asked for reimbursement from the federal government. After a brief debate in the Senate, Alexander Barrow of Louisiana declared that if the government would not defend Southern rights, the South should destroy Nassau. Now it was the *Creole*—but for the first time in cases concerning British violations of America's domestic slave trade, mutiny and loss of life were involved. The London government had made reparation for the *Comet* and the *Encomium* because the incidents had occurred before the British Emancipation Act of 1833, but refused to indemnify the *Enterprise* because it had happened afterward. The *Formosa* affair remained unresolved, and there appeared little hope for the *Creole*.

Southerners nonetheless continued to complain about the *Creole* case. They recalled that in the late 1830's, the former American minister to London, Andrew Stevenson of Virginia, had followed the instructions of Secretary of State John Forsyth of Georgia in protesting British efforts to employ visit-and-search tactics in suppressing the African slave trade. In addition to the usual praise given Stevenson by the Richmond *Enquirer*, the Baltimore *Sun* and the *National Intelligencer* acclaimed his defense of America's honor. In reply, the antislavery Portsmouth *Journal* of New Hampshire proclaimed that Stevenson's argument was satisfactory only to a "Virginia abstractionist and slave-breeder" and disgustedly denied that the Minister's purpose was to protect America's integrity. The South's only aim, the *Journal* declared, was to defend the slave trade. Unexpected encouragement for the Southern position then came from Lewis Cass of Michigan, American minister to France and prominent candidate for the Democratic nomination for the Presidency in 1844. An outspoken critic of England, he published a pamphlet in February 1842 which denounced British search and warned of a resurgence of impressment. Thus by early 1842, spokesmen for the South had resurrected warnings of infringements of America's freedom of the seas, including impressment, and proclaimed that Great Britain again was trying to dominate the ocean trade.

The issue of national honor raised by the *Creole* affair had obscured the fact that for social, political, and economic reasons, England's best interests lay in good relations with the United States. It should have been clear that impressment had become unnecessary after conditions in the Royal Navy had been improved, that its exercise in peacetime was purposeless, and that no law could stop Great Britain from using it in war. On the visit-and-search controversy, the British government many times had assured the United States that it could not trust the American flag as proof of a ship's nationality, and that its naval officers had to examine the ship's papers if they were going to suppress the African slave trade. In fact, Lord Palmerston, the British foreign secretary, had argued in 1841 that there was a difference between a "visit" and a "search." Examination of a ship's papers, he said, constituted a visit, while examination of its cargo, an action not followed by the British navy, was a search. To no one's surprise, however, the State Department had not been convinced by his logic. Lord Aberdeen, successor to Palmerston in the Foreign Office, assured Stevenson that if injury occurred during the visit, London would grant compensation. In addition, private letters among British leaders in the early 1840's show they were not trying to insult America or to gain commercial supremacy. The London government simply wanted to halt the African slave trade.

Despite the arguments involving America's maritime rights, it appears that the central concern of at least some Southerners in the *Creole* controversy was the effect such British actions could have on encouraging slave rebellions and damaging the domestic slave trade itself. The Mobile *Register & Journal* warned that the result of British interference with the coasting trade would be to establish a place of refuge in the neighboring islands for runaway slaves. The Baltimore *Sun* presented a similar argument, while the New Orleans *Picayune* at first argued questions of national honor, but finally declared that Great Britain was inducing the South's slaves to commit mutiny and murder in order to win freedom. Northern abolitionists warned the South not to use the argument of national honor to protect the trade. The Boston *Liberator*, for example, dared the United States to go to war with England over the "hellish slave trade," while the Worcester *Spy* of Massachusetts could not believe the North would go to war "to DEFEND OUR AMERICAN SLAVE TRADE."

Excitement continued to rise in the United States as abolitionists broadened their criticisms of the South's behavior to attack slavery itself. In early 1842 abolitionists from both the United States and England, including Theodore Weld, Joshua Leavitt of the *Emancipator*, and Lord Morpeth of the British and Foreign Anti-Slavery Society, had gathered in Washington to work with John Quincy Adams and other antislavery Congressmen in presenting petitions denouncing slavery. James Birney, Liberty party candidate for the presidency in 1840 and 1844, wrote an article for the New York *American* which called for the slaves of the *Creole* to be freed. The renowned New England author, John Greenleaf Whittier, editor of the Pennsylvania *Freeman*, informed the chairman of the British and Foreign Anti-Slavery Society in London about the uproar in the United States caused by the *Creole* incident. In a letter to this same British anti-slavery group, the corresponding secretary of the American and Foreign Anti-Slavery Society approved the British government's decision not to surrender the blacks, either as fugitives or as slaves. Abolitionist Lewis Tappan, instrumental with other members of the American Society in securing legal counsel for the blacks of the *Amistad*, warned of trouble if either government granted compensation to the owners of the *Creole*'s slaves. The American Society urged the British government to refuse to make reparation; otherwise London would become insurer of the American domestic slave trade against both shipwreck and revolt.

In the House of Representatives the outspoken abolitionist from Ohio, Joshua Giddings, praised the *Creole*'s blacks for winning freedom. On March 21 and 22 he presented resolutions written by Weld, which argued that a state had exclusive authority over slavery within its territory, but that the Constitution gave the federal government jurisdiction over commerce and navigation upon the high seas. Since slavery abridged the natural rights of man, he said, it could exist only by sufferance of municipal law in areas within a slave state's jurisdiction. When a ship entered the high seas, persons on board were answerable only to national law. Blacks of the *Creole* were not liable for punishment; the Constitution did not require the federal government to regain possession of liberated slaves, he argued, nor was it to seek redress.

The *Creole* affair afforded Giddings an opportunity, which he took, to launch another attack on the "gag rule" against antislavery discussions in the House, and to show the support of his home district for his antislavery stand. As is well-known, House members declared that Giddings' pronouncements, if approved, would deepen division in the country and endanger Anglo-American relations. Though Southerners in the House considered presenting resolutions on the *Creole* matter, they decided not to—probably because of the threat such action would present to the gag rule, and perhaps because abolitionists could gain from discussions about slavery. Some Southerners outside of Congress warned that passage of Giddings' resolutions would ensure more slave revolts. The Baltimore *Sun* stated that if they passed, the Congress would be placing a knife in the hands of every slave and encouraging him to commit murder. Since the Representative from Ohio condoned mutiny and murder, the *Sun* argued, his behavior deserved condemnation. Though Giddings asked for time to prepare his defense, the House on March 22 voted 125 to 69 to adopt a resolution of censure. The following day he announced his resignation, but his antislavery constituency in Ohio returned him to the House by a majority of 3,500 votes in a special election in April.

For both the American and British governments there were problems. President John Tyler, titular head of the Whig party and a slaveholder from Virginia, could not establish a convincing legal basis for demanding the surrender of the nineteen mutineers as fugitives, for the only Anglo-American extradition agreement (part of Jay's Treaty) had expired in 1807. The British minister in Washington, Henry Fox, quickly showed that in 1838 federal officials had intervened to prevent the state of New York from surrendering two British subjects accused of murder. Two years later the Supreme Court had decided in *Holmes* v. *Jennison* that the American government should not surrender a murderer who had escaped from Canada. To be sure, legal opinion in both nations at this time held that when a matter affected peace and order there existed a right, independent of treaty, to surrender fugitives, and a right of comity under international law, which called for a nation to assist a foreign vessel that involuntarily entered its port. Fox recognized these rights but declared that if England delivered the blacks to the United States their status would revert to slavery. Though he did not say it, the truth was that no British ministry could do this or even make reparation for the freed slaves without causing a wrathful public outburst at home.

Secretary of State Daniel Webster, a Whig whose views were cautiously antislavery, feared the outcome of the *Creole* case more than British seizures of American vessels illegally engaged in the African slave trade. Whether his conciliatory actions were motivated by a desire to placate the South and revive his waning chances for the Presidency, or simply by a wish to avoid trouble with England, it appears that he hoped to tie the incident to legalities and to exchanges of diplomatic notes, and allow time to calm emotions. He appealed to the principle of comity. British officials in Nassau, he decided, had not followed the understandings of hospitality; reparation was required, he explained in instructions to the American minister in London, Edward Everett. The *Creole* had been passing from one American port to another on a lawful voyage and had carried a cargo of slaves whom the Constitution recognized as property in slaveholding states. Because the mutineers forced the vessel into Nassau it was the duty of British authorities to help it resume its voyage. The Secretary said that according to a contention of Foreign Secretary Palmerston in 1837, claimants should receive compensation when officials interfered with another country's slaves, even if in British territory. British municipal law, Webster declared, had no bearing on a person who entered the empire because of "disaster and distress."

While Webster explained the Tyler administration's stand on the *Creole* incident to Everett, the London government, now under the leadership of Sir Robert Peel, was uncertain about a course of action and asked for an opinion from the Crown's law officers. The latter unanimously opposed giving up the nineteen blacks accused of mutiny and murder because there were no municipal laws or treaty provisions establishing extradition. As for the blacks not involved in the revolt, the legal advisers saw the case of the *Enterprise* furnishing precedent for their release by island officials.

Both abolitionists and non-abolitionists in Parliament agreed with the legal opinion. Abolitionist Henry Brougham, after conferring with members of the British and Foreign Anti-Slavery Society, argued in the Lords that even if there were a treaty providing for extradition of criminals, a municipal law would be necessary to execute that treaty. Lord Thomas Denman, also an abolitionist, cited Sir Edward Coke's opinion—that nations were sanctuaries for subjects fleeing for safety from one to another. He even showed that Justice Story of the United States Supreme Court, in a recent edition of his *Conflict of Laws* (1841), cited Coke as authority. Lord John Campbell, mildly opposed to slavery, showed that the then American minister in Berlin, the distinguished lawyer Henry Wheaton, had asserted in his book on international law that no nation had to surrender fugitives unless by special agreement. In the *Creole* affair, Campbell concluded, the United States government could not expect compensation, for the slaves had become free upon their arrival in British territory.

This opinion, as well as approval of the London *Times*, stiffened the Peel ministry. To no one's surprise Foreign Secretary Aberdeen told the Lords that England would not try the mutineers of the *Creole* and would not turn over the other blacks to the United States government. In agreement with a petition from the Hibernian Anti-Slavery Society in Dublin and with a memorial presented him a few days earlier by the British and Foreign Anti-Slavery Society, he told

Everett that the colonial courts could not try the blacks accused of mutiny and murder because the acts had occurred outside British jurisdiction, and that it was impossible to transfer them to the American courts because there was no extradition law. They had to go free. If the mutineers had been accused of piracy, he said, the colonial courts could have handled the case. In fact, the British government had offered its local tribunals to the American consul at Nassau if he had wanted to bring the nineteen blacks to trial for piracy. The consul, Aberdeen said, had shown no interest in the suggestion. Nassau's chief justice ruled soon after that because of lack of evidence the nineteen prisoners were free.

Webster must have expected this decision, for he never instructed Everett to demand the return of the mutineers. The Minister tried in vain to persuade Aberdeen to support reparation for the blacks of the *Creole*. After a long examination of the issues, he concluded in a note to the Foreign Secretary that Nassau officials should have brought the mutineers to justice and helped the ship resume its voyage. As for the attorney general's claim that the slaves' overseer, Merritt, gave "seeming consent" to their release, Everett maintained that the presence of the black islanders around the *Creole* had caused the man to acquiesce. He added that it was incongruous for Great Britain to argue for the unconditional liberation of American slaves when it had only just established conditional emancipation (with compensation) within its own territory. Everett's protest was perfunctory, for the Peel ministry's decision was final.

By early 1842 several issues other than the *Creole* also threatened the tenuous Atlantic connection, and the Peel government sent a special mission to the United States to try to resolve all differences between the countries. Leading the small delegation was a friend and former business acquaintance of Secretary of State Webster's, the retired head of the banking firm of Baring Brothers and Company of London, the elderly Alexander Baring, Lord Ashburton. For him the *Creole* incident seemed of lesser importance than the northeastern boundary and the African slave trade, but he soon came to realize how vital national honor was to the South. He also learned how the peculiar institution would prove a major obstacle to settlement of maritime issues, because it had worked its way into the question of national honor. In fact, as Webster and Ashburton talked in Washington during that hot summer of 1842, they feared that the slavery question might disrupt progress on all issues—even the Maine boundary. Ashburton regretted the *Creole* incident but believed the English people so warmly approved Peel's antislavery policy that there could be no compensation for slaves freed from the vessel. Yet the Minister had no instructions on the *Creole*, for Everett's formal request for reparation did not arrive until April—after the Britisher had departed for the United States. Even later Aberdeen told him only to do his best to eliminate hard feelings.

Before Ashburton arrived in the United States, Webster privately asked his friend, Justice Story, for advice on the *Creole* affair. Webster often had turned to Story on legal matters—most notably the Alexander McLeod case—and the Judge usually had been helpful. Story, a conservative from Massachusetts, was moderate in his antislavery beliefs and concurred with Webster that protection of property, including slaves, was basic to society. Their common philosophy made it unlikely there would be a confrontation with England over the *Creole* affair.

Story agreed with Webster's original stand: The return of slaves who involuntarily entered a foreign port depended upon comity and not duty. The United States therefore could only appeal to the Peel government to turn over the mutineers, for without an extradition treaty it had no legal argument. In addition, according to international law, persons committing offenses on the high seas could be tried only in municipal courts of the country to which the ship belonged. The *Amistad* decision of 1841 supported his position, he thought, for in it he himself had stated the majority opinion of the United States Supreme Court that the ship's blacks had violated no law or treaty in winning freedom. But in the *Creole* case, Story surmised, laws had been violated. The legalistic stand on extradition adopted by Webster and Story thus acknowledged the freedom of the blacks.

Ashburton wanted to conciliate the United States by offering reparation for the *Creole*, but he was not authorized to do so. He was convinced that his government must promise some security from interference with America's coastal trade, for the reefs and bars between the Bahamas and Florida made the waters perilous and made it likely there would be other incidents like that of the *Creole*. Ashburton believed London should instruct the Bahamas governor to disallow direct communication between islanders and those persons aboard American ships driven into port by distress or mutiny. Violations like that of the *Creole*, he warned Aberdeen, might inflame the South. But the Foreign Secretary replied that it was impossible to guarantee security and repeated that slaves became free when they entered British territory. When Ashburton then suggested to Webster that perhaps the United States should convoy slave ships along the coast, the Secretary was astounded. It was ridiculous to convoy American ships in peacetime, he declared. Besides, how could the mere addition of ships prevent accidents at sea?

Ashburton realized the United States government had not retreated from its stand of late 1841 and that this stubbornness might wreck negotiation of the other issues between the nations. By mid-July 1842, President Tyler had become so "sore and testy" about the *Creole* case that the Minister worried lest the President hold back on a convention to halt the African slave trade until Southerners were satisfied about the *Creole*. Indeed, there was danger that Southern Senators might seek revenge for British refusal to surrender the mutineers by defeating the entire treaty he was negotiating with Webster.

Aberdeen's initial misunderstanding of the Tyler administration's reaction to the *Creole* incident contributed to the confusion. The Foreign Secretary had wrongly assumed that Webster would demand surrender of the slaves as fugitives, and the result was that Parliament criticized the United States for a stand never adopted. Abolitionists were incensed at Webster's moderation and his reliance upon the law of nations. A call for indemnification, they declared, was approval of slavery itself. The Boston *Liberator* denounced him, the Massachusetts Anti-Slavery Society passed resolutions of condemnation, and William Channing of Massachusetts criticized the Secretary's instructions as "morally unsound" and in violation of the "law of humanity." Yet even though Webster never demanded return of the blacks, many Southern spokesmen surprisingly approved—perhaps because continuing excitement over such a divisive issue could disrupt trade, or perhaps because they knew England would refuse a demand for the blacks' release, thereby throwing the questions of national honor or slavery—or both—into open debate. Tyler's attorney general, Hugh Legaré of South Carolina, believed Webster's action would discourage fanatics in the United States, and would not embarrass the new and conciliatory Peel ministry in England. The Mobile *Register & Journal,* pleased that Webster had adopted the revised Southern view, was nonetheless apprehensive that his evasive stand could encourage more *Creole* revolts. Webster, however, believed that a demand for the blacks' release would be pointless. Either the British would free them in the Caribbean islands, or, even if the blacks were turned over to the United States, it would be impossible to have a fair trial. Though even Tyler was doubtful about the Secretary's position, Webster never demanded delivery of the blacks.

By the end of July, Ashburton was so disgusted with the *Creole* affair that he decided to act on his own. The Minister thought that since the incident had caused so much public feeling and involved both national and international law he should refer it back to London. There, he hoped, the two governments might link an extradition convention with satisfaction on the *Creole* case. After Webster reiterated the administration's view in an elaborate note, Ashburton promised without authorization that the English government would instruct its island officials to observe hospitality and to enforce municipal law in a way to "maintain good neighborhood" with the United States by avoiding "officious interference" [i.e., unauthorized or unofficial] with ships driven by necessity into British ports. The basis for Ashburton's assurance may have lain in Aberdeen's private note of May 26, where the Foreign Secretary claimed England would "certainly do nothing to encourage mutiny either among slaves or Freemen."

Tyler and Webster regretted that Ashburton was unable to settle the *Creole* affair by treaty, and regarded the promise against officious interference as less than satisfactory, but they agreed to send the problem to London for consideration. The President wanted Ashburton's note to read that English officials would not interfere with vessels brought in by "any uncontrollable occurrence," rather than by accident; he believed "officious interference" was a poor term because that offense was "universally reprehended" and meant nothing special in this case. Yet the words remained, even though Tyler succeeded in having "or by violence" follow "accident" in instructions to British colonial governors.

Ashburton was relieved to dispose of the *Creole* affair; it had been his "great plague" during the negotiations. He had sought a dozen times to settle it, but Tyler's "garrulous" and "foolish" stand, Ashburton said, prevented an understanding until August. As it was, the President received the Minister's proposal "sulkily." But for the popularity of the special mission in the United States, Ashburton believed, there would have been no agreement at all on the *Creole* case. Yet Article X of the Webster-Ashburton Treaty did not guarantee against future *Creole* cases. It provided only for extradition of individuals accused of seven nonpolitical crimes: "murder, or assault with intent to commit murder, or Piracy, or arson, or robbery, or Forgery, or the utterance of forged paper." Without much argument Webster had incorporated much of the extradition proviso of Jay's Treaty. When he had tried to add mutiny and revolt to the list, Ashburton at first had seemed amenable—until he understood the ramifications of the *Creole* case. Then he balked, and agreed to the compromise settlement only with great reluctance. So did President Tyler. As late as two days before the negotiators signed the treaty, Tyler doubted the wisdom of an extradition article because he thought British authorities might not surrender a slave who had killed his master and escaped; a jury or court could call the act self-defense.

Reaction to the *Creole* settlement varied. Senator William Cabell Rives of Virginia, chairman of the Committee on Foreign Relations and spokesman for the Tyler administration, defended the treaty, while Benton, a Democrat, bitterly attacked it as a betrayal of American interests and an invitation to England to continue violating the American coasting trade. Though the *Creole* agreement was not part of the treaty, the Senate's approval by a strict partisan vote of 39 to 9 (all opponents except one were Democrats) suggests acceptance of all parts of the negotiations. Most important, only two Southern Senators voted against the treaty. Calhoun, perhaps speaking the thoughts of many Southerners, was satisfied with the exchange of notes on the *Creole* incident—perhaps because the procedure would bury the issue and allow peaceful continuation of trade with England. Though he would have preferred a treaty article, he was pleased that Ashburton had approved Webster's interpretation of the law of nations, and that the British Minister had promised instructions would go to island officials. John Quincy Adams was furious with Calhoun and with the settlement in the negotiations. After calling the South

Carolinian the "embodied spirit of slavery," Adams denounced the treaty as a "ticklish truce" between freedom and slavery. He was disgusted with Calhoun's temperance, for it was obviously designed "to conciliate the Northern political sopranos, who abhor slavery and help to forge fetters for the slave."

Abolitionists in both the United States and England would have misgivings about the possibility of having to extradite fugitive slaves. In September 1842, after the Senate had approved the treaty, a group of abolitionists met with Ashburton in Boston to express concern. The Britisher explained that in framing the extradition article, he had been careful, despite Webster's objections, that inferior officials in Canada would have no authority to surrender fugitives; the governor alone had extradition power. Ashburton also assured them that the taking of articles considered necessary to a slave's escape into Canada would not be criminal, and that if the extradition provision proved injurious to American blacks, the British government would terminate it. The delegation left, wholly satisfied. On the other side of the Atlantic, there was delay in Parliament's approval of extradition, as Aberdeen predicted, for Ashburton was unable to offer adequate assurances to British abolitionists. The antislavery committee in Parliament urged by abolitionists, tried to revise the extradition article to guarantee safety for fugitive slaves, but it failed. Though still suspicious of the treaty, one member of the antislavery cause in England, the Reverend J. H. Hinton, eventually admitted that he and others were somewhat mollified by the provision that application for surrender of alleged fugitives had to come from the United States government—not from states involved. A year passed before extradition went into effect in England. In actual practice, however, extradition under the treaty was not enforced against runaway slaves.

The *Creole* case finally was closed in 1855 when an Anglo-American claims commission awarded $110,330 to owners of the liberated slaves, thereby vindicating the Southern position (and that of the Tyler administration) in the controversy. The umpire, Joshua Bates, Boston banker and partner in the House of Baring, declared that even though slavery was contrary to humanity, the law of nations did not prevent a country from establishing it by law. The *Creole* had been on a lawful voyage, he said. When "unavoidable necessity" drove it into Nassau, it had the right to expect shelter from a friendly power. As for the other slaves, the governor should have helped officers of the *Creole* regain command. Bates ruled that the British Emancipation Act had no bearing on the case, inasmuch as no municipal law could authorize armed force in boarding the ship of another country. Since Nassau officials had violated international law, the British government had to compensate owners of the *Creole's* slaves.

Controversy over the *Creole* affair thus dissipated. Despite its potential for trouble, it did not become a crisis between England and the United States for several reasons. Especially important was the unsettled political situation in the United States. Even if the Tyler administration had been able to act forcefully, it would have been almost impossible to adopt a policy toward London which might have satisfied Anglophobes on the one hand, without provoking the abolitionists on the other. President Tyler and Secretary of State Webster were without a party. Though Tyler had been part of the states' rights wing in Congress which helped establish the Whig party, as President his opposition to the nationalist ideas of Clay and other Whigs soon put him at odds with almost everyone in Washington. When he vetoed Clay's national bank bill in August 1841 and there was pressure from Whig leaders for the Cabinet to resign, Webster, explaining that he wanted to complete settlement of the northeastern boundary question, had been the only member to stay. It is likely that Tyler was correct when he later said that Webster chose to remain because he wanted to be in a position to prevent Clay from becoming too powerful. Though Webster also might have considered his decision to be helpful in a run for the Presidency in 1844, his chances had diminished greatly by his decision to stay with Tyler. Economic ties with England probably were a key factor in the Whigs' decision to temporarily forget party quarrels and support the Webster-Ashburton Treaty.

There were other reasons for the treaty's acceptance. One was that the subject of slavery itself did not emerge as an issue. As might have been expected, Southern protests against British interference with the domestic slave trade failed to arouse much sympathy north of the Potomac. Not only did many of the strongest antagonists of England hesitate to help slavery interests indirectly, many antislavery advocates apparently had not decided whether they hated England or slavery more and were cautious about criticizing one adversary and helping the other. Perhaps the reason why the Peel ministry did not raise the question of slavery was because the effect on Anglo-American relations could have been injurious. After all, even though England had moved strongly in an antislavery direction, it also had become heavily dependent upon the South's cotton by the 1840's. Time also worked for a peaceful solution. News of the *Creole* incident arrived in the two capitals some weeks after its occurrence; the act of compensation did not occur until fourteen years later. For these reasons, the *Creole* affair never achieved the prominence it might have had under different circumstances and at a different time in American history.

While the *Creole* affair was a relatively minor incident in American history, it deserves more than minor consideration. One reason is that it had held great potential for trouble. Besides raising maritime and legal questions that involved America's honor, the incident had had three unexpected results: It appalled abolitionists in the United States, uniting them even more in their opposition to slavery; it encouraged closer contact between abolitionists on both sides of the Atlantic; it momentarily threatened Anglo-American relations. The *Creole* revolt also helps make it clear that there was slave unrest in the antebellum South. The question still remains, however, as to how widespread that discontent was. In addition to the plots and rumors of plots within the Southern states before 1861, the *Creole* revolt was one of at least fifty-five slave insurrections at sea from 1699 to the 1840's. Yet in relation to the number of slave ships involved in America's domestic trade, the rate of incidence was small. The question, however, does not seem to be whether rebellions actually occurred in the South. More important is the fact that several times before the Civil War—especially in the 1830's—the Lower South experienced near hysteria about the possibility of slave revolts. It appears, however, that this fear was not confined to any particular region. Southern newspapers indicate that strong protests against British interference with America's coastal trade came from the Upper South as well as from the Lower South. From colonial times to the Civil War, discontent on occasion had swelled into insurrection, and just as often rumors of conspiracy created an atmosphere of terror among some whites which made them careful not to mention the subject of abolitionism for fear of encouraging more slaves to rebel. One has to admit that the *Creole* affair was an isolated incident in the history of slavery, and that the overwhelming majority of slaves on the ship refused to take part in the mutiny; yet when freedom became certain, only five were determined to return to the United States.

Perhaps it is significant that after their initial protests Southern newspapers toned down their reactions to the *Creole* case and accepted the treaty settlement; such moderation supports the feeling that the most important desire by some Southerners was to prevent more slave insurrections. It is possible that much of the South's show of Anglophobia was sincere, that its maritime grievances were real, and that its call for respect for national honor was genuine. But if that section's spokesmen were politically astute—and there is good reason to believe they were—it seems one can raise several questions. Southerners like Calhoun had to have realized that the British government valued its economic ties with the United States, and that in peacetime it would not have risked alienating Americans by using outmoded and pointless practices like impressment or an alleged right of search. Aberdeen was antislavery in view and might have wanted to denounce slavery during the *Creole* controversy, but in 1842 he and Peel considered good relations with *both* North and South to be even more important than an antislavery crusade. Domestic pressures in England encouraged the ministry to uphold its stand on the *Creole* affair—at least until the 1850s—but it did so on other than humanitarian grounds. Similarly, the South never got involved in a predicament that could have caused a confrontation with both England and Northern abolitionists on the question of slavery.

The *Creole* revolt should not be ignored. Rather, it should be regarded as indicative of unrest among slaves; of the common goal of both Americans and Englishmen to resolve their differences amicably; and of the South's fear that continual British interference with its domestic institutions could endanger Anglo-American relations. For Southerners, as well as those who agreed with Webster's stand during the *Creole* controversy, the most important issue at that time was British respect for America's honor.

14

American Imperialism and the Mexican War

RAMÓN EDUARDO RUIZ

• *The history of United States–Mexican relations fills a long
and occasionally shameful chapter in American history. Mexico first emerged as an independent country in the first quarter of the nineteenth century, and since then it has had to
contend with the policies and ambitions of a northern neigh-
bor that was stronger, richer, more populous, and more advanced. Consequently, every Mexican government has been
forced to adjust its plans and goals to the colossus of the
North.*

*The decisive military encounter that ratified this unequal
relationship was the Mexican War. In May 1846, President
James K. Polk asked Congress for a declaration of war because
the Mexican government refused to pay the claims—totally
legitimate—of American citizens against Mexico. Armed conflict culminated a long campaign by certain groups—particularly strong in the South—to encourage American expansion
to the south and west and thus make possible the prosperity
of the slave economy.*

*The immediate provocation of the war was a Mexican at-
tack on advancing American troops in a disputed territory between the Rio Grande and Nueces rivers. Subsequent accounts by United States historians have tended to lay the
blame on Mexico for this incident. But the account by Ramón
Eduardo Ruiz, by juxtaposing the antiwar views of Congressman Abraham Lincoln with those of historian Justin H.
Smith, takes the opposite side.*

*There is less dispute about the results of the war. In a series
of thrusts toward Monterrey, Vera Cruz, and Mexico City,
Generals Winfield Scott and Zachary Taylor, supported by*

From "A Commentary on Morality: Lincoln, Justin H. Smith, and the Mexican War," by Ramón Eduardo Ruiz, *Journal of the Illinois State Historical
Society* 69 (February 1976): 26–34.

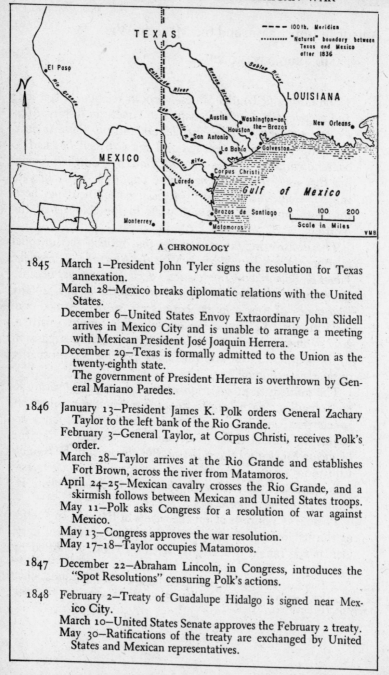

A CHRONOLOGY

1845 March 1—President John Tyler signs the resolution for Texas annexation.

March 28—Mexico breaks diplomatic relations with the United States.

December 6—United States Envoy Extraordinary John Slidell arrives in Mexico City and is unable to arrange a meeting with Mexican President José Joaquin Herrera.

December 29—Texas is formally admitted to the Union as the twenty-eighth state.

The government of President Herrera is overthrown by General Mariano Paredes.

1846 January 13—President James K. Polk orders General Zachary Taylor to the left bank of the Rio Grande.

February 3—General Taylor, at Corpus Christi, receives Polk's order.

March 28—Taylor arrives at the Rio Grande and establishes Fort Brown, across the river from Matamoros.

April 24-25—Mexican cavalry crosses the Rio Grande, and a skirmish follows between Mexican and United States troops.

May 11—Polk asks Congress for a resolution of war against Mexico.

May 13—Congress approves the war resolution.

May 17-18—Taylor occupies Matamoros.

1847 December 22—Abraham Lincoln, in Congress, introduces the "Spot Resolutions" censuring Polk's actions.

1848 February 2—Treaty of Guadalupe Hidalgo is signed near Mexico City.

March 10—United States Senate approves the February 2 treaty.

May 30—Ratifications of the treaty are exchanged by United States and Mexican representatives.

the United States Navy, easily disposed of Mexican opposition and made it possible for President Polk to dictate the terms of the peace. In one swift stroke, legalized by the Treaty of Guadalupe Hidalgo, the United States seized almost half of Mexico's entire territory, including most of what is now California, New Mexico, Arizona, Utah, and Nevada. Moreover, the division between Mexico and Texas was set at the Rio Grande River. There were even some expansionists who argued that the United States should simply follow its "destiny" and annex all of Mexico.

Mexico emerged from the peace of Guadalupe Hidalgo of 1848, the last chapter in the war with the United States, shorn of nearly half of its national domain, a beaten and emotionally exhausted country. With the passage of time, explains Armando Ayala Anguiano, a Mexican historian, the "shame" of the catastrophe "became insupportable, not only to the soldiers who lost . . . but to all Mexicans." Few American historians, however, voiced doubt about the justice of the immense territorial conquest. Recently, historian Seymour V. Connor, who stamps Mexico with the stigma of the aggressor, compiled a quantitative analysis of historians' opinions on the conflict. Of the 766 pamphlets and articles written between 1846 and 1970 (more than four-fifths of which had the imprint of American publishers), a bare 16 per cent fixed responsibility for the war on the United States. On the question of culpability, 75 per cent equivocated.

Only one writer in six, apparently, had taken to heart Abraham Lincoln's censure of his government's war policy. Lincoln, revered as the savior of the Union and remembered as the Great Emancipator, enjoyed scant prestige, among students of the war, as a historian. Instead, most scholars have followed Justin H. Smith, author of *The War with Mexico*, an eloquent defense of American innocence and winner of the Pulitzer Prize in 1920. Smith dismissed Lincoln's verdict with one terse comment. Lincoln, he wrote, wished to distinguish himself "before the home folks . . . by revealing, in a manner suited to his [youthful] years, that since Mexico . . . exercised jurisdiction on the northern bank of the Rio Grande . . . American blood must have been shed on Mexican . . . soil." As late as 1968, Kenneth M.

Stampp, C. Vann Woodward, Arthur M. Schlesinger, Jr., Edmund S. Morgan, Bruce Catton, and John M. Blum, six leading historians who collaborated on *The National Experience*, lauded Smith's study as "the fullest and most authoritative . . . on the Mexican War." But according to Frederick Merk, a distinguished scholar and author of *The Monroe Doctrine and American Expansion*, it was Lincoln, not Smith, who spoke with objectivity. It is Lincoln's view of the immediate cause of hostilities—the invasion by an American army of lands in dispute—that stands the scrutiny of time.

The controversy over culpability began with President James K. Polk, who asked Congress on May 11, 1846, to vote a resolution of war against the Republic of Mexico. In that address Polk outlined the events leading to his call for the resolution. After the rupture of diplomatic relations over United States annexation of Texas in March 1845, the United States had taken no action in response to the "wrongs and injuries committed by the Mexican Government on citizens of the United States." In September 1845, hoping "to establish peace with Mexico on liberal and honorable terms, and . . . to regulate and adjust our boundary and other causes of differences . . . on fair and equitable principles," Polk dispatched an envoy to Mexico with authority to settle all disputes. John Slidell, the emissary, landed at Veracruz on November 30 but never stepped inside the presidential palace. Mexican President José Joaquín de Herrera, cowed by the danger of a military uprising if he met to discuss Texas, refused to see Slidell. Herrera's prudence failed, however, to save him from his enemies. On December 29 an army under General Mariano Paredes toppled Herrera from power. Paredes, the new chief of the Republic, also rebuffed Slidell, who demanded his passport the following March. In Polk's words, Mexico thereby brushed aside "the offer of . . . peaceful adjustment."

Polk, meanwhile, had ordered General Zachary Taylor and his army into the region lying between the Nueces River and the Rio Grande in order "to meet a threatened invasion of Texas by . . . Mexican forces." To defend Texas, duty had called on Polk "to extend our protection over her citizens and soil." But Taylor's troops, quartered at Corpus Christi, were not ordered south, Polk said, until he "received such information from Mexico as rendered it probable, if not certain, that the Mexican government would refuse to receive our envoy."

According to Polk, Texas had declared the Rio Grande its border, with "jurisdiction . . . extended and exercised beyond the Nueces." Congress, in addition, on December 31, 1845, had "with great unanimity . . . recognized the country beyond the Nueces as a part of our territory," thus making its defense "urgent." Taylor received Polk's order on February 3 and began to march south on March 8. On April 24 Mexican cavalry forded the Rio Grande and began killing, wounding, and capturing soldiers of the United States Army.

Mexico, declared Polk, by crossing "the boundary of the United States, had invaded our territory and shed American blood upon the American soil." To Polk, moral responsibility rested squarely on Mexican shoulders. "War exists," he told Congress, "notwithstanding all our efforts to avoid it . . . by act of Mexico herself." Clearly, the truth of Polk's version of war guilt hung in balance on his assertion that the rightful boundary of Texas was the Rio Grande and not, as Mexico claimed, the Nueces River, 150 miles to the north: the Mexican assault on Taylor's troops was therefore an invasion of American territory.

Polk's justification for war perturbed Lincoln, who took his seat in Congress on December 6, 1847. As a freshman congressman from Illinois, a state pledged to the war, Lincoln initially kept his thoughts to himself. In that strategy he had abundant company; only two senators and fourteen congressmen had voted against the war resolution. Eventually, nonetheless, Lincoln did speak out, and supported all resolutions censuring Polk's conduct of the war. As he told William H. Herndon, his friend and law partner, "The war was unnecessarily and unconstitutionally commenced by the President." He labeled Polk's claim "a lie." Just two options existed, Lincoln explained, "To . . . tell the *truth*, or tell a foul, villainous, and bloody falsehood."

In Lincoln's mind, Polk was waging "a war of conquest." Had Polk and the expansionists not coveted Mexico's western provinces, the dispute could have been settled "in an amicable manner." Else, Lincoln pondered upon hearing of the terms of peace, why does Polk wish for territory beyond what is necessary to secure "indemnity for the past and security for the future?" Lincoln put little stock in Polk's assertion of Mexican unwillingness to negotiate. Paredes and his coup had not dashed hopes for peace. To the contrary, Lincoln pointed out, Polk had dispatched Taylor's army south before learning of Herrera's fall. Polk chose to wage war without regard to political events in Mexico.

Lincoln also discounted Polk's explanation for the outbreak of war. The insistence of the White House on a Mexican attack on American soil troubled Lincoln because Polk had never adequately explained how the lands between the Nueces and the Rio Grande, the scene of the first armed clash, belonged to the United States. The official message lacked the ring of truth. On December 7, 1846, Polk had charged that Mexico struck "the first blow" by spilling American blood on "our own soil." One day later, he alleged that there was ample cause for war "long before the breaking out of hostilities" inasmuch as Mexican leaders had rejected every overture for a peaceful accord and refused to see Slidell "or listen to his propositions." Even then, according to Polk, the United States "forbore to take redress . . . until Mexico herself became the aggressor by invading *our soil* in hostile array, and shedding the blood of our *citizens.*"

In his Spot Resolutions of December 22, 1847, Lincoln for the first time expressed his skepticism in public. In a series of questions, he challenged Polk to prove the American claim to lands between the Nueces and the Rio Grande. Had Spain not controlled the territory since the Adams-Onís Treaty of 1819, and afterwards the Mexican Republic? he asked. Did Taylor's men not drive from their homes the Mexican inhabitants of villages that antedated the Texas split with Mexico? Was not the American blood shed, Lincoln asked, in truth that of "*armed* officers, and *soldiers*" invading Mexican settlements? Lincoln amplified his charges in a speech to the House on January 12, 1848. When, he asked, was the Rio Grande ever the boundary of Texas? How could General Antonio López de Santa Anna, defeated in 1836 by Sam Houston and held as a prisoner of war, have conceded to Texas all lands north of the Rio Grande? Had Texas or the United States, either before or after annexation, exercised control beyond the Nueces? By what manner could Congress justify the claim to the Rio Grande boundary?

Unlike other war critics who put the boundary of Texas at the Nueces, Lincoln argued that neither the Rio Grande nor the Nueces divided Texas from Mexico. As he informed Horace Greeley, the boundary was determined by the presence of American settlements, which did extend beyond the Nueces "but not anywhere near the Rio Grande at any point." From his perspective, the " 'stupendous desert' between the valleys of those two rivers," and not the rivers themselves, separated Texas and Mexico. The United States Army had stepped into an area crying for demarcation. On the approach of the troops, the Mexicans fled their villages, forsaking their crops. "It is a fact," Lincoln wrote John Mason Peck, "that the United States Army, in marching to the Rio Grande, marched into a peaceful Mexican settlement." Taylor, for his part, had built Fort Brown "within a Mexican cottonfield, on which . . . a young cotton crop was growing." And the clash between American dragoons and Mexican cavalry had taken place on yet "another Mexican field." To Lincoln, these transgressions appeared anything but "amiable" or "peaceful."

Nor had the Rio Grande marked the western boundary of Louisiana, acquired by the United States in 1803. According to Lincoln, Polk had admitted United States relinquishment to Spain of all lands west of the Sabine River in the Adams-Onís Treaty of 1819. Even if the Rio Grande was accepted, for the sake of discussion, as the border of Louisiana, mused Lincoln, how could a line "that once divided your land from mine . . . *still* be the boundary between us, *after* I have sold my land to you?" Such a proposition, Lincoln believed, was "beyond all comprehension." Texas, moreover, even in its constitutions, had not always regarded the Rio Grande as its border. Conversely, Mexico had considered its border at the Nueces. Clearly, the question of ownership required careful study. Lincoln said further that a careful reading of the 1836 agreement revealed nothing about the Rio Grande as the boundary of Texas. On the contrary, Santa Anna made no promise to end the war and rebuffed questions about boundaries. Despite the section calling for withdrawal of Mexican forces "to the other side of the Rio Grande" in evacuating the territory of Texas, one stipulation required the troops of Texas to keep five leagues away from the enemy. Thus, by the singular terms of the 1836 agreement with Santa Anna, Texas promised to stay five leagues north of the boundary Polk later claimed for it. Polk also hedged on his view of jurisdiction, both for Texas and for the United States. While maintaining that the boundary extended beyond the Nueces, he refrained from saying it went to the Rio Grande. Nor did Congress, in annexing Texas, view the Rio Grande as the border. On the contrary, to cite Lincoln, Congress left "all questions of boundary to future adjustment." In its state constitution of 1845, Texas accepted the position of Congress.

By "design," concluded Lincoln, Polk had falsified the record. Notwithstanding his assertions, Polk had "sent the army into the midst of a settlement of Mexican people, who had never submitted, by consent or by force, to the authority of Texas or of the United States, and that *there*, and *thereby*, the first blood of the war was shed." Lincoln, in the often-quoted passage from his speech to the House, challenged the President to prove title to the disputed boundary. "But if he *can* not, or *will* not do this," concluded Lincoln, "if on any pretence, or no pretence, he shall refuse or omit it, then I shall be fully convinced, of what I more than suspect already, that he is deeply conscious of being in the wrong—that he feels the blood of this war, like the blood of Abel, is crying to Heaven against him."

The historian Justin H. Smith, writing some seventy years later, had a perplexing time with the boundary issue and labored assiduously to uphold Polk's interpretation. On February 3, 1846, according to Smith, Taylor received orders, sent to him nearly a month earlier, to leave Corpus Christi and camp on the Rio Grande "at whatever point he should consider most advantageous." The United States, "by stationing troops peaceably . . . between the Nueces and the Rio Grande . . . placed [itself] on an equality with Mexico." Taylor's presence was justified on "the principle of pacific joint-occupation." Mexico, conversely, "had no occasion to send an army into that region for defensive purposes," and if a Mexican army was dispatched "across the Rio Grande," that meant war. President Polk, Smith asserted, did not expect a Mexican declaration of war "to precede a blow."

The United States and not Mexico, Smith added, held a legitimate claim to the disputed territory. According to the State Department, "If an official demarcation had existed, the war between Texas and the mother-country had rubbed it out." Even though Texas had not effectively occupied the land claimed as far as the Rio Grande, the American claim nevertheless had ample justification. Until 1819, Americans had believed that the Louisiana Purchase of 1803 included Texas and the Rio Grande boundary. While the United States, in the Adams-Onís Treaty of 1819, ceded "whatever possessions we had west of the

Sabine . . . we did not withdraw from our position." Texas therefore "appeared to border on the Rio Grande [in 1845] not less truly than before, for no other line became established." By annexing Texas, then, the United States resurrected its "old claim." Polk, meanwhile, had given his word to Texas to uphold the claim.

Smith was not yet out of the woods, however. His account ran into trouble with Taylor's departure from Corpus Christi on March 8. To anyone who studies the record, it is clear that the villages called American by Polk were actually inhabited by Mexicans. Taylor encountered Mexicans on at least three occasions during his trek southward. "In some places," Smith acknowledged, "Mexicans had burned the herbage"; at Arroyo Colorado, troops under General Francisco Mejía (the commander at Matamoros) nearly ambushed the advancing Americans; and approximately ten miles north of the Rio Grande, Taylor's men stumbled upon "cabins in the midst of corn, cotton and pomegranates." Mexico, after all, could lay claim to the disputed territory by right of previous conquest and settlement.

Nor could Smith ignore the implications of Taylor's military activities, because Taylor, after setting up headquarters across from Matamoros and hoisting the Stars and Stripes at a site baptized Fort Brown, installed a battery of cannon aimed at the Mexican settlement. When the Mexican commander ordered Taylor to fall back to the Nueces, Smith went on, Taylor "retaliated by requesting" the American naval force, then lying off the mouth of the Rio Grande, to blockade the river. Without supplies coming in by sea, Smith conceded, "a large force could not remain long in Matamoros." Armed hostilities did not begin until April 25, when Mexican cavalry ambushed American dragoons sent out to reconnoiter.

Despite the "tragic and most regrettable" clash, Smith nonetheless believed that Polk could not be held responsible, for he had advocated peace until news of the Mexican attack "burst upon Washington like a rocket." How could anyone castigate Polk for sending troops into a region claimed by the United States? Conversely, to cite Smith, "Mexican occupation above the Rio Grande was merely by sufferance." Neither could Taylor be censured for his "provocative act" in pointing guns at Matamoros, which Smith viewed as "a defensive measure adopted . . . for military reasons in conjunction with pacific assurances and proposals." Taylor's fort on the Rio Grande did not invite the outbreak of hostilities. By Smith's logic, "joint occupation" could have proceeded peacefully "but for a distinctly aggressive step on the part of Mexico." The "hostilities," according to him, "were deliberately precipitated by the will and act of Mexico."

Strangely enough, Smith told another story in his footnotes, in which he stated that the boundary pretensions of Polk and the Texans had no validity. "Mere assertion of a boundary," he stressed, "proved nothing." The United States, he recalled, had quickly disregarded the Texas claim to Santa Fe. Texas, in reality, had not established jurisdiction beyond the Nueces. The agreement with Santa Anna only appeared to make the Rio Grande the boundary. The General, a prisoner of war at the time, did not wield presidential authority; moreover, Texas later broke the agreement and Mexico repudiated it. As to Polk's views of the boundary, "the author regards the American claim and all conclusions based upon it as unsound."

At that juncture in his analysis, Smith confronted a vexing problem. Having dismissed as false Polk's claim to the region between the Nueces and the Rio Grande, he needed additional justification for his version of American innocence and Mexican guilt. He must demonstrate that, regardless of certain inconsistencies and weaknesses in Polk's argument, Mexicans either wanted war or, because of their traits, stumbled into war. At the start of his discussion of relations between the two countries, Smith warned that "we must beware of carrying prejudice with us." But he himself had already decided that Mexican "authorities were generally unbusinesslike, often unjust or tricky, and on too many occasions positively dishonorable in their dealings with foreigners." To lay the foundations for this unflattering picture, Smith devoted much of the first two chapters to a study of Mexico and its people. He painted Mexican society in somber colors; the final subheading of Chapter II, for example, is titled "Deplorable State of Mexico." Smith spoke of demagogues, self-indulgence, contemptible politicians, graft, dishonesty, and immorality in public life. In his eyes, laws and constitutions meant little to "such a wilful, passionate race." All Mexicans, regardless of social class, "lived in the senses." Only a tiny minority enjoyed "a taste for reading books," most of which were "shockingly partisan, irresponsible and misleading." On the Mexican character, Smith waxed eloquent. A mule-driver, he cautioned, could be trusted "with anything you please, and it will surely be delivered." But if he lost at cards or lost his job, "he might rob you on the next day." Rancheros, who loved gambling and cockfighting, could lose all worldly goods, including a wife, and then light a cigarette and saunter off "without a sign of regret." Indolence and good nature characterized Mexicans, unless something excited "their passions." Of the women, he wrote, "Their forte is not conversation, for they seldom read and never think." Temperament, environment, and education blocked all dispassionate and intellectual activity. Passionate men and women, raised "in traditions of idleness and self-indulgence," could hardly be expected to practice self-restraint. Because Mexicans had few of the "qualifications for self-government," and handled poorly matters that required good judgment and self-control, "misunderstandings between them and a nation like the United States were not only sure to arise but sure to prove troublesome." Clearly, Smith implied, the people of Mexico, whom he brushed off as "children," must be held accountable. Unable to support the war on grounds of logic or law, Smith fell back on a polemical analysis of defects in the Mexican national character.

In 1966, in *The Monroe Doctrine and American Expansionism,* Frederick Merk, a Harvard historian, boldly tackled Smith's thesis. Merk demolished Polk's boundary pretension and, by implication, conferred new validity on Lincoln's views.

Merk asserted that the Sabine River traditionally marked the eastern limits of Texas. The southern boundary was fixed by Spain at the Nueces in 1816. In 1819 the United States relinquished all rights to lands west of the Sabine. On maps and atlases of the era, the Texas boundary uniformly ended at the Nueces. The three maps drawn by Stephen F. Austin, the patron of Texas, put the boundary there. A leading Philadelphia publisher twice reprinted one of the maps. European maps and atlases, as well as American ones drawn in 1830, 1834, and 1835, included in Texas only lands to the Nueces. Both John Quincy Adams and the expansionist Andrew Jackson concurred.

Neither, continued Merk, had Texas established a sacred right to the disputed area. One of the claims had been negotiated with a prisoner of war, and was never submitted to the Mexican Congress, which had ultimate authority. In addition, Texas and Santa Anna put little

stock in the 1836 agreement; both David G. Burnet, first president of
Texas, and Austin, his secretary of state, thought of it mainly for use
in future negotiating with Mexico or the United States. In 1836 the
Texans themselves agreed to accept the Nueces as their boundary if
their claim to the Rio Grande was the issue blocking recognition by,
or annexation to, the United States. Less than a decade later Texas
planned to negotiate boundaries with Mexico in return for a recognition of independence. The abortive treaty with the Tyler administration in 1844 set no boundary; and the joint congressional resolution
of 1845, which formally invited Texas to enter the Union, carefully
set aside boundary difficulties for future negotiations with "other
governments."

Despite that ambiguity and uncertainty, Polk sent Taylor to the
Rio Grande where, across from Matamoros, he planted cannon. Senator John M. Clayton of Delaware, to cite one of Polk's critics, considered Taylor's march and his blockade of the Rio Grande "as much
an aggression as pointing a pistol at a man's breast." Only then, however, Merk said, did a Mexican force fall on Taylor's men.

Merk also thought that Polk exaggerated other disputes with Mexico,
especially the amount of money owed Americans. A neutral commission had fixed Mexican indebtedness at one-fourth the figure submitted by American claimants. But Mexico, after paying three install-
ments, defaulted. Polk claimed that the unpaid balance, eventually
set at $3,250,000 by the American government, was a major grievance.
Yet, as Merk declared, American states and corporations had defaulted
on $200,000,000 of British bonds—a fact kept before the administra-
tion by critics of the war.

The Democratic majority in the House of Representatives limited
debate on the war resolution to two hours on May 11, 1846; and the
vote in the Senate took place on May 12, after only one day of debate. In Merk's opinion, Polk employed an attack on the flag to
"stampede the country into war." Still, in the end, the nation heard
the critics, perhaps lessening the harshness of the peace settlement
with Mexico. Without the dissent of Congressman Lincoln—a reflection of some of the leading opinions of the era—Polk and his allies
might have taken a larger slice of Mexico. On reflection, it appears,
the "youthful" Lincoln has proved more the historian than Smith—if
search for objectivity and veracity are the scholar's trademark.

15

Women and Their Families on the Overland Trail to California and Oregon, 1842–1867

JOHNNY FARAGHER AND CHRISTINE STANSELL

• The image of wagon trains crawling across vast plains has been entrenched in our minds by frequent movie and television westerns. Yet despite this popular treatment, the day-to-day reality of the way west remains shrouded in mystery. What impact those miles of desolation had on the minds and the lifestyles of families has rarely been explored in a serious way.

Each family that risked the dangerous trip brought with them not only physical reminders of home but in addition an entire way of viewing the world and their place in it. This viewpoint was necessarily based on a quite different reality from the one they would face during endless days of travel as well as in future places of settlement.

The frontier experience challenged in particular the basis of many of the values that characterized nineteenth-century "civilized society." An important part of this value system dealt with "the woman's place." From the 1840s on, the women's rights movement was making progress, and in that same decade the first settlers crossed into Nebraska to begin the trek to the Pacific. For the women who went west in the 1840s and thereafter, the new life was a mixture of incredible deprivation and quiet anticipation of the "great day a-comin.'" They literally put so many miles between themselves and their sisters and mothers back east that the established society of the settled country never fully caught up with them. Their very scarcity gave women a special prestige. The 1865 bylaws of Yellowstone City, Montana, for example, stated that death

This article is reprinted from *Feminist Studies*, 2 (1975): 150-162 by permission of the publisher, *Feminist Studies, Inc.*, c/o Women's Studies Program, University of Maryland, College Park, MD 20742. Please consult original article for footnotes.

was to be the penalty for "murder, thieving, or for insulting a woman." Not surprisingly, there were just fifteen women in the town and three hundred men.

Johnny Faragher and Christine Stansell explore not only how life on the Western trails affected the women's roles but also how the women themselves reacted to such changes. In addressing themselves to such issues, the authors raise an important question of historical writing. How effectively can anyone put himself into the minds of people who lived more than a century ago? Does the fact that historians are usually limited to written records substantially affect the accuracy of their conclusions?

> I am not a wheatfield
> nor the virgin forest
>
> I never chose this place
> yet I am of it now
>
> —Adrienne Rich
> "From an Old House in America"

From 1841 until 1867, the year in which the transcontinental railroad was completed, nearly 350,000 North Americans emigrated to the Pacific coast along the western wagon road known variously as the Oregon, the California, or simply the Overland Trail. This migration was essentially a family phenomenon. Although single men constituted the majority of the party which pioneered large-scale emigration on the Overland Trail in 1841, significant numbers of women and children were already present in the wagon trains of the next season. Families made up the preponderant proportion of the migrations throughout the 1840s. In 1849, during the overwhelmingly male Gold Rush, the number dropped precipitously, but after 1851 families once again assumed dominance in the overland migration. The contention that "the family was the one substantial social institution" on the frontier is too sweeping, yet it is undeniable that the white family largely mediated the incorporation of the western territories into the American nation.

The emigrating families were a heterogeneous lot. Some came from farms in the Midwest and upper South, many from small Midwestern towns, and others from Northeastern and Midwestern cities. Clerks and shopkeepers as well as farmers outfitted their wagons in Independence, St. Louis, or Westport Landing on the Missouri. Since costs for supplies, travel, and settlement were not negligible, few of the very poor were present, nor were the exceptionally prosperous. The dreams of fortune which lured the wagon trains into new lands were those of modest men whose hopes were pinned to small farms or larger dry-goods stores, more fertile soil or more customers, better market prospects and a steadily expanding economy.

For every member of the family, the trip west was exhausting, toilsome, and often grueling. Each year in late spring, west-bound emigrants gathered for the journey at spots along the Missouri River and moved out in parties of ten to several hundred wagons. Aggregates of nuclear families, loosely attached by kinship or friendship, traveled together or joined an even larger caravan. Coast-bound families traveled by ox-drawn wagons at the frustratingly slow pace of fifteen to twenty miles per day. They worked their way up the Platte River valley through what is now Kansas and Nebraska, crossing the Rockies at South Pass in southwestern Wyoming by mid-summer. The Platte route was relatively easy going, but from present-day Idaho, where the roads to California and Oregon diverged, to their final destinations, the pioneers faced disastrous conditions: scorching deserts, boggy salt flats, and rugged mountains. By this time, families had been on the road some three months and were only at the midpoint of the journey; the environment, along with the wear of the road, made the last months difficult almost beyond endurance. Finally, in late fall or early winter the pioneers straggled into their promised lands, after six months and over two thousand miles of hardship.

As this journey progressed, bare necessity became the determinant of most of each day's activities. The primary task of surviving and getting to the coast gradually suspended accustomed patterns of dividing work between women and men. All able-bodied adults worked all day in one way or another to keep the family moving. Women's work was no less indispensable than men's; indeed, as the summer wore on, the boundaries dividing the work of the sexes were threatened, blurred, and transgressed.

The vicissitudes of the trail opened new possibilities for expanded work roles for women, and in the cooperative work of the family there existed a basis for a vigorous struggle for female-male equality. But most women did not see the experience in this way. They viewed it as a male enterprise from its very inception. Women experienced the breakdown of the sexual division of labor as a dissolution of their own autonomous "sphere." Bereft of the footing which this independent base gave them, they lacked a cultural rationale for the work they did, and remained estranged from the possibilities of the enlarged scope and power of family life on the trail. Instead, women fought *against* the forces of necessity to hold together the few fragments of female subculture left to them. We have been bequeathed a remarkable record of this struggle in the diaries, journals, and memoirs of emigrating women. In this study, we will examine a particular habit of living, or culture, in conflict with the new material circumstances of the Trail, and the efforts of women to maintain a place, a sphere of their own.

The overland family was not a homogeneous unit, its members imbued with identical aspirations and desires. On the contrary, the period of westward movement was also one of multiplying schisms within those families whose location and social status placed them in the mainstream of national culture. Child-rearing tracts, housekeeping manuals, and etiquette books by the hundreds proscribed and rationalized to these Americans a radical separation of the work responsibilities and social duties of mothers and fathers; popular thought assigned unique personality traits, spiritual capacities, and forms of experience to the respective categories of man, woman, and child. In many families, the tensions inherent in this separatist ideology, often repressed in the everyday routines of the East, erupted under the strain of the overland crossing. The difficulties of the emigrants, while inextricably linked to the duress of the journey itself, also revealed family dynamics which had been submerged in the less eventful life "back home."

A full-blown ideology of "woman's place" was absent in pre-industrial America. On farms, in artisan shops, and in town marketplaces, women and children made essential contributions to family income and subsistence; it was the family which functioned as the basic unit of production in the colony and the young nation. As commercial exchanges displaced the local markets where women had sold surplus dairy products and textiles, and the workplace drifted away from the household, women and children lost their breadwinning prerogatives.

In Jacksonian America, a doctrine of "sexual spheres" arose to facilitate and justify the segregation of women into the home and men into productive work. While the latter attended to politics, economics, and wage-earning, popular thought assigned women the refurbished and newly professionalized tasks of child-rearing and housekeeping. A host of corollaries followed on the heels of these shifts. Men were physically strong, women naturally delicate; men were skilled in practical matters, women in moral and emotional concerns; men were prone to corruption, women to virtue; men belonged in the world, women in the home. For women, the system of sexual spheres represented a decline in social status and isolation from political and economic power. Yet it also provided them with a psychological power base of undeniable importance. The "cult of true womanhood" was more than simply a retreat. Catharine Beecher, one of the chief theorists of "woman's influence," proudly quoted Tocqueville's observation that "in no country has such constant care been taken, as in America, to trace two clearly distinct lines of action for the two sexes, and to make them keep pace with the other, but in two pathways which are always different." Neither Beecher nor her sisters were simply dupes of a masculine imperialism. The supervision of child-rearing, household economy, and the moral and religious life of the family granted women a certain degree of real autonomy and control over their lives as well as those of their husbands and children.

Indeed, recent scholarship has indicated that a distinctly female subculture emerged from "woman's sphere." By "subculture" we simply mean a "habit of living"—as we have used "culture" above—of a minority group which is self-consciously distinct from the dominant activities, expectations, and values of a society. Historians have seen female church groups, reform associations, and philanthropic activity as expressions of this subculture in actual behavior, while a large and rich body of writing by and for women articulated the subcultural impulses on the ideational level. Both behavior and thought point to child-rearing, religious activity, education, home life, associationism, and female communality as components of women's subculture. Female friendships, strikingly intimate and deep in this period, formed the actual bonds. Within their tight and atomized family households, women carved out a life of their own.

At its very inception, the western emigration sent tremors through the foundations of this carefully compartmentalized family structure. The rationale behind pulling up stakes was nearly always economic advancement. Since breadwinning was a masculine concern, the husband and father introduced the idea of going west and made the final decision. Family participation in the intervening time ran the gamut from enthusiastic support to stolid resistance. Many women cooperated with their ambitious spouses: "The motive that induced us to part with pleasant associations and the dear friends of our childhood days, was to obtain from the government of the United States a grant of land that 'Uncle Sam' had promised to give to the head of each family who settled in this new country." Others, however, only acquiesced. "Poor Ma said only this morning, 'Oh, I wish we never had started,'" Lucy Cooke wrote her first day on the trail, "and she looks so sorrowful and dejected. I think if Pa had not passengers to take through she would urge him to return; not that he should be so inclined." Huddled with her children in a cold, damp wagon, trying to calm them despite the ominous chanting of visiting Indians, another woman wondered "what had possessed my husband, anyway, that he should have thought of bringing us away out through this God forsaken country." Similar alienation from the "pioneer spirit" haunted Lavinia Porter's leave-taking:

> I never recall that sad parting from my dear sister on the plains of Kansas without the tears flowing fast and free. . . . We were the eldest of a large family, and the bond of affection and love that existed between us was strong indeed . . . as she with the other friends turned to leave me for the ferry which was to take them back to home and civilization, I stood alone on that wild prairie. Looking westward I saw my husband driving slowly over the plain; turning my face once more to the east, my dear sister's footsteps were fast widening the distance between us. For the time I knew not which way to go, nor whom to follow. But in a few moments I rallied my forces . . . and soon overtook the slowly moving oxen who were bearing my husband and child over the green prairie . . . the unbidden tears would flow in spite of my brave resolve to be the courageous and valiant frontierswoman.

Her dazed vacillation soon gave way to a private conviction that the family had made a dire mistake: "I would make a brave effort to be cheerful and patient until the camp work was done. Then starting out ahead of the team and my men folks, when I thought I had gone beyond hearing distance, I would throw myself down on the unfriendly desert and give way like a child to sobs and tears, wishing myself back home with my friends and chiding myself for consenting to take this wild goose chase." Men viewed drudgery, calamity, and privation as trials along the road to prosperity, unfortunate but inevitable corollaries of the rational decision they had made. But to those women who were unable to appropriate the vision of the upwardly mobile pilgrimage, hardship and loss only testified to the inherent folly of the emigration, "this wild goose chase."

If women were reluctant to accompany their men, however, they were often equally unwilling to let them go alone. In the late 1840s, the conflict between wives and their gold-crazed husbands reveals the determination with which women enforced the cohesion of the nuclear family. In the name of family unity, some obdurate wives simply chose to blockbust the sexually segregated Gold Rush: "My husband grew enthusiastic and wanted to start immediately," one woman recalled, "but I would not be left behind. I thought where he could go I could and where I went I could take my two little toddling babies." Her family departed intact. Other women used their moral authority to smash the enterprise in its planning stages. "We were married to live together," a wife acidly reminded her spouse when he informed her of his intention to join the Rush: "I am willing to go with you to any part of *God's Foot Stool* where you think you can do best, and under these circumstances you have no right to go where I cannot, and if you do you need never return for I shall look upon you as dead." Roundly chastised, the man postponed his journey until the next season, when his family could leave with him. When included in the plans, women seldom wrote of their husbands' decisions to emigrate in their diaries or memoirs. A breadwinner who tried to leave alone, however, threatened the family unity upon which his authority was based; only then did a wife challenge his dominance in worldly affairs.

There was an economic reason for the preponderance of families on the Trail. Women and children, but especially women, formed an essential supplementary work force in the settlements. The ideal wife in the West resembled a hired hand more than a nurturant Christian housekeeper. Narcissa Whitman wrote frankly to aspiring settlers of the functional necessity of women on the new farms: "Let every young man bring a wife, for he will want one after he gets here, if he never did before." In a letter from California, another seasoned woman warned a friend in Missouri that in the West women became "hewers of wood and drawers of water everywhere." Mrs. Whitman's fellow missionary Elkanah Walker was unabashedly practical in beseeching his wife to join him: "I am tired of keeping an old bachelor's hall. I want someone to get me a good supper and let me take my ease and when I am very tired in the morning I want someone to get up and get breakfast and let me lay in bed and take my rest." It would be both simplistic and harsh to argue that men brought their families West or married because of the labor power of women and children; there is no doubt, however, that the new Westerners appreciated the advantages of familial labor. Women were not superfluous; they were workers. The migration of women helped to solve the problem of labor scarcity, not only in the early years of the American settlement on the coast, but throughout the history of the continental frontier.

In the first days of the overland trip, new work requirements were not yet pressing and the division of labor among family members still replicated familiar patterns. Esther Hanna reported in one of her first diary entries that "our men have gone to build a bridge across the stream, which is impassable," while she baked her first bread on the prairie. Elizabeth Smith similarly described her party's day: "rainy . . . Men making rafts. Women cooking and washing. Children crying." When travel was suspended, "the men were generally busy mending wagons, harnesses, yokes, shoeing the animals etc., and the women washed clothes, boiled a big mess of beans, to warm over for several meals, or perhaps mended clothes." At first, even in emergencies, women and men hardly considered integrating their work. "None but those who have cooked for a family of eight, crossing the plains, have any idea of what it takes," a disgruntled woman recalled: "My sister-in-law was sick, my niece was much younger than I, and consequently I had the management of all the cooking and planning on my young shoulders." To ask a man to help was a possibility she was unable even to consider.

The relegation of women to purely domestic duties, however, soon broke down under the vicissitudes of the Trail. Within the first few weeks, the unladylike task of gathering buffalo dung for fuel (little firewood was available *en route*) became women's work. As one traveler astutely noted, "force of surroundings was a great leveler"; miles of grass, dust, glare, and mud erased some of the most rudimentary distinctions between female and male responsibilities. By summer, women often helped drive the wagons and the livestock. At one Platte crossing, "the men drawed the wagons over by hand and the women all crossed in safety"; but at the next, calamity struck when the bridge collapsed, "and then commenced the hurry and bustle of repairing; all were at work, even the women and children." Such crises, which compounded daily as the wagons moved past the Platte up the long stretches of desert and coastal mountains, generated equity in work; at times of Indian threats, for example, both women and men made bullets and stood guard. When mountain fever struck the Pengra family as they crossed the Rockies, Charlotte relieved her incapacitated husband of the driving while he took care of the youngest child. Only such severe afflictions forced men to take on traditionally female chores. While women did men's work, there is little evidence that men reciprocated.

Following a few days in the life of an overland woman discloses the magnitude of her work. During the hours her party traveled, Charlotte Pengra walked beside the wagons, driving the cattle and gathering buffalo chips. At night she cooked, baked bread for the next noon meal, and washed clothes. Three successive summer days illustrate how trying these small chores could be. Her train pulled out early on a Monday morning, only to be halted by rain and a flash flood; Mrs. Pengra washed and dried her family's wet clothes in the afternoon while doing her daily baking. On Tuesday the wagons pushed hard to make up for lost time, forcing her to trot all day to keep up. In camp that night there was no time to rest. Before going to bed, she wrote, "Kept busy in preparing tea and doing other things preparatory for the morrow. I baked a cracker pudding, warm biscuits and made tea, and after supper stewed two pans of dried apples, and made two loaves of bread, got my work done up, beds made, and child asleep, and have written in my journal. Pretty tired of course." The same routine devoured the next day and evening: "I have done a washing. Stewed apples, made pies and baked a rice pudding, and mended our wagon cover. Rather tired." And the next: "baked biscuits, stewed berries, fried meat, boiled and mashed potatoes, and made tea for supper, afterward baked bread. Thus you see I have not much rest." Children also burdened women's work and leisure. During one quiet time, Helen Stewart retreated in mild defiance from her small charges to a tent in order to salvage some private time: "It exceeding hot . . . some of the men is out hunting and some of them sleeping. The children is grumbling and crying and laughing and howling and playing all around." Although children are notably absent in women's journals, they do appear, frightened and imploring, during an Indian scare or a storm, or intrude into a rare and precious moment of relaxation, "grumbling and crying."

Because the rhythm of their chores was out of phase with that of the men, the division of labor could be especially taxing to women. Men's days were toilsome but broken up at regular intervals with periods of rest. Men hitched the teams, drove or walked until noon, relaxed at dinner, traveled until the evening camp, unhitched the oxen, ate supper, and in the evening sat at the campfire, mended equipment, or stood guard. They also provided most of the labor in emergencies, pulling the wagons through mires, across treacherous river crossings, up long grades, and down precipitous slopes. In the pandemonium of a steep descent,

> you would see the women and children in advance seeking the best way, some of them slipping down, or holding on to the rocks, now taking an "otter slide," and then a run til some natural obstacle presented itself to stop their accelerated progress and those who get down safely without a hurt or a bruise, are fortunate indeed. Looking back to the train, you would see some of the men holding on to the wagons, others slipping under the oxen's feet, some throwing articles out of the way that had fallen out, and all have enough to do to keep them busily occupied.

Women were responsible for staying out of the way and getting themselves and the children to safety, men for getting the wagons down. Women's work, far less demanding of brute strength and endurance, was nevertheless distributed without significant respite over all waking hours: mealtimes offered no leisure to the cooks. "The plain fact of the matter is," a young woman complained,

> we *have no time for sociability*. From the time we get up in the morning, until we are on the road, it is hurry scurry to get break-

fast and put away the things that necessarily had to be pulled out last night—while under way there is no room in the wagon for a visitor, nooning is barely long enough to eat a cold bite— and at night all the cooking utensils and provisions are to be gotten about the camp fire, and cooking enough to last until the next night.

After supper, the men gathered together, "lolling and smoking their pipes and guessing, or maybe betting, how many miles we had covered during the day," while the women baked, washed, and put the children to bed before they finally sat down. Charlotte Pengra found "as I was told before I started that there is no rest in such a journey."

Unaccustomed tasks beset the travelers, who were equipped with only the familiar expectation that work was divided along gender lines. The solutions which sexual "spheres" offered were usually irrelevant to the new problems facing families. Women, for example, could not afford to be delicate: their new duties demanded far greater stamina and hardiness than their traditional domestic tasks. With no tradition to deal with the new exigencies of fuel-gathering, cattle-driving, and cooking, families found that "the division of labor in a party . . . was a prolific cause of quarrel." Within the Vincent party, "assignments to duty were not accomplished without grumbling and objection . . . there were occasional angry debates while the various burdens were being adjusted," while in "the camps of others who sometimes jogged along the trail in our company . . . we saw not a little fighting . . . and these bloody fisticuffs were invariably the outcome of disputes over division of labor." At home, these assignments were familiar and accepted, not subject to questioning. New work opened the division of labor to debate and conflict.

By mid-journey, most women worked at male tasks. The men still retained dominance within their "sphere," despite the fact that it was no longer exclusively masculine. Like most women, Lavinia Porter was responsible for gathering buffalo chips for fuel. One afternoon, spying a grove of cottonwoods half a mile away, she asked her husband to branch off the trail so that the party could fell trees for firewood, thus easing her work. "But men on the plains I had found were not so accomodating, nor so ready to wait upon women as they were in more civilized communities." Her husband refused and Porter fought back: "I was feeling somewhat under the weather and unusually tired, and crawling into the wagon told them if they wanted fuel for the evening meal they could get it themselves and cook the meal also, and laying my head down on a pillow, I cried myself to sleep." Later that evening her husband awakened her with a belated dinner he had prepared himself, but despite his conciliatory spirit their relations were strained for weeks: "James and I had gradually grown silent and taciturn and had unwittingly partaken of the gloom and somberness of the dreary landscape." No longer a housewife or a domestic ornament, but a laborer in a male arena, Porter was still subordinate to her husband in practical matters.

Lydia Waters recorded another clash between new work and old consciousness: "I had learned to drive an ox team on the Platte and my driving was admired by an officer and his wife who were going with the mail to Salt Lake City." Pleased with the compliment, she later overheard them "laughing at the thought of a woman driving oxen." By no means did censure come only from men. The officer's wife as well as the officer derided Lydia Waters, while her own mother indirectly reprimanded teen-aged Mary Ellen Todd. "All along our journey, I had tried to crack that big whip," Mary Ellen remembered years later:

> Now while out at the wagon we kept trying until I was fairly successful. How my heart bounded a few days later when I chanced to hear father say to mother, "Do you know that Mary Ellen is beginning to crack the whip." Then how it fell again when mother replied, "I am afraid it isn't a very lady-like thing for a girl to do." After this, while I felt a secret joy in being able to have a power that set things going, there was also a sense of shame over this new accomplishment.

To understand Mrs. Todd's primness, so incongruous in the rugged setting of the Trail, we must see it in the context of a broader struggle on the part of women to preserve the home in transit. Against the leveling forces of the Plains, women tried to maintain the standards of cleanliness and order that had prevailed in their homes back East:

> Our caravan had a good many women and children and although we were probably longer on the journey owing to their presence— they exerted a good influence, as the men did not take such risks with Indians . . . were more alert about the care of teams and seldom had accidents; more attention was paid to cleanliness and

sanitation and, lastly, but not of less importance, meals were more regular and better cooked thus preventing much sickness and·there was less waste of food.

Sarah Royce remembered that family wagons "were easily distinguished by the greater number of conveniences, and household articles they carried." In the evenings, or when the trains stopped for a day, women had a chance to create with these few props a flimsy facsimile of the home.

Even in camp women had little leisure time, but within the "hurry scurry" of work they managed to recreate the routine of the home. Indeed, a female subculture, central to the communities women had left behind, reemerged in these settings. At night, women often clustered together, chatting, working, or commiserating, instead of joining the men: "High teas were not popular, but tatting, knitting, crochetting, exchanging recipes for cooking beans or dried apples or swopping food for the sake of variety kept us in practice of feminine occupations and diversions." Besides using the domestic concerns of the Trail to reconstruct a female sphere, women also consciously invoked fantasy: "Mrs. Fox and her daughter are with us and everything is so still and quiet we can almost imagine ourselves at home again. We took out our Daguerrotypes and tried to live over again some of the happy days of 'Auld Lang Syne.'" Sisterly contact kept "feminine occupations" from withering away from disuse: "In the evening the young ladies came over to our house and we had a concert with both guitars. Indeed it seemed almost like a pleasant evening at home. We could none of us realize that we were almost at the summit of the Rocky Mountains." The hostess added with somewhat strained sanguinity that her young daughter seemed "just as happy sitting on the ground playing her guitar as she was at home, although she does not love it as much as her piano." Although a guitar was no substitute for the more refined instrument, it at least kept the girl "in practice with feminine occupations and diversions": unlike Mary Ellen Todd, no big whip would tempt her to unwomanly pleasure in the power to "set things going."

But books, furniture, knick-knacks, china, the daguerrotypes that Mrs. Fox shared, or the guitars of young musicians—the "various articles of ornament and convenience"—were among the first things discarded on the epic trash heap which trailed over the mountains. On

long uphill grades and over sandy deserts, the wagons had to be lightened; any materials not essential to survival were fair game for dis-
posal. Such commodities of woman's sphere, although functionally
useless, provided women with a psychological lifeline to their abandoned homes and communities, as well as to elements of their identities which the westward journey threatened to mutilate or entirely
extinguish. Losing homely treasures and memorabilia was yet another
defeat within an accelerating process of dispossession.

The male-directed venture likewise encroached upon the Sabbath,
another female preserve. Through the influence of women's magazines, by mid-century Sunday had become a veritable ladies' day;
women zealously exercised their religious influence and moral skill on
the day of their families' retirement from the world. Although parties
on the Trail often suspended travel on Sundays, the time only provided the opportunity to unload and dry the precious cargo of the
wagons—seeds, food, and clothing—which otherwise would rot from
dampness. For women whose creed forbade any worldly activity on
the Sabbath, the work was not only irksome and tedious but profane.

> This is Sabath it is a beautiful day but indeed we do not use it
> as such for we have not traveled far when we stop in a most
> lovely place oh it is such a beautiful spot and take everything out
> of our wagon to air them and it is well we done it as the flower
> was damp and there was some of the other ones flower was rot-
> ten . . . and we baked and boiled and washed oh dear me I did
> not think we would have abused the sabeth in such a manner. I
> do not see how we can expect to get along but we did not in-
> tend to do so before we started.

Denied a voice in the male sphere that surrounded them, women
were also unable to partake of the limited yet meaningful power of
women with homes. On almost every Sunday, Helen Stewart lamented the disruption of a familiar and sustaining order of life, symbolized by the household goods strewn about the ground to dry: "We
took everything out the wagons and the side of the hill is covered
with flower biscuit meat rice oat meal clothes and such a quantity of
articles of all discertions to many to mention and childre[n] included
in the number. And hobos that is neather men nor yet boys being in
and out hang about."

The disintegration of the physical base of domesticity was symptomatic of an even more serious disruption in the female subculture. Because the wagon trains so often broke into smaller units, many women were stranded in parties without other women. Since there were usually two or more men in the same family party, some male friendships and bonds remained intact for the duration of the journey. But by midway in the trip, female companionship, so valued by nineteenth-century women, was unavailable to the solitary wife in a party of hired men, husband, and children that had broken away from a larger train. Emergencies and quarrels, usually between men, broke up the parties. Dr. Powers, a particularly ill-tempered man, decided after many disagreements with others in his train to make the crossing alone with his family. His wife shared neither his misanthropy nor his grim independence. On the day they separated from the others, she wrote in her journal: "The women came over to bid me goodbye, for we were to go alone, all alone. They said there was no color in my face. I felt as if there was none." She perceived the separation as a banishment, almost a death sentence: "There is something peculiar in such a parting on the Plains, one there realizes what a goodbye is. Miss Turner and Mrs. Hendricks were the last to leave, and they bade me adieu the tears running down their sunburnt cheeks. I felt as though my last friends were leaving me, for what—as I thought then—was a Maniac." Charlotte Pengra likewise left Missouri with her family in a large train. Several weeks out, mechanical problems detained some of the wagons, including those of the other three women. During the month they were separated, Pengra became increasingly dispirited and anxious: "The roads have been good today—I feel lonely and almost disheartened. . . . Can hear the wolves howl very distinctly. Rather ominis, perhaps you think. . . . Feel very tird and lonely—our folks not having come—I fear some of them ar sick." Having waited as long as possible for the others, the advance group made a major river crossing. "Then I felt that indeed I had left all my friends," Pengra wrote, "save my husband and his brother, to journey over the dreaded Plains, without one female acquaintance even for a companion—of course I wept and grieved about it but to no purpose."

Others echoed her mourning. "The whipporwills are chirping," Helen Stewart wrote, "they bring me in mind of our old farm in pensillvania the home of my childhood where I have spent the happiest days I will ever see again. . . . I feel rather lonesome today oh solitude how I love it if I had about a dozen of my companions to enjoy it with me." Uprootedness took its toll in debilitation and numbness. After a hard week, men "lolled around in the tents and on their blankets seeming to realize that the 'Sabbath was made for man,' " resting on the palpable achievements of miles covered and rivers crossed. In contrast, the women "could not fully appreciate physical rest, and were rendered more uneasy by the continual passing of emigrant trains all day long. . . . To me, much of the day was spent in meditating over the past and in forebodings for the future."

The ultimate expression of this alienation was the pressure to turn back, to retrace steps to the old life. Occasionally anxiety or bewilderment erupted into open revolt against going on.

> This morning our company moved on, except one family. The woman got mad and wouldn't budge or let the children go. He had the cattle hitched on for three hours and coaxed her to go, but she wouldn't stir. I told my husband the circumstances and he and Adam Polk and Mr. Kimball went and each one took a young one and crammed them in the wagon, and the husband drove off and left her sitting. . . . She cut across and overtook her husband. Meantime he sent his boy back to camp after a horse he had left, and when she came up her husband said, "Did you meet John?" "Yes," was the reply, "and I picked up a stone and knocked out his brains." Her husband went back to ascertain the truth and while he was gone she set fire to one of the wagons. . . . He saw the flames and came running and put it out, and then mustered spunk enough to give her a good flogging.

Short of violent resistance, it was always possible that circumstances would force a family to reconsider and turn back. During a cholera scare in 1852, "women cried, begging their men to take them back." When the men reluctantly relented, the writer observed that "they did the hooking up of their oxen in a spiritless sort of way," while "some of the girls and women were laughing." There was little lost and much regained for women in a decision to abandon the migration.

Both sexes worked, and both sexes suffered. Yet women lacked a sense of inclusion and a cultural rationale to give meaning to the suffering and the work; no augmented sense of self or role emerged from augmented privation. Both women and men also complained, but women expanded their caviling to a generalized critique of the whole enterprise. Margaret Chambers felt "as if we had left all civilization behind us" after crossing the Missouri, and Harriet Ward's cry from South Pass—"Oh, shall we ever live like civilized beings again?"—reverberated through the thoughts of many of her sisters. Civilization was far more to these women than law, books, and municipal government; it was pianos, church societies, daguerrotypes, mirrors—in short, their homes. At their most hopeful, the exiles perceived the Trail as a hellish but necessary transition to a land where they could renew their domestic mission: "Each advanced step of the slow, plodding cattle carried us farther and farther from civilization into a desolate, barbarous country. . . . But our new home lay beyond all this and was a shining beacon that beckoned us on, inspiring our hearts with hope and courage." At worst, temporary exigencies became in the minds of the dispossessed the omens of an irrevocable exile: "We have been travelling with 25–18–14–129–64–3 wagons—now all alone—how dreary it seems. Can it be that I have left my quiet little home and taken this dreary land of solitude in exchange?"

Only a minority of the women who emigrated over the Overland Trail were from the Northeastern middle classes where the cult of true womanhood reached its fullest bloom. Yet their responses to the labor demands of the Trail indicate that "womanliness" had penetrated the values, expectations, and personalities of midwestern farm women as well as New England "ladies." "Woman's sphere" provided them with companionship, a sense of self-worth, and most important, independence from men in a patriarchal world. The Trail, in breaking down sexual segregation, offered women the opportunities of socially essential work. Yet this work was performed in a male arena, and many women saw themselves as draftees rather than partners.

Historians have generally associated "positive work roles" for women with the absence of narrowly defined notions of "woman's place." In the best summary of literature on colonial women, for example, the authors of *Women in American Society* write: "In general, neither men nor women seemed concerned with defining what women were or what their unique contribution to society should be. . . . Abstract theories about the proper role of women did not stand in the way of meeting familial and social needs." Conversely, the ascendancy of "true womanhood" and the doctrine of sexual spheres coincided with the declining importance of the labor of middle- and upper-class women in a rapidly expanding market economy. On the Overland Trail, cultural roles and self-definitions conflicted with the immediate necessities of the socioeconomic situation. Women themselves fought to preserve a circumscribed role when material circumstances rendered it dysfunctional. Like their colonial great-grandmothers on pre-market subsistence farms, they labored at socially indispensable tasks. Yet they refused to appropriate their new work to their own ends and advantage. In their deepest sense of themselves they remained estranged from their function as "able bodies."

It could be argued that the time span of the trip was not long enough to alter cultural values. Yet there is evidence that the tensions of the Trail haunted the small and isolated market farms at the journey's end. Women in the Western settlements continued to try to reinstate a culture of domesticity, although their work as virtual hired hands rendered obsolete the material base of separate arenas for women and men.

The notion of subculture employed in this and other studies of nineteenth-century women is hazy and ill-defined. We need to develop more rigorous conceptions of society, culture, and subculture, and to clarify the paradoxes of women's position, both isolated and integrated, in the dominant social and cultural movements of their time. Nonetheless, the journals of overland women are irrefutable testimony to the importance of a separate female province. Such theorists as Catharine Beecher were acutely aware of the advantages in keeping life divvied up, in maintaining "two pathways which are always different" for women and men. The women who traveled on the Overland Trail experienced firsthand the tribulations of integration which Beecher and her colleagues could predict in theory.

16

Only His Stepchildren:

Lincoln and the Negro

DON E. FEHRENBACHER

• *The social and political upheavals that began with the Montgomery (Alabama) Bus Boycott in 1956 and subsided after the withdrawal of United States forces from Vietnam and the resignation of President Richard Nixon in 1974 left few areas of American life untouched. One important consequence was a reappraisal of the nation's history from the perspective of the black minority. Although the work never took the form of one unified school of thought, it effectively challenged many of the assumptions in the standard texts.*

These reappraisals reached figures such as Woodrow Wilson and Franklin D. Roosevelt, but even more importantly they touched Abraham Lincoln himself. No other American, living or dead, has ever won more universal respect or worldwide adulation than the man who epitomized the dream of "log cabin to White House," the man who in his words and actions seemed to represent all that was good and decent in the American character.

Yet the black power movement of the 1960s, which was understandably critical of patronizing, well-intentioned white liberals, noticed anew that even the Great Emancipator was a condescending savior. President Lincoln specifically affirmed that his desire was to save the Union, not to destroy slavery; and even when the famous Emancipation Proclamation was issued, it did not apply to the border states or to those sections of the Confederacy that had already been overrun by federal troops. In other words, it did not immediately free even a single slave.

Cooler heads have prevailed, and have noted that to term Abraham Lincoln a "racist" is to take the man out of his time

Reprinted from *Civil War History* 20, no. 4: Copyright © 1974 by the Kent State University Press.

and place. In his own day, the Illinois lawyer was considered a radical on the race question, and his very election was sufficient to drive the Southern states out of the Union. Professor Don E. Fehrenbacher offers a reasoned analysis of the shifting view of Lincoln and points out that there are solid reasons why the shift is back toward a more adulatory view of the wartime President.

If the United States had a patron saint it would no doubt be Abraham Lincoln; and if one undertook to explain Lincoln's extraordinary hold on the national consciousness, it would be difficult to find a better starting-point than these lines from an undistinguished poem written in 1865:

> One of the people! Born to be
> Their curious epitome;
> To share yet rise above
> Their shifting hate and love.

A man of the people and yet something much more, sharing popular passions and yet rising above them—here was the very ideal of a democratic leader, who in his person could somehow mute the natural antagonism between strong leadership and vigorous democracy. Amy Lowell, picking up the same theme half a century later, called Lincoln "an embodiment of the highest form of the typical American." This paradox of the uncommon common man, splendidly heroic and at the same time appealingly representative, was by no means easy to sustain. The Lincoln tradition, as a consequence, came to embrace two distinct and seemingly incompatible legends—the awkward, amiable, robust, rail-splitting, story-telling, frontier folklore hero; and the towering figure of the Great Emancipator and Savior of the Union, a man of sorrows, Christlike in his character and fate.

Biographers have struggled earnestly with this conspicuous dualism, but even when the excesses of reminiscence and myth are trimmed away, Lincoln remains a puzzling mixture of often conflicting qualities—drollness and melancholy, warmth and reserve, skepticism and piety, humbleness and self-assurance. Furthermore, he is doubly hard to get at because he did not readily reveal his inner self. He left us no diary or memoirs, and his closest friends called him "secretive" and "shut-mouthed." Billy Herndon in one of his modest moods declared, "Lincoln is unknown and possibly always will be." Plainly, there is good reason for scholarly caution in any effort to take the measure of such a man.

No less plain is the intimate connection between the Lincoln legend and the myth of America. The ambiguities in his popular image and the whisper of enigma in his portraits have probably broadened the appeal of this homespun Westerner, self-made man, essential democrat, and national martyr. Almost anyone can find a way to identify with Lincoln, perhaps because "like Shakespeare . . . he seemed to run through the whole gamut of human nature." Whatever the complex of reasons, successive generations of his countrymen have accepted Abraham Lincoln as the consummate American—the representative genius of the nation. One consequence is that he tends to serve as a mirror for Americans, who, when they write about him, frequently divulge a good deal about themselves.

Of course the recurring election of Lincoln as *Representative American* has never been unanimous. There was vehement dissent at first from many unreconstructed rebels, and later from iconoclasts like Edgar Lee Masters and cavaliers of the Lost Cause like Lyon Gardiner Tyler. In the mainstream of national life, however, it became increasingly fashionable for individuals and organizations to square themselves with Lincoln and enlist him in their enterprises. Often this required misquotation or misrepresentation or outright invention; but lobbyists and legislators, industrialists and labor leaders, reformers and bosses, Populists, Progressives, Prohibitionists, and Presidents all wanted him on their side. New Deal Democrats tried to steal him from the Republicans, and the American Communist party bracketed him with Lenin. Lincoln, in the words of David Donald, had come to be "everybody's grandfather."

Most remarkable of all was the growing recognition of Lincoln's greatness in the eleven states of the Confederacy, ten of which had never given him a single vote for President. This may have been a necessary symbolic aspect of sectional reconciliation. Returning to the Union meant coming to terms with the man who had saved the Union. No one took the step more unequivocally than Henry W. Grady, prophet of the New South, who told a New York audience in

1886 that Lincoln had been "the first typical American, the first who comprehended within himself all the strength and gentleness, all the majesty and grace of this Republic." When Southerners talked to Southerners about it, they were usually more restrained. Nevertheless, by the early twentieth century, the Lincoln tradition was becoming a blend of blue and gray, as illustrated in *The Perfect Tribute*, a story from the pen of an Alabama woman about a dying Confederate soldier's admiration for the Gettysburg Address.

Bonds of sympathy between Lincoln and the South had not been difficult to find. He was, after all, a native Southerner—implacable as an enemy, but magnanimous in victory and compassionate by nature. In his hands, nearly everyone agreed, the ordeal of Reconstruction would have been less severe. Even Jefferson Davis concluded that his death had been "a great misfortune to the South."

In addition, Lincoln seemed to pass the supreme test. He could be assimilated to the racial doctrines and institutional arrangements associated with the era of segregation. The historical record, though not entirely consistent, indicated that his opposition to slavery had never included advocacy of racial equality. With a little editing here and some extra emphasis there, Lincoln came out "right" on the Negro question. This was a judgment more often understood than elaborated in Southern writing and oratory, but certain self-appointed guardians of white supremacy were sometimes painfully explicit in claiming Lincoln as one of their own. He had been willing, they said, to guarantee slavery forever in the states where it already existed. He had issued the Emancipation Proclamation with great reluctance. He had opposed the extension of slavery only in order to reserve the Western territories exclusively for white men. He had denied favoring political and social equality for Negroes, had endorsed separation of the races, and had persistently recommended colonization of Negroes abroad. This was the Lincoln eulogized by James K. Vardaman of Mississippi, perhaps the most notorious political racist in American history, and by the sensational Negrophobic novelist, Thomas Dixon. In his most famous work, *The Clansman*, Dixon had Lincoln as President parody himself during a discussion of colonization:

> We can never attain the ideal Union our fathers dreamed, with millions of an alien, inferior race among us, whose assimilation is neither possible nor desirable. The Nation cannot now exist half

white and half black, any more than it could exist half slave and half free.

When one remembers that all this time millions of black Americans were still paying homage to the Great Emancipator, dualism begins to seem pervasive in the Lincoln tradition. Racist elements, to be sure, were never very successful in promoting the image of Lincoln as a dedicated white supremacist, but support from an unlikely quarter would eventually give the idea not only new life but respectability in the centers of professional scholarship.

During the first half of the twentieth century, Lincoln studies became a functional part of the literature of the Civil War, in which the problem of race was present but not paramount. Titles of the 1940s indicate the general bent of interest: *Lincoln and His Party in the Secession Crisis; Lincoln and the Patronage; Lincoln's War Cabinet; Lincoln and the Radicals; Lincoln and the War Governors; Lincoln and the South.* There was, it should be observed, no *Lincoln and the Negro.* That would come, appropriately, in the 1960s.

The sweep of the modern civil rights movement, beginning with the Supreme Court's anti-segregation decision in 1954, inspired a new departure in American historical writing. Never has the psychological need for a usable past been more evident. Black history flourished and so did abolitionist history, but the most prestigious field of endeavor was white-over-black history. Attention shifted, for example, from slavery as a cause of the Civil War to slavery as one major form of racial oppression. With this change of emphasis, the antebellum years began to look different. A number of monographs appearing in the 1960s, such as Leon F. Litwack's *North of Slavery,* demonstrated the nationwide prevalence of white-superiority doctrines and white-supremacy practices. Many Republicans and even some abolitionists, when they talked about the Negro, had sounded curiously like the slaveholders whom they were so fiercely denouncing. In fact, it appeared that the North and the South, while bitterly at odds on the issue of slavery, were relatively close to one another in their attitudes toward race. And Lincoln, according to Litwack, "accurately and consistently reflected the thoughts and prejudices of most Americans."

The racial consensus of the Civil War era made it easy enough to understand why black Americans failed to win the equality implicit in emancipation, but certain other historical problems became more difficult as a consequence. For instance, if most Northerners in 1860 were indeed racists who viewed the Negro with repugnance as an inferior order of creation, then why did so many of them have such strong feelings about slavery? And why did racist Southerners fear and distrust racist Republicans with an intensity sufficient to destroy the Union? And does not the achievement of emancipation by a people so morally crippled with racism seem almost miraculous—like a one-armed man swimming the English Channel? No amount of talk about overwrought emotions or ulterior purposes or unintended consequences will fully account for what appears to be a major historical paradox, with Lincoln as the central figure.

When the civil rights struggle got under way in the 1950s, both sides tried to enlist Lincoln's support, but the primary tendency at first was to regard desegregation as a belated resumption of the good work begun with the Emancipation Proclamation. Many leading historians agreed that during the Presidential years there had been a "steady evolution of Lincoln's attitude toward Negro rights." The changes carried him a long way from the narrow environmental influences of his youth and made him, in the words of Richard N. Current, more relevant and inspiring than ever "as a symbol of man's ability to outgrow his prejudices."

This was the liberal interpretation of Lincoln's record on racial matters. It came under attack from several directions, but especially from the ranks of intellectual radicalism and black militancy, both academic and otherwise. New Left historians, many of them activists in the battle for racial justice, could find little to admire in Abraham Lincoln. Compared with abolitionists like William Lloyd Garrison and Wendell Phillips, he seemed unheroic, opportunistic, and somewhat insensitive to the suffering of black people in bondage. He was "the prototype of the political man in power, with views so moderate as to require the pressure of radicals to stimulate action." His pre-war opposition to slavery, embracing the Republican policy of nonextension and the hope of ultimate extinction, reflected a "comfortable belief in the benevolence of history." It amounted to a "formula which promised in time to do everything while for the present risking nothing."

Election to the Presidency, in the radical view, produced no great transformation of his character. "Lincoln grew during the war—but he didn't grow much," wrote Lerone Bennett, Jr., a senior editor of

Ebony. "On every issue relating to the black man . . . he was the very essence of the white supremacist with good intentions." He moved but slowly and reluctantly toward abolishing slavery, and his famous Proclamation not only lacked "moral grandeur," but had been drafted "in such a way that it freed few, if any, slaves." His reputation as the Great Emancipator is therefore "pure myth." Most important of all, Lincoln probably believed in the inferiority of the Negro and certainly favored separation of the races. He was, in Bennett's words, "a tragically flawed figure who shared the racial prejudices of most of his white contemporaries."

This, then, was the radical interpretation of Lincoln's record on racial matters, and what strikes one immediately is its similarity to the views of professional racists like Vardaman and Dixon. The portrait of A. Lincoln, Great White Supremacist, has been the work, it seems, of a strange collaboration.

No less interesting is the amount of animus directed at a man who died over a hundred years ago. In the case of black militants, hostility to Lincoln has no doubt been part of the process of cutting loose from white America. Thus, there is little history but much purpose in the statement of Malcolm X: "He probably did more to trick Negroes than any other man in history."

For white radicals, too, rejection of Lincoln signified repudiation of the whole American cultural tradition, from the first massacre of Indians to the Vietnam War. In what might be called the "malign consensus" school of United States history, Lincoln remained the Representative American, but the America that he represented was a dark, ugly country, stained with injustice and cruelty. Plainly, there is much more at stake here than the reputation of a single historical figure.

James K. Vardaman, it is said, used to carry with him one particular Lincoln quotation that he would whip out and read at the slightest opportunity. This excerpt from the debate with Douglas in 1858 at Charleston, Illinois, is now fast becoming the most quoted passage in all of Lincoln's writings, outstripping even the Gettysburg Address and the Second Inaugural. Pick up any recent historical study of American race relations and somewhere in its pages you are likely to find the following words:

> I will say then that I am not, nor ever have been in favor of bringing about in any way the social and political equality of the

white and black races,—that I am not nor ever have been in favor of making voters or jurors of negroes, nor of qualifying them
to hold office, nor to intermarry with white people; and I will
say in addition to this that there is a physical difference between
the white and black races which I believe will for ever forbid
the two races living together on terms of social and political
equality. And inasmuch as they cannot so live, while they do remain together there must be the position of superior and inferior, and I as much as any other man am in favor of having the
superior position assigned to the white race.

It is, of course, a quotation that bristles with relevancy. Problems that
once preoccupied Lincoln's biographers, such as his part in bringing
on the Civil War and the quality of his wartime leadership, have been
more or less pushed aside by a question of newer fashion and greater
urgency. It is well phrased in the Preface to a collection of documents
titled *Lincoln on Black and White* (1971): "Was Lincoln a racist?
More important, how did Lincoln's racial views affect the course of
our history?"

Anyone who sets out conscientiously to answer such a query will
soon find himself deep in complexity and confronting some of the fundamental problems of historical investigation. In one category are various questions about the historian's relation to the past: Is his task
properly one of careful reconstruction, or are there more important
purposes to be served? Does his responsibility include rendering moral
judgments? If so, using what standards—those of his own time or those
of the period under study? Then there are all the complications encountered in any effort to read the mind of a man, especially a politi-
cian, from the surviving record of his words and actions. For instance,
what he openly affirmed as a youth may have been silently discarded
in maturity; what he believed on a certain subject may be less significant than the intensity of his belief; and what he said on a certain occasion may have been largely determined by the immediate historical
context, including the composition of his audience.

Terminological difficulties may also arise in the study of history,
and such is the case with the word "racist," which serves us badly as a
concept because of its denunciatory tone and indiscriminate use. Con-
ducive neither to objectivity nor to precision, the word has been employed so broadly that it is now being subdivided. Thus we are invited
to distinguish between ideological racism and institutional racism, be-

tween scientific racism and folk racism, between active racism and inactive racism, between racism and racial prejudice, between racism and racialism, between hierarchical racism and romantic racialism. In its strictest sense, racism is a doctrine, but by extension it has also come to signify an attitude, a mode of behavior, and a social system. The *doctrine,* a work of intellectuals, is a rationalized theory of inherent Negro inferiority. In a given person, however, it can be anything from a casual belief to a philosophy of life. As an *attitude,* racism is virtually synonymous with prejudice—an habitual feeling of repugnance, and perhaps of enmity, toward members of another race. It can be anything from a mild tendency to a fierce obsession. Racism as a *mode of behavior* is prejudice activated in some way—a display of racial hostility that can be anything from mere avoidance of the other race to participation in a lynching. Racism as a *social system* means that law and custom combine to hold one race in subordination to another through institutional arrangements like slavery, segregation, discrimination, and disfranchisement. Individuals can help support such a system with anything from tacit acquiescence to strenuous public service in its defense. These multiple and graduated meanings of the word "racism" are important to remember in exploring the historical convergence of Abraham Lincoln and the American Negro.

"One must see him first," says Bennett, "against the background of his times. Born into a poor white family in the slave state of Kentucky and raised in the anti-black environments of southern Indiana and Illinois, Lincoln was exposed from the very beginning to racism." This is a familiar line of reasoning and credible enough on the surface. Any racial views encountered during his youth were likely to be unfavorable to the Negro. But more important is the question of how *often* he encountered such views and how *thoroughly* he absorbed them. Besides, the assumption that his racial attitudes were shaped more or less permanently by his early social environment does not take into account the fact that youth may rebel against established opinion. Lincoln did in a sense reject his father's world, leaving it behind him forever soon after reaching the age of twenty-one. Certainly his personal knowledge of black people was very limited. After catching a few glimpses of slavery as a small boy in Kentucky, he had little contact with Negroes while growing up in backwoods Indiana or as a young man in New Salem, Illinois. Those first twenty-eight years of his life take up just three pages in Benjamin Quarles's book, *Lincoln and the Negro*.

If Lincoln entered manhood with strong feelings about race already implanted in his breast, one might expect to find indications of it in his earlier letters and speeches. For instance, on a steamboat carrying him home from a visit to Kentucky in 1841, there were a dozen slaves in chains. They had been, literally, sold down the river to a new master, and yet they seemed the most cheerful persons on board. Here was inspiration for some racist remarks in the "Sambo" vein, but Lincoln, describing the scene to a friend, chose instead to philosophize about the dubious effect of "condition upon human happiness." That is, he pictured Negroes behaving, as George M. Fredrickson puts it, "in a way that could be understood in terms of a common humanity and not as the result of peculiar racial characteristics." Although one scholar may insist that Lincoln's racial beliefs were "matters of deep conviction," and another may talk about "the deep-rooted attitudes and ideas of a lifetime," there is scarcely any record of his thoughts on race until he was past forty years of age. Long before then, of course, he had taken a stand against slavery, and it was the struggle over slavery that eventually compelled him to consider publicly the problem of race.

There is no escape from the dilemma that "relevance" makes the past worth studying and at the same time distorts it. We tend to see antebellum race and slavery in the wrong perspective. Race itself was not then the critical public issue that it has become for us. Only widespread emancipation could make it so, and until the outbreak of the Civil War, that contingency seemed extremely remote. Our own preoccupation with race probably leads us to overestimate the importance of racial feeling in the antislavery movement. In fact, there is a current disposition to assume that if a Republican did not have strong pro-Negro motives, he must have acted for strong anti-Negro reasons, such as a desire to keep the Western territories lily-white.

Actually, much of the motivation for antislavery agitation was only indirectly connected with the Negro. For example, the prime target often seemed to be, not so much slavery as the "slave power," arrogant, belligerent, and overrepresented in all branches of the Federal government. In Lincoln's case, no one can doubt his profound, though perhaps intermittent, sympathy for the slave. Yet he also hated slavery in a more abstract way as an evil principle and as a stain on the national honor, incompatible with the mission of America.

It is a mistake to assume that Lincoln's actions in relation to the Negro were determined or even strongly influenced by his racial outlook. He based his antislavery philosophy, after all, squarely upon perception of the slave as a man, not as a Negro. According to the Declaration of Independence, he declared, all men, including black men, are created equal, at least to the extent that none has a right to enslave another. This became a point at issue in the famous debates with Stephen A. Douglas, who vehemently denied that the Declaration had anything to do with the African race. Lincoln, in turn, accused his rival of trying to "dehumanize" the Negro. But he had constructed an argument against slavery which, carried to its logical conclusion, seemed to spell complete racial equality. So Douglas insisted, anyhow, while Lincoln protested: "I do not understand that because I do not want a negro woman for a slave I must necessarily want her for a wife."

Opponents of slavery everywhere had to contend with the charge that they advocated Negro equality. In the Democratic press, Republicans almost invariably became "Black Republicans," and political survival more often than not appeared to depend upon repudiation of the epithet. Thus the race question was most prominent in the antebellum period as a rhetorical and largely spurious feature of the slavery controversy.

Lincoln's first general remarks about racial equality on record were made in 1854, when the repeal of the Missouri Compromise drew him back to the center of Illinois politics. What to do, ideally, with Southern slaves, he pondered in a speech at Peoria. "Free them, and make them politically and socially our equals? My own feelings will not admit of this; and if mine would, we well know that those of the great mass of white people will not." More often that year, however, he talked about the humanity of the Negro in denouncing the extension of slavery. Then came the election of 1856 and Frémont's defeat, which Lincoln analyzed with some bitterness: "We were constantly charged with seeking an amalgamation of the white and black races; and thousands turned from us, not believing the charge . . . but *fearing* to face it themselves." It was at this point, significantly, that he became more aggressive and explicit in disavowing racial equality. He began using census figures to show that miscegenation was a by-product of slavery. He spoke of the "natural disgust" with which most white people viewed "the idea of indiscriminate amalgamation of the white and black races." And, under heavy pounding from Douglas during the senatorial campaign of 1858, he answered again and again in the manner of the notorious Charleston passage quoted above. Indeed, his strongest feeling about race appears to have been his vexation with those who kept bringing the subject up. "Negro equality! Fudge!!" he scribbled on a piece of paper. "How long, in the government of a God great enough to make and maintain this Universe, shall there continue knaves to vend and fools to gulp, so low a piece of demagoguism as this?"

Most of Lincoln's recorded generalizations about race were public statements made in the late 1850s as part of his running oratorical battle with Douglas. Furthermore, nearly all of those statements were essentially disclaimers rather than affirmations. They indicated, for political reasons, the *maximum* that he was willing to deny the Negro and the *minimum* that he claimed for the Negro. They were concessions on points not at issue, designed to fortify him on the point that *was* at issue—namely, the extension of slavery. If he had responded differently at Charleston and elsewhere, the Lincoln of history simply would not exist. And words uttered in a context of such pressure may be less than reliable as indications of a man's lifetime attitude.

At least it seems possible that Lincoln's remarks in middle age on the subject of race were shaped more by his political realism than by impressions stamped on his mind in childhood. The principal intellectual influence, as Frederickson has demonstrated, was Henry Clay, Lincoln's political hero, whom he studied anew for a eulogy delivered in 1852. Clay, in his attitude toward slavery, represented a link with the Founding Fathers. A slaveholder himself who nevertheless believed that the institution was a "curse," he began and ended his career working for a program of gradual emancipation in Kentucky. He helped found and steadily supported the American Colonization Society. In his racial views, moreover, Clay emphasized the Negro's humanity and reserved judgment on the question of innate black inferiority. Lincoln not only adopted Clay's tentative, moderate outlook but extensively paraphrased and sometimes parroted his words.

Considering, then, the peculiar context of his most significant remarks on the subject of race, and considering also his dependence on Clay, it seems unwise to assert flatly, as some scholars do, that Lincoln embraced the doctrine of racism. Not that it would be astonishing to find that he did so. The assumption of inherent white superiority was almost universal and rested upon observation as well as prejudice. Comparison of European civilization and African "savagery" made it extremely difficult to believe in the natural equality of white and black races. Yet Lincoln's strongest statements, even if taken at face value and out of context, prove to be tentative and equivocal. He conceded that the Negro *might not* be his equal, or he said that the Negro *was not* his equal *in certain respects*. As an example, he named *color*, which certainly has a biological implication. But we cannot be certain that he was not merely expressing an aesthetic judgment or noting the social disadvantages of being black. He never used the word "inherent," or any of its equivalents, in discussing the alleged inferiority of the Negro, and it is not unlikely that he regarded such inferiority as resulting primarily from social oppression. In 1862, he compared blacks whose minds had been "clouded by slavery" with free Negroes "capable of thinking as white men." His last recorded disclaimer appears in a letter written as President-elect to a New York editor. He did not, it declared, "hold the black man to be the equal of the white, unqualifiedly." The final word throws away most of the declaration and scarcely suits a true ideological racist. Here there is a doubleness in the man as in the legend. It appears that he may have both absorbed and doubted, both shared and risen above, the racial doctrines of his time.

Lincoln, who had four sons and no other children, was presumably never asked the ultimate racist question. He did indicate a disinclination to take a Negro woman for his wife, agreeing with most of his white contemporaries in their aversion to miscegenation. Otherwise, there is little evidence of racism as an attitude or racism as a mode of behavior in his relations with Negroes. Frederick Douglass, sometimes a severe critic of his policies, said emphatically: "In all my interviews with Mr. Lincoln I was impressed with his entire freedom from popular prejudice against the colored race." During the war years in Washington, the social status of Negroes underwent a minor revolution, exemplified in the arrival of a black diplomat from the newly-recognized republic of Haiti. Lincoln, according to Current, "opened the White House to colored visitors as no President had done before, and he received them in a spirit which no President has matched since." Douglass and others appreciated not only his friendliness but his restraint. There was no effusiveness, no condescension. "He treated Negroes," says Quarles, "as they wanted to be treated—as human beings."

On the other hand, Lincoln in the 1850s did plainly endorse the existing system of white supremacy, except for slavery. He defended it, however, on grounds of expediency rather than principle, and on grounds of the incompatibility rather than the inequality of the races. Assuming that one race or the other must be on top, he admitted preferring that the superior position be *assigned* to the white race. Thus there was little association of institutional racism with ideological racism in his thinking.

Although Lincoln was by no means insensitive to the deprivation suffered by free Negroes, he saw little hope of improving their condition and in any case regarded slavery as a far greater wrong. Moreover, it appeared that any serious attack on institutional racism would raise the cry of "Negro equality," and thereby damage the antislavery cause.

But then, if he hated slavery so much, why did Lincoln not become an abolitionist? There are several obvious reasons: fear for the safety of the Union, political prudence, constitutional scruples, a personal distaste for extremism, and perplexity over what to do with freed slaves. In addition, it must be emphasized that Lincoln, as Lord Charnwood observed, "accepted the institutions to which he was born, and he enjoyed them." Social reform was a fairly new phenomenon in antebellum America. Only a relatively small number of persons had adopted it as a lifestyle, and Lincoln cannot be counted among them. This author of the greatest reform in American history was simply not a reformer by nature. He even acquiesced in the retention of slavery, provided that it should not be allowed to expand. For him, the paramount importance of the Republican anti-extension program lay in its symbolic meaning as a commitment to the principle of ultimate extinction. Some later generation, he thought, would then convert the principle into practice. What this amounted to, in a sense, was antislavery tokenism, but it also proved to be a formula for the achievement of political power, and with it, the opportunity to issue a proclamation of emancipation.

Of course, it has been said that Lincoln deserves little credit for emancipation—that he came to it tardily and reluctantly, under Radical duress. "Blacks have no reason to feel grateful to Abraham Lincoln," writes Julius Lester in *Look Out, Whitey! Black Power's Goin' Get Your Mama!* "How come it took him two whole years to free the slaves? His pen was sitting on his desk the whole time. All he had to do was get up one morning and say, 'Doggonnit! I think I'm gon' free the slaves today.' " But *which* morning? That turned out to be the real question.

Lincoln, it should be remembered, was under strong pressure from *both* sides on the issue of emancipation, and so the Radical clamor alone will not explain his ultimate decision. Nevertheless, when the war began, many Americans quickly realized that the fate of slavery might be in the balance. Veteran abolitionists rejoiced that history was at last marching to their beat, and Lincoln did not fail to read what he called "the signs of the times." Emancipation itself, as he virtually acknowledged, came out of the logic of events, not his personal volition, but the time and manner of its coming were largely his choice.

There had been enough Republicans to win the presidential election, but there were not enough to win the war. They needed help from Northern Democrats and border-state loyalists, who were willing to fight for the Union, but not for abolition. A premature effort at emancipation might alienate enough support to make victory impossible. It would then be self-defeating, because there could be no emancipation without victory. Lincoln's remarkable achievement, whether he fully intended it or not, was to proclaim emancipation in such a way as to minimize disaffection. He did so by allowing enough time for the prospect to become domesticated in the public mind, and by adhering scrupulously to the fiction that this momentous step was strictly a military measure. Much of the confusion about the Emancipation Proclamation results from taking too seriously Lincoln's verbal bowings and scrapings to the conservatives, while all the time he was backing steadily away from them.

The best illustration is his famous reply of August 22, 1862, to the harsh criticism of Horace Greeley, in which he said that his "paramount object" was to save the Union. "What I do about slavery, and the colored race," he declared, "I do because I believe it helps to save the Union; and what I forbear, I forbear because I do *not* believe it would help to save the Union." The most striking thing about the entire document is its dissimulation. Although Lincoln gave the impression that options were still open, he had in fact already made up his mind, had committed himself to a number of persons, had drafted the Proclamation. Why, then, write such a letter? Because it was not a statement of policy but instead a brilliant piece of propaganda in which Lincoln, as Benjamin P. Thomas says, "used Greeley's outburst to prepare the people for what was coming."

There were constitutional as well as political reasons, of course, for casting the Proclamation in military language and also for limiting its scope to those states and parts of states still in rebellion. In a sense, as historians fond of paradox are forever pointing out, it did not immediately liberate any slaves at all. And the Declaration of Independence, it might be added, did not immediately liberate a single colony from British rule. The people of Lincoln's time apparently had little doubt about the significance of the Proclamation. Jefferson Davis did not regard it as a mere scrap of paper, and neither did that most famous of former slaves, Frederick Douglass. He called it "the greatest event in our nation's history."

In the long sweep of that history, emancipation had come on, not sluggishly, but with a rush and a roar—over a period of scarcely eighteen months. Given more time to reflect on its racial implications, white America might have recoiled from the act. Lincoln himself had never been anything but a pessimist about the consequences of emancipation. Knowing full well the prejudices of his countrymen, he doubted that blacks and whites could ever live together amicably and on terms of equality. Over a century later, it is still too early to say that he was wrong.

With stark realism, Lincoln told a delegation of free Negroes in August 1862: "On this broad continent, not a single man of your race is made the equal of a single man of ours. Go where you are treated the best, and the ban is still upon you." And while blacks suffered from discrimination, whites suffered from the discord caused by the presence of blacks. "It is better for us both, therefore, to be separated," he said. But Lincoln apparently never visualized a segregated America. For him, separation meant colonization, which, as a disciple of Henry Clay, he had been advocating at least since 1852. Perhaps the strangest feature of Lincoln's presidential career was the zeal with which he tried to promote voluntary emigration of free Negroes to Africa or Latin America. He recommended it in his first two annual messages, urged it upon Washington's black leadership, and endorsed it in his Preliminary Emancipation Proclamation. He had foreign capitals circulated in a search for likely places of settlement. Furthermore, with funds supplied by Congress, he launched colonization enterprises in Haiti and Panama, both of which proved abortive.

What surprises one the most about these almost frantic activities is their petty scale. Lincoln implored the delegation of Washington Negroes to find him a hundred, or fifty, or even twenty-five families willing to emigrate. The Haitian project, if completely successful, would have accommodated just five thousand persons—about the number of Negroes born every two weeks in the United States. It would have required an enormous effort even to hold the black population stable at four and one-half million, let alone reduce it appreciably. Back in 1854, Lincoln had admitted the impracticability of colonization as anything but a long-range program. Why, then, did he betray such feverish haste to make a token beginning in 1862?

One interesting answer emerges from the chronology. Most of the colonization flurry took place during the second half of 1862. After that, Lincoln's interest waned, although, according to the dubious testimony of Benjamin F. Butler, it revived near the end of the war. After issuing the Emancipation Proclamation on January 1, 1863, Lincoln never made another public appeal for colonization. It appears that his spirited activity in the preceding six months may have been part of the process of conditioning the public mind for the day of jubilee. The promise of colonization had always been in part a means of quieting fears about the racial consequences of manumission. Offered as the ultimate solution to the problem of the black population, it could also serve as a psychological safety valve for the problem of white racism. This combination of purposes had inspired a number of Republican leaders to take up the cause of colonization in the late 1850s. One of them, the brother of his future postmaster-general, had told Lincoln then that the movement would "ward off the attacks made upon us about Negro equality."

In his second annual message of December 1, 1862, Lincoln said, "I cannot make it better known than it already is, that I strongly favor colonization." Then he continued in a passage that has received far less attention: "And yet I wish to say there is an objection urged against free colored persons remaining in the country, which is largely imaginary, if not sometimes malicious." He went on to discuss and minimize the fear that freedmen would displace white laborers, after which he wrote:

> But it is dreaded that the freed people will swarm forth, and cover the whole land? Are they not already in the land? Will liberation make them any more numerous? Equally distributed among the whites of the whole country, and there would be but one colored to seven whites. Could the one, in any way, greatly disturb the seven? There are many communities now, having more than one free colored person, to seven whites; and this, without any apparent consciousness of evil from it.

Here, along with his last public endorsement of colonization, was an eloquent plea for racial accommodation at home. The one might remain his ideal ultimate solution, but the other, he knew, offered the only hope in the immediate future.

Yet, if his plans for Reconstruction are an accurate indication, Lincoln at the time of his death had given too little consideration to the problem of racial adjustment and to the needs of four million freedmen. How much that would have changed if he had not been killed, has been the subject of lively controversy. Certainly his policies by 1865 no longer reflected all the views expressed in 1858, when he had repudiated both Negro citizenship and Negro suffrage. Now, by fiat of his administration in defiance of the Dred Scott Decision, blacks were citizens of the United States, and he had begun in a gentle way to press for limited black enfranchisement. He had overcome his initial doubts about enlisting Negroes as fighting soldiers, was impressed by their overall performance, and thought they had earned the right to vote.

Lincoln once told Charles Sumner that on the issue of emancipation they were only four to six weeks apart. The relative earliness of his first favorable remarks about Negro enfranchisement suggests that he had again read the "signs of the times." It is not difficult to believe that after the war he would have continued closer to the Sumners than to the conservatives whom he had placated but never followed for long. And one can scarcely doubt that his postwar administration would have been more responsive to Negro aspirations than Andrew Johnson's proved to be.

But for several reasons Lincoln's role was likely to be more subdued than we might expect from the Great Emancipator. First, during peacetime, with his powers and responsibilities as Commander-in-Chief greatly reduced, he probably would have yielded more leadership to Congress in the old Whig tradition. Second, at the time of his death, he still regarded race relations as primarily a local matter, just as he had maintained during the debates with Douglas: "I do not understand there is any place where an alteration of the social and political relations of the Negro and white man can be made except in the State Legislature." Third, Negroes as Negroes were nearly always connotative in Lincoln's thinking. Their welfare, though by no means a matter of indifference to him, had never been, and was not likely to become, his "paramount object." They were, in the words of Frederick Douglass, "only his stepchildren."

Finally, in his attitude toward the wrongs of the free Negro, Lincoln had none of the moral conviction that inspired his opposition to slavery. He never seems to have suspected that systematic racial discrimination might be, like slavery, a strain on the national honor and a crime against mankind. Whether that is the measure of his greatness must be left to each one's personal taste. Of Copernicus we might say: What a genius! He revolutionized our understanding of the solar system. Or: What an ignoramus! He did not understand the rest of the universe at all.

17

Jefferson Davis—Leader Without Legend

FRANK E. VANDIVER

● Jefferson Davis was the only President the Confederacy ever had. In April 1865, when General Robert E. Lee informed him that Richmond could no longer be held, Davis fled southward with his cabinet in hopes of reaching Texas and continuing the fight west of the Mississippi River. While disguised as a woman, he was captured by the Union Army, placed in irons, and imprisoned for two years in Fort Monroe. The former chief executive was indicted for high treason against the United States but never actually brought to trial. Almost alone among Southern leaders he never asked for amnesty and was never restored to American citizenship. (Congress finally restored him to citizenship in the 1970s.) An unreconstructed Confederate who never gave up his belief in the Lost Cause, Davis died in New Orleans in 1889 as a man without a country.

Historians have been deeply divided about Davis's effectiveness as Confederate President. Everyone agrees that the tall, slender, and handsome West Point graduate was strong-willed and articulate. Some add that he was nation-minded and world-minded, a natural leader of integrity, virtue, and high principle who was misunderstood because of the prejudice of Northerners and because of the need of Southerners to find a scapegoat. Others argue that his reputation as a bungler and incompetent is well-deserved and that his constant interference in military matters undermined his generals and seriously compromised the effectiveness of his armies. Frank Vandiver, a noted military analyst who has written of many Civil War campaigns, traces the popular and

Frank E. Vandiver, "Jefferson Davis—Leader Without Legend," *Journal of Southern History*, XLIII (1977), 3–18. Copyright 1977 by the Southern Historical Association. Reprinted by permission of the Managing Editor. Footnotes have been omitted.

professional assessments of Davis and concludes with a generally favorable estimate of the tragic figure who has been
called "the most misunderstood man in history."

No saintly aura buffers Jefferson Davis from the barbs of judgment.
Precious little that he did as President of the Confederate States of
America is sanctified. So he stands from the past as the most curious
of chieftains—a man without legend in the *Oxford English Dictionary*
sense of legend as the life of a saint. He is not, to be sure, a man
without account. More cold dissection, carping, rebuke, harsh study,
critical interpretation, has been aimed at him than at perhaps any
other leader of the modern era. He is worn by analysis beyond reality.
Minute scrutiny has denied legend and has wrought a Davis of myth
and mystery. Something of his mythic future might have been
glimpsed forming during the war, especially in the first of the "histories" of the Confederacy.

Edward Alfred Pollard, curmudgeon extraordinary, Richmonder,
editor of the *Examiner*, early rejected hope for Davis and prophesied
doom for a cause trusted to him. Dislike and suspicion poisoned Pollard's eye and cost some of the impact of his occasionally valid criticism. But things he saw wrong with the President had the power of
popularity and the ring of repetition. Davis clearly aimed at des-
potism; his judgment erred everywhere; as a diplomat he lacked
suavity; as an administrator, reality; as a war leader, sense; as a man,
charity. Pollard's convictions grew as the war progressed, and he
advanced them beyond his newspaper. In 1862 his *First Year of the
War* appeared, followed by annual volumes, each more anti-Davis than
the last. In 1866 Pollard culled his multivolume diatribe into one,
The Lost Cause. Now the world could read of a cause elevated by the
sacrifices of southern women, by the heroism of all gray-clad soldiers
and lost by the perfidy of Jefferson Davis.

Pollard carried his indictment further in 1869 with his *Life of
Jefferson Davis, with a Secret History of the Southern Confederacy,
Gathered "Behind the Scenes in Richmond,"* Jefferson Davis should
have a truthful and acute biographer," Pollard allows in his preface,
and then boasts of his impartiality. Once accused of "hostility" to

Davis, he now "is able and willing to do exact justice" to his subject. In addressing the main question of *"Who were responsible for the failure of the Southern Confederacy?"* Pollard argues that "Responsibility must rest somewhere in hsitory" and sees it rising naturally to higher officials. Consequently, "in regarding Mr. Davis as the prime cause of the failure of the South in the late war, the author has but simply recognized and submitted to the great law of logic in historical composition:—that, in political affairs, where a certain result is clearly not an accident or misadventure, but must have come from a well defined cause, that cause ultimately and inevitably rests in the head of the government." Never had logic been so convenient. Davis led the Confederacy and lost; ergo, he engineered defeat. The interpretation stuck.

Later students who approached Davis favorably were finally engulfed by Pollard's lingering prejudice. Elisabeth Brown Cutting's *Jefferson Davis, Political Soldier* is an example. Cutting writes almost sentimentally about much of Davis's life, maintains a casual detachment amid some of the thornier Confederate problems, waxes almost maudlin at the end of her story. Davis's courage, his willed triumph over pain, his constancy under stress all find echo in her pages. And yet, at the end, there is an eight-page "Epilogue" which rejects sympathy and calls up once more all the faults and flaws, the lapses and misdeeds, in the manner of Pollard redivivus. "Loyalty" and "devotion" were allowed Davis. "Affairs of state were his occupation," Cutting asserts, "but only in a restricted sense was he a statesman."

> He was not a great executive. He could not delegate power, but he could heed the representations of the man who best understood that his vanity must be fed. . . . Davis was neither resourceful nor foresighted in his capacity of Commander-in-Chief of his army. He was unequal to dealing in large figures for the magnitude of the task demanded. . . . He had always the recourse of the egoist, an immovable faith in his own decisions. . . . His vanity admitted of no rebuke, and he recognized a mental equal only when their ideas coincided. . . . He was a leader of a cause but not of men.

Cutting suffered divided sentiments throughout her book. Good things somehow had to be balanced against "objective" things lest Davis loom beyond the dim confines of his reality. Her struggle and her perception show some growth beyond Pollard's simple venom. Yet her try for scholarly impartiality worked its own distortion. The illusion of new fairness gave added credence to old criticisms. The chilly near-statesman made reckless by ambition and aloof by hauteur stood revealed now by records, a creature made real by research.

As any scholar could have guessed, research revealed a fuller man than Pollard's shabby mannequin. Details of Davis's life fleshed him for history and offered glimpses of a nimble mind and a curiously difficult personality. Davis's character obviously had vast impact on the Confederacy, but his soul lacked some evoking spark—he was an incomplete man, flawed beyond success. That discovery was to prove crucial in carving Davis's special niche in history.

Cutting's work had added importance since it was based not only on new research in foreign archives, but also on three earlier books— William E. Dodd's near classic *Jefferson Davis*, Hamilton J. Eckenrode's strange Nordic polemic, *Jefferson Davis, President of the South*, and Allen Tate's *Jefferson Davis: His Rise and Fall*. Dodd's still rings truer than most studies of Davis in its unadorned try for the truth. Dodd ground no axes, simply tried to see the man lurking in the dusty myths of losing. In that quest he came close to giving Davis a history. Both Eckenrode and Tate use Davis for their own purposes. Eckenrode sees Davis as the leader of a failed racial crusade and hence as bearing guilt far beyond his time. All the old charges are leveled and an old conclusion reached: "Jefferson Davis was a great man, even if he was not great enough to triumph." Tate, too, sees the end of the Confederacy as the end of the original America; out of the cauldron of Civil War came a new alignment of Union, one different in tone and temperament, in soul and substance from the hope of the Founding Fathers. Tate assigns Davis less perfidy in engineering the loss of American innocence. He glosses his criticism—which reads familiarly —in kindness. Yet it was Davis who lost a world he lacked the vision to grasp. Pollard's old stamp prevailed; Cutting followed in a well-cut scholarly wake.

Robert McElroy, in his two-volume *Jefferson Davis: The Unreal and the Real*, labeled the role historians were giving Davis—"The Scapegoat." McElroy's impressive sifting of Dunbar Rowland's ten-volume collection of Davis letters, papers, and documents seemed to confirm an awful sterility of achievement. In an episodic, oddly discursive book McElroy gives Davis a new patriotism—that of defender of an older Union. Davis's views of America, of the right of secession, were of lasting value in McElroy's eyes; the defeat of the South damaged the ideas not a whit. The war McElroy treats almost as an anticlimax. He believes that the scapegoat's mantle was thrown over Davis by a frustrated Southland unable to accept reality. This perception, doubtless, is partly sound, but McElroy misses an important point of his own work: he, too, makes Davis a scapegoat, makes him the stout champion of dying ideals dear to McElroy. Davis's postwar life stretched in dusty tedium as he guarded the ghosts of the past.

What makes Davis so ready a scapegoat? What makes him so malleable a subject for historical role-givers? The fact that his cause was lost? Possibly. But the most likely reason is his utter lack of legend. Lincoln suffers from "picklock biographers" more fearsomely by far than Davis, yet his legend only increases his identity. Davis has lost his identity—he is virtually a historical nonperson. So he easily fits any role historians may devise for him.

Pollard and most of his successors have allowed Davis scarcely even a loser's mite. They dissect the dry bones of his Confederate administration, the symmetry of his prewar years, to find out how he lost the war, the South, Camelot, the future—whatever they happen to lament. They have, of course, made him more than a scapegoat—he is a kind of southern Barabbas. Sharp analysis of his poor humanity simplifies history. Davis's contemporaries, represented by Pollard, needed to fix blame on the President lest they confront their own failures.

Historical fads change. In the cascades of good, bad, and indifferent studies emerging during the Civil war Centennial, a new Jefferson Davis made a shadowy appearance. Simplistic symbolism, simplistic causation, eroded under the impact of the consensus school of historical studies. Davis as a single cause of defeat no longer seemed reasonable. He might well have contributed to the South's losing, but he was surely just one of multiple causes. This view gained some headway in the works of Allan Nevins and David M. Potter. Some historians still recall the old Davis—Bell I. Wiley and Clifford Dowdey come to mind—but Shelby Foote's monumental *Civil War* pretty well sets the new Davis mold. In this mold he ceases to be a surrogate of failings and begins to stand for himself. Thomas B. Alexander and

Richard E. Beringer's important *Anatomy of the Confederate Congress* tends to confirm the new image of Davis.

Fortunately, the emerging Davis appears to escape mawkishness. The idolatry of early Civil War days, when he was heroically distorted in schoolbooks for little Rebels, the cloying regret of a thousand funeral orations, the venom of Pollard, all are fading in a new awareness of complex causes of behavior. There is, to be sure, the ne'er-do-wrong view of Hudson Strode, but his work has become almost a benchmark of excess. The new Davis is a flawed man, too finely haughty for charisma, who holds his opinions too well for fair argument, and who stands too lofty for affection. But he comes now as a real leader, even a strong President. David Herbert Donald, in the most recent edition of his and James Garfield Randall's admirable *Civil War and Reconstruction*, gives the new Davis full play and concludes that "much of the criticism of the Confederate President fails to take into account the insuperable difficulties of his position and to realize that no other Southern political leader even approached Davis in stature."

A conviction that Davis somehow failed of fair treatment at history's hands led the late Allan Nevins to support a proposal to collect and publish the papers of the Confederate President anew. True, Dunbar Rowland had published ten volumes of papers in the 1920s, but a careful check of his pages against originals in the Huntington Library convinced Nevins that deliberate distortion marked the earlier collection; and he believed also that much new material must have been discovered since Rowland's work. He was right. The Jefferson Davis Association, a nonprofit organization chartered in Texas, started collecting in 1964, has developed sources of collections beyond Rowland's, and has issued two volumes of what may well be an endless series. This new Davis scholarship, focused as it is on sources, is beginning to take Davis on his own terms and reinforces the recent imagery. The man he thought he was is sometimes the man of his critics, but not often; nor is he often the man of his admirers. He shows early some irritating qualities that would have pleased Pollard. A whiff of legalism tinges his West Point career, but his vaunted prissiness is softened by troubles at Benny Haven's tavern. Legalism tinges his early army service, legalism infected by a love of regulations—Davis may even have liked filling out forms! His early Mississippi

political career shows growing interest in issues, a flair for public
speaking, and a tendency toward rigid conviction. Honesty and a
fair mind are hallmarks from the start.

From the early evidence, what are likely to be the full lineaments
of this newer Davis? Documents already on hand tend to confirm his
punctilio, his statesman's dismissal of petty politicking, his finely tuned
sense of constitutionalism, his complex nature. These documents, from
far-scattered hoards, dimly show a Davis different from any yet revealed. This emerging Davis may force a legend of his own. Its full
outline cannot be predicted, but some elements may be guessed from
established evidence.

Old flaws will be granted. Davis will stand aloof, restive, above the
haggling of part-time patriots, yet "sensitive" to critics who failed
to see devotion in every act and screed. Misplaced friendship he
will still hold beyond the public good, and his brittlely legalistic
arguments will continue to alienate men of goodwill and many future
historians.

Much of the new Davis will have to come from shadings, from
analyses of things he did that were untypical, either of himself or of
his fellow southrons. Throughout the years of his presidential service
he ranked as a "doer." Business came first with him; hours were
spent in his office in the Confederate White Houses, in the executive
offices, reading the whelm of correspondence, reports, summaries,
orders, which daily cascaded across his desks. The Confederate President found, as did Lincoln, that Americans had little hesitation in
bombarding their leader with wartime's every problem. Davis probably spent too much time wrestling with trivia better handled by a
cabinet member or by some other functionary. Awkwardness in delegation made up a good deal of Davis's business. But much that came
to him did require presidential notice. Military and legal matters
claimed most of his attention. A Pollard might suggest that Davis's
fetish with details led him to sign commissions even for second
lieutenants, but the charge ignores duty.

Business of the President came often from constitutional obligation.
Matters of strategy, logistics, important personnel questions, all filtered
to his office. Each item received at least a glance, often a long endorsement which might analyze complex constitutional issues. Hours were
spent simply seeing people. Again, some Pollards suggest that Davis

shut himself away from the citizenry, even from Congress, that he hid in his book-strewn "snuggery" to cherish the portents of fame—but the streams of casual callers, the crowds of congressmen trooping to his office or to the White House belie the accusation. Special-interest groups visited in numbers; special pleaders often arrived alone. Cabinet members were at least weekly visitors to the White House. Those who saw Davis in relative privacy saw an executive different from the marble man of Pollard's projection. In the comfort of a closed circle Davis waxed warm, witty, and charmed visitors into zealots. In his special diction Davis made pure reason into patriotism.

Something of that witchery Davis worked in extemporaneous remarks before large audiences—it was a talent he scarcely knew he had until the inaugural trip to Montgomery, Alabama. In countless talks from his railroad car Davis found a different oratory and the people a different man—fire from such calm touched hearers with hope. But before Congress, where events so much demanded suasion, Davis stood often like a preacher. Why? Did the Confederate Congress overawe a longtime United States senator? No, he was not overawed. He simply expected quick support and understanding from fellow patriots. And he went to Congress filled with an anguished love for his country and his cause, a love as deep as Lincoln's for the Union, a love that somehow parched his eloquence and made him a strangely muffled leader. He learned much in office; the need to cajole Congress he could not bring himself to learn.

Davis and the Confederate Congress came to an unfortunate mutual disbelief—they stared at each other across a widening gulf of troubles. Distrust grew in direct ratio to bad news about the war. Davis thought congressmen should do what was right simply because it was right; congressmen thought the President should explain himself and his program of emergency nationalism so that state-rights constituents would know the need for temporary revolution. Instead of communication—to use a modern word—both sides got declamations.

Davis could persuade individual congressmen; he should have brought small groups to the White House on a regular basis—for discussions, briefings, for mutual complaint. This smacked too much of politicking to a statesman who knew his country's needs. Articulate with a few, even with many, Davis seemed dumb to his Congress. It was a grievous fault, surely, but his willingness to go to the people of the Confederacy, his increasingly passionate correspondence, his public exhortations, were marks of growth in a highly private person. They were hallmarks, too, of a working President, who realized he had to grow into a different man to fill a different role.

Evidence of Davis's hard work came in every facet of his job. If southerners were indolent, as so many Yankees said, Davis seemed hardly a southerner. In his role as chief administrator of the government he lavished hours on filling offices, setting precedents, hearing plans and programs, dictating policy. Early he confronted the cabinet problem. Ability he wanted as the foremost quality of cabinet members, but politics dictated state representation as the first consideration in cabinet making. Even so, Davis picked men better than his critics admit. Far from a cranky lot of marplots, the cabinet was made of men of goodwill and competence, who managed a far-flung line, a disparate country, a tiny fleet for four years. Changes came in the membership, but mainly men of accomplishment aided Davis. Much administrative success came from lower-level management in each of the departments. A civil service, which relied only slightly on experienced exiles from Washington, developed early. Davis, like Lincoln, found energetic bureaucrats vital to the war. He managed them well enough, or rather, he allowed his cabinet to manage them. Clusters of government workers moved into Montgomery, thence to Richmond, and their numbers grew with war's complexities.

These workers, ferreting papers in all bureaus, did the daily business of government. Their doings pretty well prove that Davis did not supervise everything—too may details were attended to by too many people for the President's total comprehension. Many good and bad things were done by the burgeoning bureaucracy. Goaded by the apparent need for security in a city teeming with every kind of human, including Yankees, Richmond at length took on some trappings of a police city-state. Special detectives under General John Henry Winder imposed varying degrees of martial and kangaroo law. The whole country suffered restrictions on civilian travel. Complaints spilled through the national press, and Davis reaped some of the blame. All misdeeds of the administration were his own; few of the good deeds went to his credit.

Davis deserves praise as an executive. His government, organized from nothing, ran midst alarms, emergencies, crises of every kind; the machinery groaned and shuddered often, but it ran for four years well enough to hold the armies and the country together.

As a war leader Davis showed courage, considerable flexibility and imagination. Contrary to long-held notions, Davis did evolve and keep a war plan consistent with southern circumstance and with sound strategic theory: the "offensive-defensive." He groped for his plan, made a serious error early in advocating state and area defense, but learned from that mistake. His strategic ideas were bold enough for Confederate practice. His organizational ideas reflected growing awareness of the different nature of mass war. Quickly he appreciated the relative isolation of Richmond and the communication problems which resulted. He sought ways to delegate management of operations. First, he tried the familiar scheme of departmental commands designed along geographical lines. When this system proved inadequate, Davis devised a novel adaptation which showed his capacity to adjust to emergencies—the idea of a theater command. Twice he sought to apply his concept; twice it failed. He was undone by the human element. General Joseph Eggleston Johnston, first offered a vast satrapy from western Georgia to the Mississippi and from the Gulf to whatever northern boundary he could reach, missed the fullness of his opportunity and sought instead traditional army command. Later Pierre Gustave Toutant Beauregard, too, missed the opportunity—strange, for so vast a chance should have piqued his Gallic verve. If either Johnston or Beauregard had grasped the chance the President offered, a bold conception in command might have shown something of the strength it gathered in the Second World War. Human frailty ruined an idea ahead of its time, an idea which shows Davis's martial innovativeness at its best.

Innovation could be seen in his earliest military notions expressed to the Confederate Congress. Asserting that "all we ask is to be let alone," the President prophesied trouble. Hints of a coming storm Davis glimpsed in Lincoln's inaugural address and thought there was every chance for a "war of extermination on both sides." Supporting his expectations, Davis asked for an impressive folio of military laws. Congress accepted his lead and created staff departments for the army and navy, authorized regular land and naval establishments, and went so far as to agree with Davis's demand for provisional forces.

The provisional force notion had merit. An army of twelve-month volunteers would have flexibility for command experiments and would avoid the problem of a large standing army. Davis urged, too, the acceptance of volunteers organized by the states, the acceptance of militia units, even on short enlistment terms, and the control by his government of all military property in the states. Congress agreed to all these requests and also gathered to Confederate control all military operations in the country.

Familiarity with martial matters gave Davis a special interest in creating the Confederacy's army. In the early weeks of nationhood he worked to push organized units to points of concentration and have them ready for shipment to threatened points on southern borders. The government had thousands, even possibly half a million, men ready for the colors—and had barely two hundred thousand arms. Davis realized that time worked against the hasty patriotism everywhere apparent. While he struggled with diplomacy in Washington to solve the touchy issue of Forts Sumter and Pickens, he worried that diplomacy lacked excitement. Zealots for war would lose interest in protracted tranquillity. By mid-April 1861 the Sumter crisis rested not only on Federal intentions but also on Rebel enthusiasm. The solemn cabinet decision to fire on the Charleston fort was forced as much by the pressure of apathy as by sovereignty. General Beauregard's first shell launched a train of events which proved quickly Davis's wisdom in military legislation. Lincoln called for 75,000 volunteers; Davis for the 100,000 authorized by Congress.

War sparked a new enthusiasm; men trooped in from the far reaches of the Confederacy. Davis, concerned especially for the border areas, funneled men northward as Virginia joined the new nation. He thought the Old Dominion would be the coming battleground. It was, and the early battles were encouraging. First Manassas in July brought a triumph with dismal results. Southerners were now convinced that latter-day minute men could lay aside the plow, take up the musket, and run the Yankees off. Victory brought happiness and dangerously lowered guard. The President, fully aware of defeat's probable effect in the North, urged redoubled efforts—but his sobriety found few adherents in the South. By winter troubles ringed the Confederacy. Bad news came in batches; curious failures dulled southern martial sheen. Early in the new year, 1862, Forts Henry and Donelson on the Tennessee and Cumberland rivers fell; next went Roanoke

Island in a clutch of ill omens. Twelve-month enlistments were about to expire; tedium and defeat eroded patriotism. How many men would reenlist? Prognostications by the War Department were not good. Volunteering yielded to anxiety. The armies might well dissolve. That looming possibility demanded the firmest executive leadership. As the permanent government went to work in Richmond in February 1862 the new Congress found the administration increasingly urging some kind of conscription law. Davis pushed hard for drafting all white men between eighteen and thirty-five, and especially for extending the service of men already in the ranks. It was a tough stand, one likely to be extremely unpopular in a laissez-faireist, extremely loose Confederacy. But the President pressed his needs, and in April the first draft law in American history was enacted—to remarkably light opposition.

As the war continued and manpower dwindled Davis increased his efforts to sustain the armies. The use of Negroes as laborers, then as special auxiliaries to the armies, he advocated, and, at last, he openly urged the drafting of blacks into Confederate ranks. His persistence in the matter of arming the slaves illustrates something of his perception in leadership. A discussion among generals of the Army of Tennessee in January 1864 centered on filling depleted legions with Negroes—and the discussion erupted into charges and counter-charges of treason, subversion, and other heinous intents. Davis, who received a bulky package of these protests, quashed the argument, refused to penalize anyone, and soothed ruffled social sensibilities. Why blacks should not be drafted for national defense he could not see, especially when the enemy used them in war against the South. In a perceptive passage to Congress he suggested that Negroes were more than chattels. "The slave . . . bears another relation to the State—that of a person. . . . In this respect [army service] the relation of person predominates so far as to render it doubtful whether the private right of property can consistently and beneficially be continued, and it would seem proper to acquire for the public service the entire property in the labor of the slave." Taking over the national slave supply would bring special confusions. "Should he [the slave] be retained in servitude," Davis asked, "or should his emancipation be held out to him as a reward for faithful service?" Davis advocated freedom after service as trained auxiliaries in supply and medical services. He went on to suggest that it might be necessary to put blacks in the ranks and explained his thinking: "A broad moral distinction exists between the use of slaves as soldiers in defense of their homes and the incitement of the same persons to insurrection against their masters. The one is justifiable, if necessary, the other is iniquitous and unworthy of a civilized people." Quietly he kept the debate going, urged discussion as he could in correspondence, and hoped that realities would change customs.

In the last months of the war he got his way as a few companies of Negroes drilled in gray uniforms and under the Stars and Bars. Their debt to servitude worried Davis, and he urged a reluctant Congress to grant freedom to every black Rebel soldier. Some of the states agreed with this highly revolutionary notion, and so did General Robert Edward Lee.

Radical change had been part and parcel of Davis's experience from his earliest days in the Confederate White House. When first he came to Montgomery he saw clearer than most the absurdity of southern circumstance. To wife Varina he noted in February 1861 that "We are without machinery, without means, and threatened by a powerful opposition." Refusing to "despond," he sought to build strength in unity—and unity seemed uncommon in a cause of confederation.

Next, certainly, to girding for war, Davis faced the task of nation-making. He had to do it almost alone—the various states pranced in high fettle, talked of the Confederacy, but acted with a truculent sense of new sovereignty.

He began the call for a country shortly after arriving in Montgomery, Alabama, on February 16, 1861. Summoned by a cheering throng to the Exchange Hotel's balcony, he spoke of a new brotherhood. "Brethren of the Confederate States of America," he labeled his listeners, "for now we are brethren, not in name, merely, but in fact—men of one flesh, one bone, one interest, one purpose." That theme he echoed again in his first inaugural address two days later. "To increase the power, develop the resources, and promote the happiness of the Confederacy," he prescribed "so much of homogeneity that the welfare of every portion shall be the aim of the whole. When this does not exist, antagonisms are engendered which . . . result in separation."

Unity ran through most of his public utterances. Stressing "common cause," Davis welcomed new states, preached the need for cohesion as he increased his private correspondence, and in several "swings around the Confederacy" he argued for nationalism. A group of western congressmen, harping on the need for separate state protection during the hectic campaigns of 1863, got the national catechism in blunt words from the President. It was a "fatal error" he said, to suppose "that this great war can be waged by the Confederate States *severally* and not *unitedly* with the least hope of success."

Just as William Gladstone could proclaim at Newcastle, England, in October 1862 that Jefferson Davis had made a country, Davis could proclaim in December 1863 that adversity had made Confederates out of southerners. "We have been united as a people never were united under like circumstances before," he boasted to Congress, and added that "the patriotism of the people has proved equal to every sacrifice demanded by their country's need."

But through the grinding year 1864—"the year the war broke up" as one anonymous Rebel put it—Davis fought growing despair from all corners of his country. Governors, influential citizens, generals, soldiers, people with boundless advice, all received presidential exhortations. Davis's eloquence grew with crisis; his letters to carpers were measured rebukes; his replies to state executives still prating state rights read like primers of federalism; his thanks for praise and comfort ran deep and sincere. But criticism mounted as the cause declined. He bore criticism poorly in the best of times; as disasters gathered his patience thinned until, at least, his acerb reaction transformed into a kind of acceptance of martyrdom—witness some sad words to General Lee on April 1, 1865: "The distrust is increasing and embarrasses in many ways." Against such old foes as Governors Joseph Emerson Brown of Georgia and Zebulon Baird Vance of North Carolina he turned almost at bay. These men were aware of the trending and still fought unity. Baffled by disloyalty he combatted it with logic—and logic rang hollowly in the dark Wilderness and was lost in the angry sieging at Petersburg. Davis became a kind of conscience of his country as he watched its substance ebb. The congealed calm so long preserved cracked at the end, and an unexpected passion spilled into his last shining vision of a future in which the South would win and be free. It was pitiful and human, and it lent nobility to his last public message. Lee had gone from Richmond, the government fled to nameless places, the enemy swarmed everywhere—and yet "Let us but will it, and we are free; and who, in the light of the past, dare doubt your purpose in the future? . . . Let us not, then, despond, my countrymen, but, relying on the never-failing mercies and protecting care of our God, let us meet the foe with fresh defiance, with unconquered and unconquerable hearts."

In the avalanche of enmity that came with defeat, most of Davis's own substance was lost. His enemies, Union and Confederate, used his errors as the stuff of myth. He symbolized everything tawdry the times and the Pollards required—sinful southern arrogance, haughty Confederate incompetence. An image he had carefully fashioned throughout his life was ignored by northerners needing a traitor and by southerners needing a scapegoat. Who cared that he wanted to be the epitome of the Southern Gentleman; who cared, for that matter, about Southern Gentlemen in the wreckage of their era? He wrapped the guise of Southern Gentleman around him, though, a cloak against fate—it was a guise he began building after Sarah Knox Taylor Davis's death. In grief and guilt, he sought to make himself something she would cherish, something his hating father-in-law might admire. The role took form in Congress, in Pierce's cabinet, especially in the United States Senate years, until, at last, Davis could stand in that forum as the full embodiment of a class. In those comfortable years he championed state rights with fiery rhetoric and firm belief. As Confederate President he turned against state rights and became a Rebel nationalist; still, though, the Gentleman incarnate.

Historians have recently noted Davis's move to nationalism—some as a sign of growth, others as a sign of expediency. But none have so far noticed the unusually revolutionary nature of Davis's shift in loyalty.

If Davis comes to have a legend it may be as a gentleman revolutionary. Traditionally pictured as a constitutionalist trapped in a revolutionary moment, he is often berated for sticking too closely to the law. He stuck to the law all right, but in his hands the constitution became a revolutionary document.

Let me try to illustrate the point by first mentioning a recent paper by my colleague, Professor Harold M. Hyman, in which he asserts "that until the American Revolution is understood more clearly as a revolution in government *procedures* and *institutions* rather than as an overturning of class, economic, racial, or sex relationships, its applicability to the present will be limited."

Davis's revolution must be seen first as one of procedures before it can be understood as one of institutions and as, finally, a full rending of a people and a way of life. He took the Confederate constitutions for what they said they were: the supreme law of the land. Under that conviction he turned the law against the states, first by creating a national army out of state forces, an army loyal to the Confederacy. Next he worked to build a sense in the southern people of a higher loyalty than state rights—a sense of Confederateness. In doing this he fought the governors on economic, military, and political issues, even, at last, on social issues; he fought, too, the natural independence of fellow southrons to devise a war plan consistent with reality and with theory; he fought himself to change his ideal Southern Gentleman into a Confederate.

Far from being a slave to the constitution, Davis early schemed to rise above it or go around it. In a message to Congress on November 18, 1861, Davis urged the building of a railroad between Danville, Virginia, and Greensboro, North Carolina. If the military necessity was accepted by Congress, Davis had no doubt that "the action of the Government will not be restrained by the constitutional objection which would attach to a work for commercial purposes." If the war demanded rationalizing the constitution, Davis rationalized. The clearest example concerns finances and came in a message to Congress in December 1863. Reviewing the general failure of war taxation to that time, Davis bluntly said that land and slaves made up roughly two-thirds of the Confederacy's taxable property, and they ought to be taxed. Constitutional objections had prevented it, he thought, objections with some validity. Taxes on land and slaves were considered direct taxes, and the constitution forbade such levies without a census on which to apportion the burden. There had been no census, and there was not likely to be one. Should the government, as a consequence, not tax land and slaves? To that question Davis aimed his nimblest analysis. "The general intent of our constitutional charter is unquestionably that the property of the country is to be taxed . . . for the common defense, and the special mode provided by levying this tax is impracticable from unforeseen causes. It is in my

judgment our primary duty to execute the general intent expressed
. . . , and we cannot excuse ourselves for the failure to fulfill this
obligation on the ground that we are unable to perform it in the
precise mode pointed out." By that later stage of the war Davis's
priorities were coming into clear focus. Nothing mattered save victory.

That certainty sparked the President's attitude toward using slaves
in the army, even if slavery went as a result, and toward reconstructing the country along industrial lines. With uncommon boldness
Davis sponsored such tough policies as the tax in kind, direct war
taxation, the full-scale use of impressments, government control of
the railroads, commandeering of cargo space on blockade runners.
He even offered to trade slavery for recognition in February 1865. He
did these things because they were necessary for the war effort. He
knew what the war was about—independence. And he knew that
old-style gentlemen were yielding to a new breed of businessmen
whose sights were on the future. He was one of them.

What substance can there be to a Davis legend? To have substance, a legend ought to be based on some kind of remarkable
achievement, some kind of heroic deed. Was he a man who rose to
challenge—as do so many American Presidents? Certainly, he rose
to crises, and they increased daily into an unrelieved wave of woe.
He bore the burden with unwavering calm. Personal and official
tragedy never induced panic in the President—in travail he found
personal triumph.

Is personal triumph sufficient for legend? Probably not, but there
is another dimension for measure. Did Davis succeed in making a
Confederate nation? If so, then he deserves rank with a handful of
legendary Americans who changed history. Gladstone thought Davis
had succeeded in 1862, and Davis himself had no doubts of success
by 1863. The world noted Confederate deeds for four years. The
Confederacy's fate was sealed in battle. Its history, though, Davis
helped preserve in the hard years after the war, and its history is re-
written afresh by each generation. Persistent history is best proof of
success. About his own role in making that lasting legacy, Davis might
say, as he once said to Beauregard, "Enough was done for glory, and
the measure of duty was full."

What more does legend need?

18

Reconstruction in Richmond

JOHN T. O'BRIEN

• The Civil War was going very badly for the Confederate States of America in early April 1865, when President Jefferson Davis, attending Sunday morning services at St. Paul's Church in Richmond, was handed an urgent message from his great strategist, Robert E. Lee. The note was brief, but the implications were enormous: the battered Army of Northern Virginia could no longer hold Petersburg and its vital railroad connections against the relentless hammer blows of General Ulysses S. Grant's mighty Army of the Potomac. With Petersburg gone, Richmond would surely follow. A reluctant Davis ordered the Confederate government to evacuate the capital.

For four years Richmond had been the symbol of secession and defiance, the target of repeated thrusts by a succession of Northern generals. Appropriately, the Southern capital was also the home of perhaps fifteen thousand blacks. When the Union Army triumphantly entered the city, the newly liberated slaves fell to their knees in thanksgiving. Deliverance was theirs. And to make the message of freedom even clearer, President Abraham Lincoln himself came to Richmond to pronounce: "Liberty is your birthright."

All across the South, black men and women were flocking to the cities, jubilant about the end of bondage but uncertain about the future. The following article considers the two crucial months immediately following the establishment of United States Army control over the defeated capital. In particular, John T. O'Brien focuses on the freedmen and their struggle for political and civil equality. Was the goal utopian and impossible of achievement because of generations of

Reprinted by permission of the editor from the *Virginia Magazine of History and Biography* 89 (1981), 259–281.

slavery? Or did national and local leadership lose a rare opportunity to bring justice to all Americans?

Several recent studies of slave life call for a reassessment of the impact of emancipation on slaves and free blacks and a reexamination of their role in reconstructing the South. Sambo has been banished to the scrapheap of discarded historiographic constructs, and with him has gone the vision of freedmen wandering throughout the South dazed by the suddenness of their emancipation and bewildered by the range of choice and weight of responsibility thrust upon them. It now appears that enslaved Afro-Americans emerged from bondage with a distinctive culture and with enduring familial and social structures, and a few historians, notably Lawrence Levine and Herbert Gutman, have begun to explore the effects of emancipation upon Afro-American culture and society. Further study of black communities in the Reconstruction period will doubtless extend and modify these historians' findings and present a fuller picture both of black life in the late antebellum period and the black response to the new conditions created by the abolition of slavery. As well, such studies should inquire whether freedmen were able to shape the tone, substances, and direction of the Reconstruction experiment where they lived. Emancipation exercised a mighty influence over the lives of Richmond, Virginia, blacks, permitting them to act openly in ways previously prohibited. Moreover, their activities as free men and women shaped the manner in which their city was reconstructed. The following paper outlines their responses to liberation from the day the shackles of bondage were broken in April 1865 to their protest in June 1865 against oppressive restoration policies. In Richmond freedmen benefited from emancipation and participated in shaping the Reconstruction experiment.

Over 14,000 blacks lived in Richmond in 1860, 2,000 more than had lived there in 1850 and several thousand less than were on hand when Union troops entered the city in 1865. Much remains to be learned about the interior life of the antebellum community, but a broad characterization of the slave and free black community can be drawn which reveals something about their lives within the peculiar institution and something of their later experiences as a free people. The oppressions and indignities heaped upon American bondsmen bore heavily on Richmond slaves: they were bought and sold, had few legal protections, could not openly organize schools or societies, and were denied freedom of movement. Free blacks, though in a less dependent and impotent position, were burdened by caste legislation and popular white prejudice, were restricted in their movements and choice of occupations, and were legally prevented from acquiring education. Yet, to paraphrase Ralph Ellison, Richmond blacks did manage to fashion a life for themselves within a white supremacist society. This can be seen by looking at their experiences as employees of tobacco factories and members of African churches, the two most important institutions in antebellum black Richmond.

The manufacture of chewing tobacco was the largest Richmond industry and one that depended almost exclusively on black male labor. By 1860 more than 3,300 blacks worked in 49 factories: most were male slaves and about 40 percent were hired. Some workers enjoyed the privileges of finding their own employers, although of course their wages went to their owners, many made their own boarding arrangements, and all could earn money by producing in excess of daily production quotas. Tobacco slaves won more privileges than slaves working in other occupations, but the others usually managed to earn a bit of money and to partake of a varied black social life that existed in the alleys, groceries, and rooms housing slaves and free blacks throughout the city. Their familiarity with the subtle techniques of bargaining, with managing their own households, and with budgeting their earnings gave them experiences they would later put to greater use as free men.

The second major black institution, the African Baptist churches, attracted about a third of the adult black population and a significant proportion of their earnings. By the mid-1850s the First African Baptist Church alone boasted more than 3,000 members, and the congregation had long since purchased its meeting house. The church's record, as well as that of the smaller Ebenezer African Baptist Church, reveals that the congregation, although supervised by white ministers and white laymen, governed itself in important ways through the agency of black deacons. The congregation elected its deacons, who were usually propertied free blacks. Blacks elevated to the diaconate gained experience as community leaders and competent administrators. The code of behavior expected of church members and enforced by the deacons valued faithful marriages and harmonious familial relations, insisted upon honesty, sobriety, Christian fellowship, and obedience to God's commandments and lawful authorities, and obligated members to be charitable to the needy. Church organizations and illegal, secret benevolent societies regularly cared for the poor, tended to the sick, and buried the dead. The God of the Old Testament and the fortunes of His Chosen People figured prominently in Afro-American religion, and when Union troops entered Richmond on April 3, many blacks rejoiced for their own deliverance which they saw as fulfilling the Scriptures.

As the last Confederate units retreated from Richmond just before daybreak, setting fire to munitions stores, warehouses, and bridges, blacks gathered outdoors awaiting their liberators. One white resident recollected that Richmond "seemed in a night to have been transformed into an African city." When the troops appeared, Nellie Grey saw the "negroes run into the street and falling on their knees before the invader hail them as their deliverers." Emmie Lightfoot noted that the "negroes were in a wild state of excitement" and that freedwomen called the soldiers "their Saviours." Mary Fontaine's servants were "completely crazed, they danced and shouted, men hugged each other, and women kissed." These public celebrations ended quickly, however, because soldiers stacked arms and began fighting the conflagration with the aid of all able-bodied men. Together they saved the city from complete destruction, but only after the fires had consumed more than 1,100 buildings and had razed most of the commercial district. The next morning blacks again took to the streets to give Abraham Lincoln an enthusiastic welcome. Thousands escorted the president on his tour of the city and assembled in Capitol Square to hear him. His words were electrifying, for they captured the feelings and longings of the audience. You "can cast off the name of slave and trample upon it; it will come to you no more," he stated. "Liberty is your birthright. God gave it to you as he gave it to others, and it is a sin that you have been deprived of it for so many years." Black spokesmen would later recast Lincoln's message by comparing emancipation to religious conversion and claiming these as their two most important experiences. Emancipation like conversion changed their lives.

Blacks returned to their homes and former masters after the public celebrations, but what occurred among them and between blacks and whites was rarely recorded. The diary of a resident from the outskirts of the city, however, provides insights into the social transformation whereby slaves became freedmen and traditional southern households fell apart. Emma Mordecai kept a record of the dissolution of her brother's household just outside Richmond. The most important black figure in her account was Cyrus Hughes, about whom little is known except that he joined the First African Baptist Church in 1848 and that he remained a slave until April 3, 1865. Hughes journeyed to Richmond with Mordecai on the day Lincoln arrived; she hastily returned home rather than suffer Lincoln's presence but he remained behind. Two days later Mordecai found Hughes sitting idly by the side of a road and asked whether he intended to live on the farm without working. Hughes answered that he would work for wages paid immediately and regularly, but that he would not work for the promise of wages paid after harvest. He explained that "there was to be no more Master and Mistress now, all was equal, he 'done heard dat read from the Court House Steps.' " He added that he planned to remain there "until I see how things is gwine to wuck. All the land belongs to the Yankees now and they gwine divide it out among de coloured people." Mordecai could offer "no redress, no refutation—so I left him and walked on." Tensions between the white family and the former slaves surfaced repeatedly during April, and several freedmen left. The major break came on May 4, when Cyrus angrily insisted that "he had a right to stay here—to bring here whom he pleased—to keep his family here." He claimed further that he was "entitled to a part of the farm after all the work he had done on it. The kitchen belonged to him because he had helped cut the timber to build it." The Mordecai faimly ordered him off their place. All the remaining servants left with Hughes the next day, many going to Richmond.

Freedmen in the city were challenging customs that had once denoted their inferior status. They invaded such exclusive white sanctuaries as Capitol Square, ceased abandoning sidewalks for white passersby, and held meetings without first securing permission from whites. Before emancipation black congregations were required to have white pastors, and afterwards they debated whether to retain their services. The first challenge to a white pastor came from black Union troops on April 9 who charged Robert Ryland of the First African Church with preaching a disloyal sermon and threatened to arrest him. The congregation protected Ryland, for he had served them since 1841, longer than any white minister in charge of a black church. Ryland subsequently resigned twice. In May the majority refused to accept his withdrawal, but in late June they consented and the congregation unanimously elected Gilbert Stockwell, a northern Baptist minister, as their pastor. During the same period congregations at the Third Street African Methodist Church and three other African Baptist churches dismissed their white pastors and replaced them with black ministers, three from the North and one from Richmond. Church property, however, remained legally owned by white trustees until much later.

Black congregations, even before choosing new pastors or gaining legal ownership of their churches, worked actively with northern schoolteachers to establish schools for their children. They met frequently with the teachers, meetings which one described as "dignified and to the point," and promoted education throughout the community. Because the congregations were willing and able to assist the school experiment, teachers were able to open classes for over 1,500 children two weeks after the occupation. This achievement led one of the teachers, Sarah Chase, a veteran teacher of blacks since 1862, to note on April 18 that "work in this Department begins under more favorable auspices than any other." Richmond blacks, she wrote, "are far more intelligent and thrifty than any I met with in the South—and though the laws against learning have been so strict, many can read and a large portion know their letters and spell a little, having been taught by the poor whites secretly and at exorbitant rates." Sarah Chase and her sister Lucy later learned that many children "had picked up one or two letters in the secret corner where the negro father kept his treasured book." Despite prohibitions against teaching blacks, they added, "nearly every colored family in Richmond has one or more members who can read." Other teachers shared the Chase sisters' assessment of the freedmen. "Cato" reported that many children, in addition to appearing neat and orderly, "knew the alphabet; many could spell, and not a few could read and write with considerable ease and correctness." They told teachers that "their mothers had taught them." On further investigation, "Cato" added, "their statements were found to be correct; and that many of the parents had actually, *under the very eye of the masters*, found means to possess themselves of that coveted knowledge, which they were now in secret imparting to their children." Many of Jennie Armstrong's 180 students were "considerably advanced in book knowledge," which she thought they had learned "by little systems of bribery, exchanging with white children a nut or an apple for a letter." Former slaves and freedmen had apparently preserved a tradition of literacy antedating the repressive laws of the 1830s or acquired it on their own from whites.

Juvenile literacy and the adult enthusiasm for education deeply impressed the teachers. Lucy Chase wrote on April 29: "I bow down in spirit before these worthy people. The mothers know their duty, and they do it." They "mean all things shall be; and their children are their faithful *mirrors* as they move about the streets." Some children and parents paid dearly for their education. "Many of our children have been driven from their homes because they came to school," Lucy Chase added, and "in some instances, *whole families* have been turned into the *streets* because they were represented in the schoolroom." Jennie W. Duncan noted that "the parents are delighted with the idea of their children learning to read, and many take great pleasure in visiting the schools, and asking the teacher to pay 'ticular pains to our children, as we wish them to get all the learning they can, 'cause you know Miss, I's got no learning myself, consequently I know how much I loses without it, so Miss, please just be mighty strict and ticular with them.'" Sarah Chase was struck by the quiet dignity of the freedmen, most of whom, though impoverished, "will not beg." Freedwomen especially searched for work and the means to support themselves. "I find very many of them living miserably," she continued, but "the house and family [are] scrupulously neat and tidy, the clothes marvelously mended, and the faces radiant with joy, thanksgiving, and hopefulness, though the larder is nearly empty, and the fireplace quite so." The freedmen's love of family, another philanthropist insisted, was "no mere figment of northern sympathy."

Like many northerners, teachers wondered whether the freedmen, still in the "infancy of the race," would mistake leisure for freedom and would fail to respond to the rewards and disciplines of the free labor system with industry. In a short time, however, their misgivings were quieted. Sarah Chase wrote on May 5 that "everyday confirms our first impressions of the superiority of the Richmond negro over all others we have had under our observation. All are eager for work." Three weeks later, Chase added that "a very little help of the right kind will advance them in a short time to an independent position." They asked only for "work and justice," she claimed. Many of her co-workers agreed that the freedmen wanted work and sought it more energetically than whites. John Dudley of the National Freedmen's Relief Association noted that urban freedmen in Virginia were "generally intelligent, industrious, economical, thriving, hopeful, and quiet: doing all the labor; are the largest customers of the merchant." "Cato" reported that the "colored people, as a body, are the only industrious persons in Richmond." S. E. Fitz, an agent for the United States Christian Commission in the city, made the same point. "The whites liked our rations, but hated our gospel. The blacks worked for their own food, while they sought the gospel from us." Two northern reporters were equally impressed by the freedmen's self-reliance and performances as free laborers. John R. Dennett noted that they "seem to look for an improvement in their condition more to their own exertions and to local actions, and less to the general Government and the people of the North." The "negro does not consider that he is fully free," John Trowbridge remarked, until he finds a job. "He has no prejudice against labor, as so many of the whites have." Black activities during April and May, so cheering to philanthropists working for a reconstruction of southern society, failed to impress either the military authorities or most local whites, for in seeking a restoration of loyalty and order they had little tolerance for black experiments with freedom or philanthropic efforts to "uplift" blacks.

The occupation army governed, policed, and fed Richmond's sorely pressed civilian population. It inherited a partially destroyed city whose economy was in a shambles and whose citizenry required emergency aid. The restoration program, inaugurated immediately after the occupation by General Godfrey Weitzel and carried on by his successors, tried to encourage loyal sentiments among the conquered whites and to elicit work from the liberated blacks. The army used its control of needed foodstuffs to extract loyalty and industry from them. Whites seeking rations had first to swear allegiance to the government before becoming eligible for them. Able-bodied blacks had to work for their rations under the quartermaster's supervision. These policies expressed the army's view of what each racial group needed to learn for there to be a return of order. The whites' abilities to support themselves were not in question, but their political loyalties were. It was thought that conciliation and material benevolence would most quickly and efficaciously nurture gratitude and loyalty. Loyalty was not seen as a pressing issue for blacks, but their willingness to labor as free persons was. The army's manipulation of relief distributions most clearly captured its evaluation of whites and blacks and expressed its understanding of the requirements of restoration.

General Weitzel believed that his policies were producing the desired effects. Thousands of blacks worked in gangs clearing debris from the streets and rebuilding walls and bridges, while thousands of whites lined up in front of provost marshals' offices to take the oath of allegiance. Others were less sanguine. Charles Dana, a special agent working for Secretary of War Edwin Stanton, claimed that the "malignity of the thorough rebel here is humbled and silenced, but seems only the more intense on that account. I do not think," he added, "the Union feeling here is half as sincere as Weitzel believes it to be, but there is a great throng of people after victuals." A black reporter for the *Philadelphia Press* complained that the high command, in an effort to appease white sensibilities, diverted black troops away from the city's center on April 3, giving white soldiers time to enter Richmond, win the honor of taking it, and form its provost guard. Neither criticism, however, damaged Weitzel nearly as much as his handling of a controversy regarding church prayer. During the first week of April several Episcopalian ministers approached the military authorities for permission to conduct church services without offering a prayer for the president of the United States, a modification of the liturgy that only their bishop, then absent from the city, could approve. A member of Weitzel's staff approved their request, delighting the clergymen by requiring them merely to pray for unnamed authorities but outraging the secretary of war. Stanton "strongly condemned" and disallowed the concession, severely chastised Weitzel, and ordered the churches closed until their ministers acknowledged Lincoln's authority by praying for him. Weitzel left Richmond on April 13 under a cloud of suspicion.

A military triumvirate, which formed in the ten days following Weitzel's departure, fashioned restoration policies for the city and the state until mid-June. General Edward O. C. Ord, commanding the Army of the James, established his headquarters in Richmond on April 13, and immediately announced his intention to "be kind to the submissive" and to make military rule acceptable to them. General Marsena R. Patrick, provost marshal general of the Army of the Potomac, took charge of the police and relief agencies on April 14. Eight days later, General Henry W. Halleck arrived as the senior military officer for the Department of Virginia and North Carolina. Halleck had attracted national fame and abolitionist wrath in 1861 when he ordered the expulsion of fugitive slaves from his lines in the Department of the Missouri. These three shared important assumptions about the nature and purpose of the occupation government. They believed that defeated whites would most quickly return to the Union fold if they were treated kindly and respectfully and that their loyalty could be measured by the degree to which they acknowledged the finality of the Confederacy's defeat and by the number who took the oath of allegiance. They wanted civilian government reestablished after a brief period of military rule, during which resistance to the government would be crushed, the integrity of the Union guaranteed, the immediate postwar emergencies met, and the private economy given necessary assistance. Finally, they wanted freedmen to resume working much as they always had with the exception that they were free to bargain for wages, support their families and dependents, and receive the fruits of their labor. The generals showed little patience for overt signs either of white disloyalty or black idleness.

The army's test of white loyalty required of the defeated little more than that they recognize the obvious realities of the Confederacy's defeat and slavery's abolition. Not surprisingly, most whites passed the test, for initially it was silent on such thorny issues as their willingness to treat freedmen fairly, to accord them any rights, or to repudiate the Confederacy's war debt. Defined so minimally, the army's loyalty program was an instant success. Halleck reported on the day he arrived in Richmond that the city "is today more loyal than Washington or Baltimore. The people acknowledge that they are thoroughly

conquered." On April 28 he claimed that whites "have thus far conducted themselves with great propriety, and are most respectful to the
United States authorities." "Rebel feeling in Virginia is utterly dead,
and, with proper management, can never be revived," he added on
April 29. To strengthen his assessment, Halleck noted that "more
than 5,000 people have offered to take the amnesty oath" and that
the "recusant clergymen have offered to pray for the President of the
United States." Halleck omitted mentioning that oath-taking was a
prerequisite for receiving rations, practicing law and the ministry, im-
porting goods, and protecting private property from government seizure, and that the "recusant clergymen" decided to pray for the president only after the authorities invited loyal ministers to take over
their pulpits. What mattered was that the whites showed no inclination to take up arms again against the government, which was to
the generals convincing proof of their loyalty. With the loyalty issue
settled satisfactorily by the end of April, the army could enlist the aid
of white civilians to solve more vexing problems.

The army reluctantly shouldered the responsibility for feeding the
destitute. It created the Richmond Relief Commission, staffed by
white civilian volunteers, which was feeding over 15,000 persons,
mostly whites, by April 21. Commission visitors gave ration tickets
to all needy whites but only to aged or infirm blacks. Able-bodied
blacks were sent to the quartermaster for work assignments and rations. Ord specifically directed the quartermaster to offer the blacks
rations only and not to pay "wages to colored men as they will leave
the country and come to the cities where they are not required." At
the same time, army officials worked to prime the city's shattered
economy. Ord reported on April 19 that he had "authorized the canal,
road, and mail companies to resume their works." He announced
plans to give free transportation back to their homes to white refugees.
Ord and Halleck repeatedly urged Stanton to revoke special trade
permits and to permit trade to flow freely. On April 25 the army permitted loyal landlords to collect rents, and a week later Halleck created a court of conciliation to adjudicate disputes over property ownership, sale, and rental. A crucial part of the plan to revive Richmond's
economy was to halt the influx of rural freedmen, to settle them in
the countryside, and to entice blacks already in the city out to the
plantations. On May 3 Ord directed sentinels guarding roads leading to

Richmond to turn back black migrants. Halleck told regional commanders two days later to use their influence to "reconcile all differences between freedmen and their former masters," and to "assure the freedmen that they will be required to labor for the support of themselves and their families, but that they are free to select their own employers and make their own bargains." The government, he emphasized, "will protect, but cannot support them." Lest freedmen dally too long bargaining for better conditions, the army cut off rations to the able-bodied.

Richmond's newspapers gushed praise for their military rulers and for the terms of the restoration. "Never was a city taken and occupied in so quiet and orderly a way as was ours by the Union soldiers," who have been "uniformly kind and polite," the *Commercial Bulletin* proclaimed on May 15. "We have nothing to complain of and much to be thankful for." The *Richmond Times* stated that all citizens conceded that "the conduct of the military authorities, since the evacuation of Richmond, has been, in forebearance, moderation, courtesy and benevolence, unprecedented in the history of civil wars." Private citizens were no less grateful. The Yankees "have behaved very well indeed," one wrote, "no private property has been touched and no insults have been offered to any of the citizens." Sallie Putnam admitted it "would be a failure of simple justice" not to accord the military "the offering of sincere gratitude, for the respect, kindness, the lenity with which the citizens were treated." White Richmonders displayed their loyalty, and the generals pronounced it genuine. All southerners, the *Richmond Times* asserted on May 16, were working "with singular unanimity" for the restoration of the old Union. Soon, it predicted, elections would be held, state representatives would return to Congress, and "all traces of the Confederacy" would disappear as though "four years of civil war had not just been brought to an end." Events seemed to bear out the paper's optimism. President Andrew Johnson recognized the unionist regime of Governor Francis H. Pierpont as Virginia's legitimate government on May 9. Upon arriving in Richmond on May 26, Pierpont promised to moderate the state's radical 1864 constitution. A week later, Pierpont restored civilian government to Richmond. Their confidence fast returning, white citizens cheered loudly as the army attacked the "Negro Problem."

Halleck reported to Stanton on May 7 that his "greatest anxiety was in regard to the crops for this year." "The planting season is so nearly over," he explained, "that I fear the colored population will not settle down to quiet and labor in time to raise grain enough for the coming year." From the countryside came complaints of a labor shortage, as numerous freedmen like Cyrus Hughes held out for better conditions than planters were offering, hoped that land might be given to them, searched for relatives, friends, and better employment possibilities, or withdrew wives and mothers from the fields. Far too many seemed headed for the cities, where work was scarce. Military officials sought first to halt the influx of rural freedmen to Richmond and later to reverse it. On May 13 Halleck ordered Patrick to "check the issues of subsistence to destitute persons." Within a week Patrick issued orders requiring blacks to carry passes signed by whites indicating who they were, whether they were employed, and who their employers were. He also imposed an evening curfew on blacks only. Soldiers swept through the city, stopping all blacks, checking their passes, and arresting those without passes or work. The Richmond press was jubilant, for this was a feature of restoration local commentators found downright sensible.

Local newspapers offered increasingly outspoken advice about the proper resolution of the "Negro Question" as their confidence in the military officials and about the direction of restoration grew. They copied stories from northern Democratic papers predicting that the freedmen, like the American Indian, would soon become extinct. "The man is an idiot or lunatic," the *Richmond Republic*, a moderate Unionist sheet, declared, "who will contend that where white skilled, energetic labor comes in free competition with the unskilled and slovenly labor of free negroes, the latter class will not go to the wall, to the gutter, and to the hovel." Since the government had broken the master-slave bond, it had the responsibility for supervising freedmen, for fending off their extinction, somewhere far from Richmond. Send them out west as railroad or mine workers, the *Republic* suggested; settle them in northern Mexico, the *Commercial Bulletin* proposed; make them till the fields, the "only work" they are "capable of performing," the *Times* added. Patrick's troops, the *Times* crowed, were at last teaching "Cuffee that liberty does not mean unlimited army rations, idleness, and vice." Freedmen, Emma Mordecai mused, "will now begin to find out how easy their lives as *slaves* had been, and to feel the slavery of their freedom."

On May 20 the *Richmond Times* warned employers to give their black employees passes if they wanted to protect them from arrest. Thereafter, cavalry patrols arrested blacks without passes, sending women and children to one depot and men to another. The military invited planters wanting laborers to bid for their services at either of the depots. The *Times* suggested that laborers could be gotten on the cheap. "From a schedule of the rations dealt out to the negroes who are quartered at these places," the paper added, "we find that they are entitled to bare enough to live on, and no inducement is held out to prevent their wishing to get homes as soon as possible." Four days later, the *Times* congratulated the army for its wisdom in invariably assigning blacks "to country employment in preference to any other, where they can be engaged in tilling the soil and developing the vast agricultural resources of the State." In the city, "most all kinds of employment will be gladly accepted by white persons and therefore it is that the blacks, who are not so well adapted to the work which is to be done here, have been hired to farmers who desire them." In the same issue, the *Times* announced that it would not publish a card from "a number of free negroes, complaining of the conduct of the authorities" because they erroneously believed that the pass requirement oppressed all blacks. "The whole object of the authorities—and a most commendable one it is," the paper lectured, "is to let no idle negroes loaf around the city, but to put them to work, and to make them earn their own living." Although far more whites than blacks received free government rations, the generals and editors accused blacks only of seeking charity and desiring freedom without work. Blacks continued to search for redress locally from an unsympathetic military regime.

Schoolteachers recoiled at the sight of Union soldiers harassing freedmen, but they were powerless to prevent it. "Our soldiers as well as the Johnnies plunder the houses of the poor blacks continually," Sarah Chase reported on May 25, "so that the colored people feel it is neither safe to go out or remain at home." Julia A. Wilbur thought that deteriorating conditions suggested that the military and white citizenry had "combined to make the situation of the colored people intolerable." Blacks said that "these soldiers of the Union Army must be *rebels disguised in Federal uniforms* or they would not cooperate so willingly with the rebel citizens of Richmond," she added. The suspension of free rations and housing for schoolteachers, which the army had previously provided, further heightened the teachers' suspicion of the local commanders. The one agency which might have come to the freedman's aid, the newly established Freedmen's Bureau, was politely but unenthusiastically welcomed to Richmond by the generals. Failing to receive staff, offices, or jurisdiction over freedmen's affairs from the army command, Captain Orlando Brown, the assistant commissioner of the Bureau for Virginia, left Richmond after a brief stay and complained of his inability to get the Bureau organized to his superior, General Oliver O. Howard. Stunned by their mistreatment at the hands of troops who only two months earlier had liberated them, blacks appealed unsuccessfully to the authorities for an end to their oppression. They took matters into their own hands at the end of the first week of June, when the restoration of civilian municipal government seemed to signal that emergency military measures had become permanent policy. The return to power by Joseph Mayo, who had served Richmond as mayor since 1853, threatened to end abruptly and unsatisfactorily the blacks' experiments with freedom, and to substitute caste discrimination, passes, curfews, and white supremacy for genuine freedom and equality.

Several blacks met on June 7, the same day Mayor Mayo reopened his court and ordered civilian police onto the streets, to compose a letter of protest to the *New York Tribune.* Richard and Madison Carter, coopers, Robert Johnson, shoemaker, Spencer Smithen, bricklayer, and N. H. Anderson signed the letter for "many others." They introduced themselves as freeborn Virginians, family men, loyal citizens, and dependable taxpayers who had "no superior save in education." Richmond "needs a decent government," they asserted, explaining that cavalrymen, "whose business is the hunting of colored people," made their lot "worse than ever we suffered before." They complained bitterly about having "to get some white person to give us passes to attend to our daily occupations, without which we are marched off to the Old Rebel Hospital, now called the negro bull pen." To carry out this "disgraceful work," the governor had reinstated the mayor and "all his former nigger hunters and whippers, and today they are going into people's houses and taking them out and confining them in the City Jail until nearly night, when they are marched off by the mounted guard to the bull pen." They closed by claiming that "All that is needed to restore Slavery in full is the auction-block as it used to be."

On the following day another group met in a private house and appointed a committee to investigate complaints of army and police persecution. Fields Cook, Nelson Hamilton, Peter Woolfolk, and Walter Snead, all former free blacks and longtime church leaders, conducted the hearings and compiled more than twenty sworn depositions. The deponents testified that soldiers punished them arbitrarily and cruelly, arrested both employed and unemployed blacks, treated all blacks disrespectfully, and sided invariably with whites in interracial disputes. Two men complained of having been hung by their thumbs for forcibly resisting a drunken white man; two northern blacks were insulted by soldiers and warned against ever contradicting whites; two young men were taken from their place of work and arrested for not having proper passes; and a visiting black artisan from Petersburg, despite telling soldiers that free men should not have to carry passes, was jailed for failing to have one. Ned Scott received the most shocking abuse. Scott's ordeal began when he reprimanded two paroled Confederate soldiers for manhandling his wife and worsened when he fought with and cut some off-duty Union soldiers who, having witnessed the confrontation between Scott and the Confederates, harassed him for his impudence. After being taken into custody, Scott was bucked and paddled, marched through the streets to the Rogue's March, encased in a casket, smeared with meal and honey to attract flies, and carted off to a military prison where, he was falsely told, he would be shot. The *Richmond Times* found Scott's humiliation and punishment amusing and claimed that white onlookers "enjoyed the spectacle hugely." Scott, "almost half dead with fright and heat," will "know how to behave himself in the future," the paper chuckled. Others, however, were not amused.

The *New York Tribune*'s local reporter called Scott's tormentors "cruel fiends" and added that such "abuses have been growing worse and worse until this last act of restoring Mayor Mayo to power, which seems to have let loose all evil passions." William Coan, a northerner in charge of Richmond's black schools, claimed that the "Devil" and, little worse, the "Copperheads" had taken over the city. Julia A. Wilbur reported that the military and police were creating a "reign of terror" for black people. A northerner who had lived in the South for twenty years told Orlando Brown that "he never saw the negroes abused as they are now." Brown received several depositions from the black investigating committee and forwarded them to Howard, noting that "these statements may seem incredible, but I fear they must be believed." Brown promised to correct abuses "when the military turn over the cares of the negroes to me," but until then "I can do but little." Frustrated in their attempts to find redress locally, black leaders called a mass meeting for June 10.

Over three thousand blacks crowded into the First African Baptist Church, listened to several addresses, and approved a protest memorial that the investigating committee had composed. C. Thurston Chase, an agent for the American Union Commission who represented Orlando Brown at this meeting, asked the people to channel their concerns and complaints through the Freedmen's Bureau. Chase later reported that he almost won the crowd over and would have succeeded had T. Morris Chester, the black reporter for the *Philadelphia Press,* not objected. Chester told the crowd that Brown "should have been here weeks ago to attend to these matters, to investigate their grievances and extend protection and afford redress." He recommended that the people avoid channels and go instead directly to the president of the United States. Such a move would immediately attract national press coverage and win speedier results. Chester's position prevailed. After approving the protest memorial, the crowd selected Chester, the local reporter for the *New York Tribune,* Van Vleet, and a representative from each of six African churches to take their case before the president. They donated money that night and on the following Sunday at their churches to defray the delegates' expenses. Before leaving for Washington, the delegates visited Governor Pierpont, presented him with their evidence, and secured his promise to depose Richmond's civilian government.

In their protest memorial, blacks described their community, listed their grievances, and requested all civil and legal rights of freemen. The petitioners claimed to represent more than 20,000 Richmond and Manchester blacks "who have ever been distinguished for their good behavior as slaves and as freedmen, as well as for their high moral and Christian character." Over 6,000 belonged to churches, between 2,000 and 3,000 were literate despite slave laws that "severely punished those who taught us to read and write," and about 2,400 owned property valued at between $200 and $20,000. They supported themselves and had always cared for the poor and sick of their community. "None of our people are in the Alms-House, and when we were slaves, the aged and infirm who were turned away from the homes of hard masters, who had been enriched by their toil, our benevolent societies supported while they lived, and buried them when they died, and comparatively few of us have found it necessary to ask for Government rations, which have been so bountifully bestowed upon the unrepentant Rebels of Richmond." The community's industrious and progressive character alone should have earned it respect instead of persecution.

Moreover, blacks were the only loyal segment of the city's population. Throughout the war blacks prayed for a Union victory and gave "aid and comfort to the soldiers of Freedom (for which several of our people of both sexes, have been severely punished by stripes and imprisonment)." While local blacks acted as "scouts" and "pilots" for the army, legions of black troops "fully established the indomitable bravery, the loyalty, and the heroic patriotism of our race." When the Union forces marched into Richmond, "we alone gave it a cordial welcome," when Lincoln arrived, "we alone hailed his advent with enthusiastic cheers of acclamation, and of all the citizens of Richmond we alone, with a few solitary exceptions, wear the exterior badges for his untimely death." Many whites "have become our enemies, who seek not only to oppress our people, but to thwart the designs of the Federal Government and benevolent Northern associations in our behalf." State law provided no protection. White trustees retained legal ownership of church buildings paid for by slaves and free blacks. The military and police "will not allow us to walk the streets by day or night, in the regular pursuit of our business or on our way to church, without a pass, and passes do not in all cases protect us from arrest, insult, abuse, violence, and imprisonment." Blacks who had come to Richmond seeking work after being evicted by their former owners had been arrested and hired out "for the most insignificant sums." Blacks seeking relatives, "who ignorantly supposed that the day of passes had passed away with the system which originated them, have been arrested, imprisoned, and hired out without their advice or consent." In addition, "some of our people have been punished in the most cruel manner, the like of which was never heard of, even in the slave pens of Southern traders."

The petitioners concluded by expressing regret for the government's use of past authorities and discredited standards to guide its Reconstruction policies. The restoration of Mayor Joseph Mayo, they claimed, was an affront both to themselves and to Union prisoners of war. "During the whole period of the rebellion," they explained, "Mr. Mayo, as the Chief Magistrate of the city, and as a private citizen, exerted all his influence to keep alive the spirit of treason and rebellion, and to urge the people to continue to contest." Mayo "openly and shamelessly approved" the cruelties perpetrated upon Union prisoners. During his long years as mayor of the city, Mayo "ordered us to be scourged for trifling offenses against slave laws and usages; and his present police, who are now hunting us through the streets, are the men who relentlessly applied the lash to our quivering flesh, and now they appear to take special pleasure in persecuting and oppressing us." A recent order issued by the commander of Lynchburg stating that freedmen had "all the rights at present that free people of color have heretofore had in Virginia" dispirited them. "We were sorry to see this announcement," they noted, "for we supposed that the recently freedmen were a class of persons unknown to the law of Virginia, or to any other State, but that they were to be subjected only to special acts of Congressional enactment." In closing, the petitioners affirmed their loyalty while reminding "your Excellency of that sublime motto once inscribed over the portals of an Egyptian temple, 'Know all ye who exercise power, that God hates injustice!' "

The delegates met Johnson on June 17 after conferring with General Howard of the Freedmen's Bureau the previous evening. Asked by the president whether they had taken their case before local military authorities, Fields Cook, the chairman of the delegation, replied that he had, "and the result had been that they had been treated very much worse than before calling General Patrick's attention to facts which has exasperated the subordinates to find they were complained of." Cook also stated that they "could not get an audience with General Halleck, though they frequently tried so to do, and so they thought best to come to the chief head of all authority." After pointing out that Governor Pierpont had already deposed Richmond's civilian government, Johnson "assured the delegation that he would do all in his power to protect them and their rights; that he would take care of the military and see they perpetrated no more wrongs upon them, while the Governor would manage the civil authorities." The delegates then retired "much pleased with the President and their interview." A week later, back in Richmond, the delegates reported on their mission and its accomplishments to a packed house at the First African Baptist Church. Richard Wells, a delegate and the pastor of the Manchester African Baptist Church, expressed sorrow at the behavior of many whites whose motto seemed to be "hickory stick growing in the ground, if you ain't got a start keep the nigger down," but he closed on a positive note, reminding the audience that they now had schools, "had at last got a start and had reached the round where they could whisper into the President's ear their wrongs."

Black Richmonders had good reason for celebrating and for judging their protest a success. All four white leaders lost their posts in Richmond during June. Mayor Mayo was hastily retired by the governor. General Patrick, already angered by criticism of his conduct and by the terms of Johnson's amnesty program, resigned in disgust on June 8. Generals Ord and Halleck were reassigned to new posts as part of a general reorganization of the army, but their transfers became public only after the black protest, giving the impression that their displacement and the protest were connected. Although it is unclear whether the choice of the new military commander for Virginia was influenced by the events in Richmond, General Alfred H. Terry was dispatched to Richmond with explicit orders to investigate the troubles there and correct injustices. Terry was ideally suited to the task. A Republican, military hero, and wartime commander of both black and white troops, Terry could be depended upon to treat blacks more fairly than his predecessors and thereby resolve a problem that clearly embarrassed the government in Washington. The protest occurred when the government was still formulating its restoration programs and while the president was still consolidating his support among northern Republicans. Aided by the notoriety of their city and its proximity to Washington, and supported by sympathetic reporting in such important Republican newspapers as the New York Tribune, the

Richmond protestors struck a responsive chord in the capital and won speedy redress.

General Terry received orders directing him to Virginia while he was preparing to attend a banquet in his honor in his native state of Connecticut. The circumstances surrounding his appointment led the *Richmond Republic* to venture that "the order assigning General Terry . . . was rather unexpected." At Washington the secretary of war instructed Terry to investigate the causes of the troubles in Richmond and to recommend the "most necessary step to remedy the existing evils." Terry reported back from Richmond on June 16. The government's first priority, he suggested, should be to "establish definitely and authoritatively the status of the freedmen." He proposed declaring that "the people of color will henceforth enjoy the same personal liberty which other citizens and inhabitants enjoy." They should be subjected to the same restraints and same punishments for crime that are imposed on whites, and no others." Although vagrancy would be suppressed, neither blacks nor whites would "be restrained from seeking employment elsewhere when it cannot be obtained with just compensation at their homes, nor from traveling from place to place on proper and legitimate business." He proposed creating military courts that would receive "the evidence of colored persons" until the civil courts were reorganized and willing to admit black testimony. Stanton approved his suggestions. In one of his first official acts as commander of Virginia, Terry abolished the pass and curfew regulations on June 17.

The protest resulted in more than removing the obstructions erected by the alliance between Richmond's military triumvirate and civilian government. True to his word, Terry established military courts which admitted black testimony and accorded blacks some legal protection. Terry proved far more sympathetic to the freedmen than his predecessors. He gave the Freedmen's Bureau the personnel and material assistance it needed to commence its land program, supervision of labor contracts, and organization of the school system. When the inadequate performance of Richmond's provost guards outraged blacks and spurred a protest, Terry received the blacks' complaints and reorganized the military police. Terry also proved far less sympathetic to the whites' avowals of loyalty than his predecessors. He voided the results of the July municipal elections when self-proclaimed Unionists suffered defeat. In addition, he suppressed several local newspapers for publishing articles that he judged disloyal. Benefiting from the protection provided by the more impartial Terry administration and from the aid and advice offered by the Bureau and northern philanthropists, freedmen entered a brief period marked by optimism and activism, if not economic prosperity.

Richmond freedmen entered the political arena in June 1865. Caught in the middle of a hurried rush to sectional reconciliation that threatened their rights, they waved the "bloody shirt" and publicly linked the previously separate issues of white loyalty and white respect for black emancipation. They demonstrated in June a capacity for acting collectively, cleverly, and effectively. In the middle of the emergency, thousands rallied in their churches behind men the community had elevated to leadership positions in the antebellum churches. They met in their churches, collected funds at church services, and elected black deacons and ministers to carry their protest to the president. Cleverly, the protestors avoided attacking the army directly, although the army had spearheaded the campaign to expel blacks from the city. They instead blasted away at their former masters and reminded the federal government of the whites' recent disloyalty. Although they successfully argued their case in Washington, Richmond blacks learned from their experience the danger of remaining without political influence locally and the probable consequences to themselves if reconstruction were left to whites alone. Gradually, increasing numbers of blacks perceived the need and expressed the demand for the vote. Richmond delegates to a statewide black convention held in Alexandria in August introduced resolutions calling for the franchise, a position reaffirmed by local black rallies held in December 1865. Their political activism and initiatives stunned their white neighbors and triggered a white reaction. Some whites, anxious to protect themselves from further federal interventions on the blacks' behalf, dusted off states' rights arguments, insisting that the federal government had no right to interfere in Virginia's internal affairs and proclaiming the state's right to defy the federal government in such matters. This resurrection of a militant states' rights position, so soon after the demise of the Confederacy, hardly srtengthened the whites' claim that as loyal and humble suppliants before the victor they deserved to be readmitted speedily into the Union. The June protest was the Richmond black community's first overtly political act after emancipation, and it was followed by a rapidly accelerating politicization of the community which shaped the course of the city's reconstruction. The ultimate failure of that experiment to guarantee black civil and political equality and to assist black economic advancement occurred despite vigorous black efforts to transform their society.